Finding the Heart of the Child

Essays on Children, Families, and Schools

To Frederick G. Tremallo,
who taught me how to write
and to
Sue, my wife,
who taught me most everything else

EMH

To my wife Theresa
and to
the memory of my former teacher
Frank W. Trevor

MGT

Finding the Heart of the Child

Essays on Children, Families, and Schools

Edward M. Hallowell, M.D.
Michael G. Thompson, Ph.D.

NATIONAL ASSOCIATION OF INDEPENDENT SCHOOLS

Finding the Heart of the Child:
Essays on Children, Families, and Schools

Published by
National Association of Independent Schools
1620 L Street, NW
Washington, DC 20036-5605

"College Admission as a Failed Rite of Passage," "Child Sexual Abuse," "Masochism in Teachers," "How Can Teachers Cope?," "Understanding School Culture," and "Normal Sexual Feelings Between Children and Adults" have previously appeared in *Independent School* magazine.

Table of Contents

Foreword

Many readers will already be thrilled at the prospect of opening *Finding the Heart of the Child* to read and savor some of the talks they have heard from Ned Hallowell and Michael Thompson at schools and conferences around the country. Such readers need no introduction to the pleasures and insights that await them. For many others – the luckiest ones – these essays will open doors to new understanding, and will introduce two exciting minds.

Ned and Michael have been working together for more than a decade. They have shared presentations, panel discussions, office complexes, and a tennis court. (Anyone you can get along with week after week on the tennis court you can get along with anywhere.)

But they share something deeper: a common vision of the work of psychological support and the role of schools in helping children and families. Both describe themselves as deeply indebted to their own schools (Ned writes about this in "Remembering My Schools"), and as great admirers of teachers. They share a normalizing rather than a pathologizing view of psychology; that is, they see behavior as occurring on a continuum, and see the possibility of drawing the most troubled child back along the route to psychic health, while reminding us that even the most normal child faces many difficult psychic challenges (see especially Michael's "Adolescence Is Hard Work"). Putting it simply, both are hopeful: they take a reassuring rather than a catastrophic view of their work and their subjects.

Where they differ markedly is in the ways they express this shared vision. Ned, the psychiatrist, dazzles us with the elegance of his prose, the range of his allusions, and the height of his vision. Michael, the psychologist, touches us with the clarity, precision, and depth of his insights. Michael's is the calm, quiet voice of a parent soothing his child after a tantrum or a nightmare, Ned's the soaring eloquence of the parent sending his child off to conquer the world. When I read each I hear their voices: Michael's soft, encouraging, often coming from somewhere in a darkened room beside a slide projector, using cartoons, comic strips, and other illustrations to get his point across; Ned's ringing out from center stage, at the podium, quoting poets and prophets, delighted to know his audience is following the flights of his thought.

Ned's writing is self-revealing in ways that would astonish a classical psychoanalyst. He shares with us his boyhood, his own learning difficulties, his family life and friendships. For Ned the story always comes first, the experience from which the theory is woven. In his essays he plays with forms, inventing characters, dialogues, dramatic scenes, even sentient rooms, in order to convey his observations about behavior. Michael's writing is more reserved, more orderly, analytical, and comprehensive. His approach is structured; he promises to explain something to you, then proceeds to do so in terms as simple as the complex topics he's chosen allows. Ned is hot, Michael warm; Ned romantic, Michael classical; Ned is literary, dramatic, passionate, Michael essayistic, expository, understated. Together they provide two paths in the journey of understanding our children and ourselves. Readers will undoubtedly find one more congenial than the other; wise readers will soon realize that the less congenial may offer them the greater, more new – to them – perspectives.

Finding the Heart of the Child is divided into three sections. "On Childhood and Adolescence" explores the common developmental issues of all young people, whether through Ned's recollections of childhood or Michael's schema of the developmental tasks of adolescence. "Disorders and Traumas" examines the broad issues of normal and abnormal behavior, along with depth studies of certain specific conditions, from learning disabilities to sexual abuse. "To Teachers and Other Adults" reminds us that we cannot understand our children, whether as their parents or their teachers, without understanding ourselves. The book makes no attempt to be exhaustive: conditions like anorexia, for example, receive little attention; others, like learning and attention difficulties, a great deal. Enthusiasts will therefore be glad to know that Michael and Ned continue to write about this all important subject of growing up and about how adults can best help children through the process. Ned has written a book on attention deficit disorder, *Driven to Distraction*, published by Pantheon Books. And Michael is hard at work on a book about boys, to be published in 1998.

That's good news, because both have far more to say than can fit between these covers. I have known Michael and Ned for thirteen years, during which I have heard them make at least twice that many presentations. Just when I think I know what they have to say, each surprises me with a new theme, a new observation, a new subject of interest.

Some have observed that our society's illness can be gauged by the fact that we now have to pay someone to listen to us for an hour, a hired confidante, as it were, to fulfill a role once taken up by clergy, friends, family members, village elders, or others in the community, I don't know if there ever was a time when those who needed a sympathetic ear or a word of advice found it as readily as this utopian recollection suggests. I do know that no society which can produce such friendly ears, such sympathetic and inspiring voices, as Ned Hallowell's and Michael Thompson's, need apologize for itself on this count. So open their book, and enjoy their presence.

Richard Barbieri
Independent school educator and consultant

Chapter One

On Childhood and Adolescence

Remembering My Schools

by Edward M. Hallowell

How far away it seems to me now. I arrived at Fessenden School in September 1960, at the age of ten. When my mother asked me if I wanted to go to boarding school, literal boards came to my mind – planks and two-by-fours. I thought she was sending me to a lumberyard. I knew I had certain problems– underachievement was the word they used – but a lumberyard seemed harsh punishment indeed. She explained that boarding had nothing to do with wood but rather referred to one's living at the school. At once I enthusiastically agreed. With perfect logic I assumed that if you lived at the school the great bane of my life, homework, would be impossible, because you never went home.

By the time I found out the truth, I was trapped. I had been dropped off and said goodbye to. The images are vivid even now: the green striped curtains that served as doors for the cubicles, the gaslights that were lit at night flickering shadows on the walls until dawn, the night watchman who walked the empty hallways, the bright sloping lawn I saw out my window, the grass the same as at home but feeling so different, the starched white coat I was given when told I would be a waiter – a waiter? Maybe this was worse than a lumberyard.

The images were lonely at first. I was afflicted with that disease no child likes to admit: homesickness. So I contrived a scheme to distract myself. I managed to buy some firecrackers through outside sources (to which, to this day, I must remain loyal) and I set them off at school. The investigation that followed was exciting, just what I needed. As each lead came up empty and I saw Mr. Cook's exasperation grow, I felt proud, as if I had duped the F.B.I.

But then came the fear – maybe he would catch me – and the threat of a school-wide search. I had hidden the last few in my trunk in the trunk room.

So, late at night, unable to sleep, I went to Mr. Cook and confessed. I didn't know what sort of punishment to expect – do they spank you at boarding school or make you do push-ups, or do they turn you out into the night? But when there was no punishment forthcoming, indeed just a friendly chat, I knew I was really trapped. I was at boarding school to stay.

The school became my home, and what a big home it was. So many siblings! So many parents! The corridors seemed enormous, the boiler room so ominous, the eighth graders, or sixth formers, so important. Would I make it that far?

I figured I had to do something to get noticed (a tendency that to this day I have not surrendered), so I gave up my underachieving ways and set to doing that homework with a vengeance. I learned what it is to be smart one day when, on the way into the dining room, I overheard some seventh graders who had just learned the miraculous fact that if two negative numbers are multiplied together they produce a positive number. It happened that I was sitting at their table when they decided to show off their new knowledge. Turning to me they asked disdainfully, "If five times five is twenty-five, what is negative five times negative five?" I, who had not known that such a quantity as negative five even existed before overhearing their conversation, replied confidently, "Positive twenty-five of course." That answer put me on the map. How could a mere fifth-grader know the mysteries of negative numbers? What a brain. I asked my friend Joe if I should have confessed; he assured me that against the seventh grade all is fair.

As our group came together and friendships grew, we began to talk to each other in earnest. Ambition may be the last infirmity of the noble mind, but to us, back then, it was the magic that could transform a boring Sunday afternoon into a time for planning kingdoms and conquests. I remember when Tommy and I asked for each other's frank assessment as to our chances of becoming president of the United States. In all candor we both agreed that we each stood a very good chance. Tommy thought my weakness would be in domestic policy – I had done poorly on a recent geography test on the Farm Belt. I thought his weakness would be in labor relations – he had been unable to negotiate a raise in his allowance. But, with a little work, it was quite likely we each could make the White House. Uh-oh. What if we both wanted it in the same year? Ah, competition. I couldn't look at Tommy the same. He might keep me out of the White House. Something had to be done. We decided that, if elected, he would name me president for foreign policy, and I would name him president for domestic policy.

My years produced many presidents and astronauts and pitchers for the Red Sox. Looking back, our dreams are just childhood fantasies, but then they were alive and real and electric. Boarding school provided the safe and caring place wherein we could build new worlds each day.

Of course, it was not all dreams and play. School was a good deal more academically rigorous than anything I encountered in college, but not rigorous in the starched collar, rote sense. The Greek myths I learned in the fifth grade are with me still, and the love of words imparted by the English department is the single most valuable academic gift I have ever received. I can remember cockily telling Mr. Gibson that diagramming sentences was easy, whereupon he told me to diagram, in front of the class, The Lord's Prayer (hint: the hard part is at the beginning if you've never encountered the subjunctive, as I had not). We took language seriously. Why must a gerund take a possessive pronoun rather than the gerund's being thought of as a participle modifying the pronoun in the objective case? We debated that point one morning, the whole class joining in, a consultant finally being brought in from across the hall to arbitrate. Can you imagine the effect of such training? Words come to life, sentences become rambunctious creatures to be mastered. Run is a verb, but not when used in the following sentence: Run is a verb. And so on. I linger over Mr. Gibson and grammar only because I think it representative of the teaching. I didn't know what was happening to me, but because of Mr. Gibson, I was falling in love with words.

Life was not without danger. There was always the danger of a surprise quiz – can presidents have flunked two history quizzes in a row? – or the delicious danger of listening to Johnny Most announce the Celtics on a concealed radio under your pillow; how loud can you have it without the masters hearing it? Occasionally, there was real danger from the world outside that we knew so little of. I am there again on the soccer field, leaves swirling through our fierce game against Belmont Hill, the autumn air as crisp and tart now as when the news was hollered from across the field, "Kennedy has been shot." The game went on, but over the next few days the carefree lilt of school life stopped, and we all learned what it is to have a death in the family. Teachers cried. We cried. I can hear the hymn for those in peril on the sea and I can remember wondering if the school would go on.

Of course, it did. How is it that I can still see the look on Mr. Cook's face when he discovered I had a pet alligator under my bed, or the look on Ed Sullivan's face when for the first time he introduced The Beatles to our dorm gathered around the TV, or my Yankee-fan friend Jeffrey's face when over the radio we heard Roger Maris take Tracy Stallard downtown for home run number sixty-one? How could I be friends with Jeffrey after that? Somehow, our friendship endured.

Friendship. Competition. Dreams. Danger. In its little details it was high adventure. One night, three of us, dressed in our pajamas, had a race to see who could go through all the tunnels of the school and back to the dorm without being caught by the night watchman or any stray master. It was 2 a.m. To be caught meant expulsion, at least. Rod and I were neck and neck when, from under the gaslight, the night watchman emerged. Rod gave himself up so I could escape. The moral dilemma. We all confessed, and our lives were spared.

By the eighth grade we had all become important. We moved through that year basking in seniority and privilege, pretending that we would not have to say goodbye in June. We were buddies, almost brothers. Fessenden had given us this great feeling called friendship and nothing would take that away. Wherever Tommy went to school next, I'd go there too, and so would Rod, and Bill, and Dominic, as in DiMaggio. We would always be a group, and our ties would bring us back, wherever we might move.

In fact, I haven't seen my friends from Fessenden since I left. Perhaps that's how it should be. You're grade school chums, you're with each other for when life starts. Then you look back from the vantage point of middle age and you see your long-forgotten buddy Sammy playing pick-up ice hockey on a patch of black ice on a secluded pond on a frosty Sunday afternoon, and the memory takes your breath away because it reminds you of what you have forgotten day-to-day, that you were young once, that you had a childhood, that you spent hours and afternoons whiling away the time or getting into mischief or just unknowingly basking in the fact of promise and hope and devil-may-care. Maybe the way you never do part with those friends and those times is by not watching each other grow old. You preserve those days intact, as they were, enameled in memory where time stops and you are always a kid, out on the fields, racing through the corridors, and all your old buddies are back there with you, young and fresh and without age or diminished expectations. You hold onto those days in memory. You're out on the playground still, still finding ways to stay up past lights out.

After Fessenden I went to Exeter, where I read for the first time those final lines of what would become my favorite novel, *The Great Gatsby*: "And so we beat on, boats against the current, borne back ceaselessly into the past," never thinking that I would now be borne back myself over those twenty years as I try to recapture the experience.

Not that I have aged. No, not that, of course. But in the years that have passed, and will pass, I am drawn back again and again to Exeter, caught up short by a memory, a scene, an image, even an odor, back to those short four years that at the time seemed endless.

The power lies in the details, of course, details that mean nothing to someone else but course through me like ice water on a hot summer day.

I can see K. Don Jacobusse, whose antique Mercedes convertible speeding along in spring will always be one of my first examples of panache. I can see one of my classmates slowly raise his hand in the middle of our first math class and observe dolefully that this wasn't French I, was it? I can hear the crunch of leaves in fall and I can see the sun filling up the quad with bright expectation. I can feel the push of bodies up against the little cubbyholes to the outside called mailboxes, and I even still dream now and then of what my combination used to be.

And I can remember Fred Buechner asking us in sermon how we would react if God walked down the aisle with two six-shooters on his hips – would that be proof, or what? And I can see the green-glass light shade over the amber bulb on the table where K. sat to check us in from vacation. And cans of Coke left on windowsills to keep cold. And little chocolates, called Ice Cubes, wrapped in gold foil, sold at Court Street Market.

And the shimmering winter mornings after a storm when the sun and the ice filled the trees with spangles of light. And the muffled sound of the bell of Phillips Church striking in the falling snow. And the lonely sight of an orange leaf frozen in black ice viewed from the bridge near the cannons.

Tame, perhaps inane details. But they surrounded a passion play. An intensity suffused those years, an awkward, unpolished intensity, the passion and intensity of so many firsts. Whether it was first looking into Fitzgerald's *Gatsby*, or first looking into my own insecure psyche, or first looking beneath the blouse of the first girl who let me clumsily, breathlessly undress her, these were years of firsts, of discovery, of passion and excitement

Now I have the terms to put it into perspective, terms like "adolescent" and "boys' boarding school," but then, although I knew the terms, I had no perspective. The world was wildly, wonderfully, frighteningly out of perspective. One day I was a budding Dostoyevsky. The next day, after watching *Wild Strawberries* in Lamont Library, I was a potential suicide. The next day I was up late into the night trying to catch smoke rings around my finger in the butt room.

We were always catching smoke rings. Our dreams would appear and disappear from week to week as the cockeyed optimist within us did battle with doubt and self-reproach. Oh, we were as hard on ourselves as we were grand, and every giddy moment of success and creation was paid for with moments in the slough of despond.

It was a cold-weather school, but there was fall to warm and crackle us into winter and spring to lift us out. We didn't have girls, and that was too bad. We had girls on the brain, that's for sure, and again, without perspective. It would be impossible to exaggerate the fantasy life of the average member of my class.

Presiding and participating was the faculty. Since I came to Exeter from a chaotic family, the debt I feel to the teachers is perhaps more extreme than others'. Fred Tremallo not only took me on an excursion through the world of ideas, he and Ellie took me into their home and gave me of their hearts in ways that have sustained me ever since. Fred, Henry Ploegstra, George Bennett, Ted Bedford, and Charlie Terry taught me about words and writing and finding ways of getting experience on a page. And they also found me ways of just getting on, of enjoying and creating, of living with loss and working with love.

I can't imagine they knew their influence. Does Dave Thomas know I can't open a window in winter without thinking of his Latin class, and that the shudder I feel is not of cold but of affection and respect? I was a scared boy when I arrived at Exeter, and although I'm not bold enough to say I became a man while there, I left the place armed with knowledge and dreams that I draw upon every hour of every day. The teachers gave me the knowledge and drew out and nourished the dreams, and they sent me off brave enough to be myself. All out of perspective, thank God.

Even as I bring the images back to mind, I can feel them taking me with them, years back. Only now, I am changed. Now when I see George Bennett, six weeks before his death, reading to us, in his offhand way, "I have been one acquainted with the night," I have some better idea what he felt. The phrase has been in my mind, like a seed, ever since he read it. When I read it, sometime near my own death, I think I will hear George Bennett's voice to help tell me the way.

And as I see him and hear his voice, and all the others, so many that as I write this, I feel I want to shake one more hand, give one more embrace before I let go, I know that I will grow old and that I once was young, and that welded into each memory is the seed of a certain growth, a certain bloom, and a certain death.

I was young. And there were Linc and Robbie, the leaders in the class, and my friend Jim and my friend Doug, and Jon a year ahead of me, and we were all young, then, weren't we, and the time is still young in our minds, and K. Don's Mercedes still speeds along, and the blouse still lifts, and *Gatsby* still reads like the book I knew I'd never forget.

It was not a perfect time by any means; the competition could be cruel and the veneer of disdain painful. We were burdened with perhaps too much sophistication too young, too much ambition, too much intellection. But it was a time of passion and of dreams and of discovery, of the self and of others, of Ice Cubes and of philosophies, of details and of ideals.

The memories weave around me as if those years were yesterday or as long ago as Kittredge. I could no more be rid of them than my skin.

I loved those years, and I love them now, not as an ideal but as any real love, full of passionate ambivalence and a hold that won't let go.

A Few Thoughts on Developmental Psychology

by Edward M. Hallowell

Author's note: This essay was written to be read to an audience of parents of elementary and middle school children.

Whatever important there is to learn about developmental psychology you laid down in your own bones once already, when you took that remarkable trek through the first part of life, the part we call childhood.

Remember when you were wearing sneakers and playing stickball and Mike Higgins managed the Red Sox and Don Buddin played short and drug stores were like clubhouses, and in winter there was black ice on ponds and you yearned to have two digits in your age and then to be a teen, and time went so slowly? Remember sleepovers and sneaking around? Remember worrying about getting caught? Remember, back then, before you were a parent, before you could even conceive of becoming a parent, remember how vast and complicated your small neighborhood was, how a walk down a street in the dark could seem like a voyage into outer space? Remember however long it took you to become a grownup, how long it took to get there, and how fast the time has passed since you arrived? Do you remember your appearance back then, how you looked in, say, the second grade? Do you remember the bureau in your bedroom or those things called sneakers? Do you remember basements, or the wide brooms they swept school corridors with and the special smell of the sweeping compound? Do you remember Adlai Stevenson and Ike? Do you remember the first person you were willing to say you actually liked romantically?

I ask you all these questions because I want to put you in touch with your local expert on child development, namely the child within you. And the family you remember growing up with. And the town, and the school. It's all there, only a few dreams and associations away. If you are like most grownups, and I certainly include myself, you don't consult with your local expert nearly often enough. He or she is there, waiting to talk, maybe down by the river or curled up in bed watching a snowstorm, or just kicking a stone along the sidewalk. Now that you've taken on the role of "authority figure" you might enjoy remembering what a great kick it was to misbehave or to bollix up the people in charge. As much as we didn't believe it then, it is a dirty rotten deal having to grow up, and it's good to know that, in fantasy at least, we can go back again.

Another way to go back, of course, is to do what all of you have done: Become a parent. I must confess to you all that although I make my living by working and playing with children and by advising parents and schoolteachers, I am not a parent myself. If God is good to me I will become a daddy in July, at which time I worry I shall have to give up giving advice because I will be bungling things so miserably myself. We'll see. *(Author's note: Since I gave this talk, my wife Sue and I have had two children: Lucy, born in 1989, and Jack, born in 1992. I'm still giving advice, but I'm also frequently seeking it!)*

In getting ready to be a father, I have received an abundance of advice from my friends who have kids, most of it thinly disguised sadistic variations on the theme of "Just you wait." I have also been advising myself, and, most of all, trying to listen ever more closely to kids, and to the kid within me. Kids have become my panel of experts on developmental psychology.

What do they have to say, this child panel of counselors? Well, if you listen to them directly, they say things like, we should have unlimited time for Nintendo, or make allowances triple daily, or do away with schoolteachers completely, or get rid of younger brothers altogether. But if you read between the lines there emerge certain themes, which I have tried to put into words even an adult can understand.

You see, we're just kids, they say. If you get nothing else across to those grownups, get that across. We're just kids, and we don't want to get cheated out of having the chance to be kids.

OK, I say. But these parents want me to tell them about the developmental tasks kids face, particularly kids in kindergarten through grade five.

Now I have to spend some time explaining to them that a developmental task is not a fancy way of saying doing the dishes and cleaning your room and doing homework and being nice to your sister but that it means, well, sort of like what you go through or what you get used to before you get used to something else. Like if you suddenly get a baby sister, what you go through to get used to her before they spring another on you, or what you have to go through to get used to school or what you have to go through before you get a room of your own or even fun things like skiing and dancing and things that have to do with sex.

Well, after some deliberation – and the way this panel deliberates could probably teach a thing or two to General Motors – the panel thinks it is pretty clear that the main developmental tasks of this period of life are leaving home, going to school, making friends, and finding out that your parents aren't perfect, which, they add, it's a good thing you weren't told in the first place because you don't win many fights in first grade by saying, "I come from a very imperfect set of parents."

That's the main stuff, they say. Leaving home, making friends, finding new heroes beyond Mom and Dad. Learning how to get along with other people, living under a non-home-rule system of justice, learning about competition. How come one person has to have more good stuff than another person, be smarter, be prettier, be more popular? Grownups probably don't have to worry about these kinds of things, the panel says, but we sure do. Grownups probably don't have to worry about envy and jealousy and clubs and being picked or being excluded. Boy, it must be fun to be a grownup and have cars and all the TV you want, and you don't get grades. How come there's such a thing as stupid, and how come it matters if you can spell, and how come people can say mean things and nobody does anything about it, and what's the deal with this Santa Claus routine anyway? Why don't they do it the other way around and tell you there isn't a Santa Claus and then let you discover that there really is? But one thing is for sure. It's friends that count. But what if nobody likes you? And what do you have to do to be liked? Some Dads say if you have enough money you never have to worry about being liked. Is that true? Who invented money anyway? Why don't we all just share everything? Except with my little brother. Sometimes moms and dads say wouldn't it be nice just to be a kid again. Boy, they don't know what we're up against. All these developmental tasks.

We've mentioned the main ones. And then there are other things that come under the heading of a sort of 007 license-to-kill kind of intellectual curiosity where it is OK to answer every statement with, "Why?" until someone threatens to knock your block off, at which point it is best to remember they are only imperfect parental units.

Also, there is a lot of other stuff, like learning how to do new things, and think new things, and think those new things in new ways. One of the panel remembers crying one morning at the airport when she was very little as she watched her grandmother take off in an airplane. As the plane climbed higher and higher into the sky, it got littler and littler until finally it disappeared. The little girl reasoned that her grandmother had shrunk as the plane had shrunk and disappeared into nothingness, and it had made her cry very hard. As she got older she found new ways of understanding this phenomenon and many others as well. She learned abstract reasoning, which added some magic to her life, and she came up against reality-testing, which took away some other magic. She said, "If the clouds from inside a plane look like pillows, but then the plane descends through the clouds I guess that means you can only lie on the clouds in your imagination, which the older I get seems to be about the only place you can do an awful lot of things."

And then the panel talked about getting bigger and all the stuff that comes with that. Which reminded them of a point they wanted me to be sure to make. In adult terms, it is that development occurs on a continuum, not in discreet packages. Which means that on your seventh birthday you don't wake up a different person than you were the night before. So you can't take a third grader and say, "Look, you're in the third grade now," as if that would awaken some sleeping neuronal circuit and, presto, the ability to speak French or make breakfast would appear. Development is like the change of seasons; there is a noticeable difference, but it doesn't happen on a specified day.

The panel also thought you'd be surprised to know that they want you to maintain law and order. They're not necessarily in favor of spanking or harsh punishments, but they do have an acute sense of justice, and they know they aren't able to enforce all the rules by themselves. Plus which, it's only if you adults are in charge that they get to have the fun of trying to outfox you. Please protect us, they said, from the scary situation where the parents look to the kids to run the show. Also, please don't ask us to make decisions we shouldn't have to make, like whether we love Mom or Dad better, or whether we should go on to the next grade or not, and please don't ask us to fix things we don't know how to fix, like Mom's depression or Dad's drinking problem or the threat of nuclear war.

While we're on nuclear war, they wanted me to mention that you have an awful lot of committees and programs and stuff like that that have to do with grownup-sounding topics like war and starvation and sex and drugs and pollution and a lot of other things that are really important and everybody should be up on, but why not have some committees on allowances and the candy shortage and the question of how to deal with your mom when she shows up at school?

Finally the panel wanted me to say something they couldn't say because they hadn't grown up yet, and so they couldn't know they would want to say it. It is to remind you that childhood nurtures dreams. Particularly during that phase of childhood that begins with going off to school and ends at the start of adolescence, we build and solidify the reservoirs of play and imagination and affiliation that will feed us for the rest of our lives.

When we look back to our school-age days we usually look back and find a self we really like and trust, a set of friends we really miss and love, a special playtime place that has all the crayons and dolls and beat-up baseballs and magic passwords we could really use right now, and we usually find a pet we loved and cried over when it died, and an old man or woman down the block we used to sneak in and drink coffee with and listen to stories, and we usually find a few horrifying memories made all the more horrifying because they mark our first encounter with what is wrong and unfair and unjust, and we find our mom and our dad before they got sick or whatever, and our schoolteachers, and we find those mementoes of an innocent time that could fill a gallery, an old bike with its squeaky horn, frayed shoelaces, ticket stubs from the bleachers, the program from the first time we saw *The Nutcracker*, the carrot we stuck in our first snowman, and the images continue to cascade down around us if we let them, until we are somewhat protected from the concerns and preoccupations of adulthood and we feel in our hearts the hope and excitement we knew from back then.

This is the message of developmental psychology I would like to leave you with: It is never developmentally necessary for the child within you to die, nor for you to kill it within your children. True, we must give up a great deal as we leave the school years behind, but we do not need to give up the best of it – the primacy of friendship, the insistence on justice, the search for heroes, and the love of adventure and romance.

We build upon the best of ourselves by preserving what we lose.

Adolescence Is Hard Work

by Michael G. Thompson

Adolescence is hard developmental work. In our culture, at this time in history, with all that we must teach children to prepare them to be competent adults in a technologically complex society, adolescence has become an extended developmental trial. Though I think life in general is difficult and involves a lot of suffering – and a lot of happiness and joy, I might add – adolescence is a particularly difficult time of life. There are five tasks that all adolescents must come to grips with and at least partially complete in order to become young adults. The tasks are: 1) adapting to puberty; 2) separating from parents; 3) finding new friends and intimates; 4) integrating lust and intimacy; and 5) forming identity and values. These tasks cannot be avoided; they cannot be gotten through quickly. There are no shortcuts. Completing the five developmental tasks is hard, hard work.

For many years I have been polling middle-aged adults and asking them whether they worried about aging and if so whether they would voluntarily choose to return to an earlier age in life. I then offer them the choice of going back to age thirteen, or sixteen, or nineteen, or twenty-one. Only a tiny minority is theoretically willing to go all the way back to thirteen. The majority doesn't want to go back any earlier than nineteen. Why is that? In part, it is a trick. We are all so proud of our development, we don't want to give up any of it. If you asked a group of ten-year-olds whether they would be seven again, they would naturally answer, "Seven!... Yuck!...They are so retarded!" Ten-year-olds don't believe they got to be ten just because they've been alive for ten years. Not at all! They are ten because they grew themselves up to be ten.

We all feel like that; our age is our personal achievement, our wisdom is hard won.

At the same time, people are willing to go back to nineteen, but not to thirteen. What does that tell us about adolescence? I think what it says is that the memories people have of early and middle adolescence are often extremely painful. The pace of change in adolescence is so rapid that it is all that an adolescent can do to keep up with herself or himself. How would you like, over the course of the next five years, to grow thirty to fifty percent larger than you are now? How would you like to have your body change radically in ways that you cannot predict, and that may make you look very different from all of your friends, at least for a period of time? How would you like to become (if you are not already) touchy, extremely self-conscious, moody, and depressed? How would you like to have to leave the most important loved people in your life, and suddenly have radically different feelings about them? How would you like to suddenly become extremely self-conscious about yourself and wonder all the time whether you will measure up in the world? How would you like to have to develop a whole new philosophy of living, one which differs from your family's and even those of your friends? And how would you like to have to do that in five years? That is an offer that any sane person would refuse, only no one can. Because it just happens to you in adolescence, whether you want it to or not.

The first task of adolescence starts for girls before age eleven, and for boys between twelve and thirteen. It is begun by the series of complex hormonal and body changes that we call puberty. Now everyone expects puberty to happen, and everyone knows it is normal, but for a moment step back and think about what an assault on the psyche puberty is. A child has a body that is more or less the same from the end of toddlerhood until the age of ten or twelve, approximately six years. During that time growth is steady and incremental and in a sense invisible to the child, expect when the apocryphal aunt comes in from out of town and makes a fuss over the child, saying, "Oh, how you've grown." Such attentions make the child uncomfortable, somehow implying that he or she is out of control. Children want to be seen to be in charge of themselves.

Suddenly, puberty hits, and you are transformed. Some parts of the body begin to grow more quickly than others: the hands, nose, feet, and jaw. Then of course there is the development of breasts or penis growth and the appearance of body hair. Beautiful children can suddenly look homely and awkward. Not many people remember with fondness the way they looked at thirteen.

Along with the body changes come changes in skin appearance; many young adolescents develop pimples. Young adolescents can spend whole days focused on their faces and be consumed by the belief that everyone is looking at them because of the zit on their nose. There is no way to overestimate the extreme self-consciousness of adolescence. Adolescents are egocentric in their thinking and behavior, beginning with the intense preoccupation with one's own body and looks. Mothers of sloppy nine-year-old boys who never want to bathe or comb their hair often pray for the onset of adolescence. When it does arrive they are soon bored by their child's self-absorption with appearance.

Naturally, the first thing you do when your body starts to change is to turn around and start comparing yourself to other kids. While there is comparison and competition between kids at younger ages, it is never so focused on physical growth as it is in early adolescence. It is not a fair competition; puberty hits some kids earlier than others. At age thirteen, three girls can have such different rates of development that one still looks like a ten-year-old, one is average for thirteen, and one is as developed as a sixteen-year-old.

These differential growth rates have a profound social impact. Adults tend to smile when they see two children in seventh grade who are a "Mutt and Jeff" combination in height; however, it was not a smiling matter for those same adults when they were children. Most adults can remember by name or by face the first-maturing child in their fifth or sixth grade classroom. Many can remember the latest-maturing adolescent in their high school class. What may not have been so evident is the pain that such children can be in.

A few years ago I was referred a tenth-grade boy who was severely depressed. He had been one of the social leaders in his middle school, but had failed to begin puberty and came from a family of short stature to begin with. By the middle of tenth grade he still looked like a sixth-grader. When he had gone on to high school, his friends, who were interested in meeting girls, had dropped him as a social friend. No high schooler wanted to be hanging out with a boy who looked that young. An enterprising wrestling coach saved the young man's freshman year by convincing the boy to wrestle at the lightest weight during ninth grade; however, in tenth grade the boy wouldn't return to the team. He was too embarrassed to shower in the locker room. With respect to puberty, children who are too far out in front of the mainstream group and children who are too far behind are psychologically at risk.

Even normally developing children worry a great deal about the process. Many are focused on breast size, penis size, or when they are going to get their period. Some women are so anxious about their first period that as adults they have no memory of the event itself, described as "menarche amnesia." Boys begin telling anxious jokes about penis size at this age, and this trend continues in men until death.

Additionally, there is the upsurge in sexual feelings that comes with puberty. Body arousal, strange and new feelings toward the opposite sex or toward the same sex, often experienced as sudden shyness and awkwardness, and finally the development of the beginnings of a conscious fantasy life, all dominate the internal experience of early adolescents. The comedian Robert Klein says that when he was thirteen he used to get an erection when he saw a bus. Indeed, both boys and girls experience their sexual feelings as sudden, out of control and embarrassing. The feelings are often so surprising and intense that a child feels suddenly transparent.

The development of a fantasy life that is explicitly sexual is a natural phenomenon that fills many children with guilt and embarrassment. For boys, fantasy plays an important role in masturbation. In girls, some of whom masturbate and some of whom don't, fantasy is always a part of their lives. Group discussions among children define what is sexual and what is not; here significant gender differences manifest themselves. Boys teach each other that what is sexual is the graphic, the pornographic, and the concept of winning – "first base, second base, and home runs." Girls teach each other that what is sexual is romantic and relationship-based, but there are detailed conversations about boys' bodies and sexuality as well. The differences in socialization in early adolescence make for difficulties later in life. What is clear is that there are no "sweet young things" – at least on a fantasy level – among boys and girls.

All of the things I have discussed so far – body changes, secondary sexual characteristics, self-consciousness, sexual feelings, and fantasy – lead to changes in relationships between children and parents, because suddenly there is a natural and inevitable wish for privacy from parents. This happens in all families, no matter how liberal or strict, or how much communication there is between children and parents. It is, I believe, a natural phenomenon that occurs for both evolutionary and individual psychological reasons.

Thus begins the second major task of adolescence: separating from parents. Transforming the relationship with parents is perhaps a better way to describe what actually occurs; however, the psychological impact is of a separation. Sexuality is not the only motor of change. Perhaps the central moving force in redefining parent-child relationships is size. There is a series of moments, which I will describe as if it were one single moment, during which a child sees herself or himself through new, "big" eyes. For example, there may be an argument between mother and daughter in which the mother is strenuously lecturing the daughter. All of a sudden, the daughter realizes that she is looking directly into her mother's eyes, and she thinks, "Why is this woman talking to me this way? She is no bigger than me. She is big, but so am I! She has no right to treat me like a little kid."

The child's wish to be treated as "big" is a significant shift in the parent-child relationship; the parents' authority is called into question in an entirely new way. What it means is that children begin to distance themselves from their parents and may begin to dislike their dependence.

The change is a radical one in a relationship that has been intensely close and loving for eleven or twelve years. All children, even children with not-so-great parents, love their parents. With very rare exceptions, children under the age of ten are among the most loyal people on earth. What every young child wants is to have two parents, to have them be perfect, and to grow up to be like them.

Young children idealize their parents and try to prop them up if they are obviously flawed, so that they can continue to idealize them. Parents also idealize their children, imagining them as full of limitless potential; they have dreams for their children.

As the child begins to psychologically separate from the parents, the parents may feel rejected and disappointed. They suddenly realize that their children are not going to be exactly like them, are not going to fulfill their dreams. And the children, who had heretofore worshipped their parents, suddenly begin finding fault with them. As one lovely seventh grader said to me, "I used to think my parents were perfect, and then I began to see little faults in them, and even though I didn't want it to happen, the faults kind of piled up." Suddenly parents don't look so great any more; they can be a source of embarrassment to their children. Seeing your parents' flaws, and feeling as unconfident and self-conscious as you feel between eleven and fifteen, children begin to take a critical stance toward their parents.

As a result of feeling rejected and criticized, parents begin to regard their children in a different light. In the parents' eyes, the child has become touchy, irrational, and untrustworthy. Parents begin to talk to their friends about their children in a way they never did before, sometimes right in front of their children. Children who have enjoyed a special relationship with one or the other parent may suddenly feel that their parents are allied against them. Parents may not respect adolescent pursuits and are inclined to extrapolate from a present preoccupying interest to a catastrophic, life-long character flaw. The "Doonesbury" cartoon character Zonker used to complain that his father was unappreciative of his highly disciplined approach to competitive tanning. Indeed, most parents would have doubts about such an enterprise. What is different about parents of early and middle adolescents is that they, unlike parents of younger children, are examining their children's behavior for signs of future outcome. The helplessness that surrounds parents as their adolescents start to separate makes them want to control what cannot be controlled and to predict the unpredictable, i.e., how their child is going to turn out.

Most parents find a graceful way to create space in the family for the emerging adolescent's autonomy and independence. They go through a period of adjustment which becomes resolved into an acceptance of their child's emergent adult status. However, parents and their adolescent children can become locked into situations of mutual distrust and anger. Much of this anger is a psychological defense against sadness: the sadness of loss.

Psychoanalytic writers have long believed that adolescence is a period of mourning for both children and parents, with each side giving up the child-parent relationship and transforming it into a more complex adult relationship.

Families who cannot make the transformation often break down into war. A particularly rigid parent or a particularly challenging child can inflame the other party. D.W. Winnicott, the English psychoanalyst, wrote that some adolescents do not see any way to grow up except over their parents' dead bodies. The proportion of adolescents who feel that way is small, but it is just such an adolescent that parents fear.

In their own grief and confusion, parents can sometimes overestimate their children's power. They forget that adolescents are usually scared underneath, and that the sullen face they are facing is often hiding fear and uncertainty. Nevertheless, adults can be fooled by the sullen face and often seriously provoked by it.

This can lead, in the most extreme cases, to what I call the paradox of power. Both adolescent and parent feel small in relation to the other, and each reacts as if the other were much larger and more powerful. Each feels disempowered in the presence of the other because the child always has a mental image of the parent of early childhood, who was much bigger and more powerful, and the parent remembers the small, compliant child who has suddenly become so large and impossible. The child has become a monster.

Occasionally, this dynamic can operate between teachers and students as well, particularly between older high school students and young teachers. In a typical confrontation, the teacher feels helpless and small; she may say, "He took over my class; I couldn't get anything done!" But the student reports, "She was humiliating me in front of everyone. I had no choice but to leave the room."

Let me emphasize that most families handle the separation of children from the family with considerable grace and flexibility. Similarly, most schools and teachers handle the growing independence of children with style and understanding. However, everyone suffers from the sadness of the process. The growing up and departure of a child from a family can feel like the end of a love relationship. Both parties can come to feel dreadfully sad and abandoned. Of course, it is not the end of the relationship at all. It is the transformation of a relationship, but it evokes the sad and angry feelings that a true separation does.

All of this sadness is no one's fault, just the natural and stressful process of growth. I believe that it is a psychological hardship for many people to achieve the level of independence our culture requires, and that much of our adolescence is spent preparing for that hardship. In this culture we equate ' independence" with true mental health. There is a strong argument to be made that our culture holds out an impossible ideal of self-sufficiency and that it causes much suffering among children and parents as they try to achieve the ideal level of separation from one another. I believe that the final goal is, in the Scottish psychoanalyst's Fairbairn's phrase, "mature interdependence." It takes adolescents a certain amount of time to be able to acknowledge their continuing need for their parents when they are trying to separate themselves out and become their own person.

What does a child do with the loneliness that comes from separating from parents and family? The child must find friends and intimates outside the family. These relationships are different from earlier play relationships with friends at school or from the neighborhood. These new friends, especially the "number one friend," become trusted confidantes to whom an adolescent child can tell her secrets. The American psychiatrist Harry Stack Sullivan called this phase of friendship the "chumship" stage. It is a quaint term; however, it captures the intensity of the period. Most adults can remember having a very important, number one friend during the period of sixth grade to eighth grade. What differentiates these special early adolescent friendships from the friendships of elementary school relationships is that the friends are entrusted with secrets about each other's families. Gone is the loyalty of the young child; adolescents tell each other about the pain in their families. Psychological research demonstrates that to have such friends and to talk to them in intimate ways is healthy and helpful. To be unable to form such friendships can mean a child is condemned to loneliness in adolescence.

Unfortunately, many children lose confidence in early adolescence – or had too little confidence to begin with. This lack of confidence can inhibit their ability to make friends. Their self-consciousness and insecurity can make may them chronically uncomfortable in groups, even when they have apparently been accepted. Adolescents are terribly aware of who is popular and why, of dress, of looks, grades, money, status, etc. I remember consulting to a wealthy private school where a girl had been terribly teased when it was discovered that she was wearing clothes from Sears, which was considered low-class by the social trendsetters. The point is, the girls were so insecure and competitive that they were checking the labels on each others' clothes for clues as to who was truly "in" and who was not.

The sense of being on the margin, not truly accepted, not glamorous or cool, is one of the most common feelings of adolescence. Thankfully, it diminishes as you grow into adulthood. It has to be lived through time and time again until you discover you can live through both the irrational feelings of being "out of it" and the actual reality of being on the margin, when it does occur.

The power of the group is a mixed blessing. It is the best cure for adolescent loneliness and depression (I rejoice when a depressed adolescent becomes involved in a team sport – it is the beginning of health). However, group values are powerful, and they can sometimes require an adolescents to go along with something that makes them uncomfortable or directly conflicts with their personal and family values. To go against the group is to risk loneliness, to go along at certain times is to risk being stampeded into doing something unfortunate. The majority of public vandalism in the United States is done by thirteen- to sixteen-year-old boys in groups. Adolescent group judgment can be so bad that it appears that the "group IQ" is twenty points lower than that of the least bright member of the group. When group values require kids to actually hurt or reject parents, it can make a child feel intensely guilty. Adolescents spend a lot of time trying to resolve conflicts between their love for their parents and their loyalty to the group. I once interviewed an eighth grade class and asked them what I could say to their parents, whom I was going to address that evening. The class, led by three boys in the back who introduced themselves as "deadheads," said, "Tell our parents to get off our backs!" Then one boy grumbled, "We hate our parents," and others chimed in. Finally, one girl raised her hand and whispered, "I still love my parents." I told her I thought most kids in the class did, but that the things kids talked about in public were their criticisms of their parents.

Most adolescents resolve the group-parent conflict by leading a double life: acting one way in front of parents and other adults and acting another with the group. Some of what kids do with the group is stuff their parents wouldn't approve of – sex, drugs, and rock and roll. But at home most kids behave and want to be loved and respected by their parents. If the discrepancy between the two lives is not too great, a double life can be a healthy solution for the family-group loyalty conflict.

The fourth developmental task of adolescence is the integration of lust and intimacy. I am indebted to Harry Stack Sullivan for these terms. Sullivan, a gifted adolescent therapist, pointed out that the needs for sexual fulfillment are some times highly separate from intimacy needs and at others highly related. Zella Luria, a professor of psychology at Tufts University, says that for the most part boys in adolescence are satisfied with masturbation and cars; they don't yet need the intimate romantic relationships with girls that girls' emotional training leads them to seek.

There is a clear difference between sexual needs and intimacy needs in early adolescence, yet these become confused in group life. An adolescent must ask himself or herself, "Am I attracted to this person because they are sexy or because I want them as a friend?" There is no ready answer to the question; the novel feelings of adolescence do not come with labels and a guidebook. What most adolescents try to do initially is divide the other gender into two different types: the sexy and the friendly. Freud called the male phenomenon of dividing all women into two camps the "Madonna-whore" complex. When I was in high school the boys would talk about "nice" girls and "good" girls, but such splitting is not just a male tendency. In any contemporary movie of teen-age life, the heroine is always faced with a choice of two possible love interests: one a clean-cut, responsible, president-of-the-student-council type who loves her but whom she regards as "being like a brother," the other a black-leather-jacketed, motor-cycle-riding guy who drives her parents crazy but whom she regards as very sexy. The resolution of such movies is always the integration of the two visions. The student council president becomes heroic and sexy, or the outlaw becomes domesticated and safe.

Every adolescent must decide whether what is operating inside himself or herself are lustful impulses or intimacy needs or both. There is no escaping the problem. And for those boys and girls who are going to be gay the problem is even more complex. They have to discover that their sexual orientation is different from the majority's, they have to try to make their peace with it, and then they have to find other adolescents with similar orientations. It can be an extremely painful and risky psychological journey for gay adolescents. Some adolescents – both straight and gay – sensibly wait to begin sexual behavior; others experiment from early on. When this issue is resolved, an adolescent or young adult is able to combine both passion and intimacy in a relationship.

The so-called sexual revolution in the United States really happened. The average age of first intercourse in this country has dropped by more than two years in the last twenty-five years. The age of first intercourse is now in the middle of the sixteenth year. Obviously, because that is an average, it means that many adolescents have become sexually active before that age. The astronomically high rates of teen-age pregnancy, as well as the threat of AIDS, make one wish that adolescents were more cautious, but they are not. Studies of inner-city adolescents reveal that the average sexually active sixteen-year-old may have had ten partners. Social psychological studies of adolescent sexuality suggest that teens no longer believe that adults have the right to tell them what or what not to do with their bodies. Peer culture creates sexual meaning in young adolescents, teaching boys and girls what they should consider sexy, and the group dictates the pace of sexual experimentation. Adults are more or less irrelevant to the process. What parents and other caretakers try to do is create a moral and non-exploitative atmosphere in which adolescents can safely find their way toward an integration of lust and intimacy, and then hope for the best.

The fifth and last task of adolescence is that of forming an identity and developing a set of values. There is great variation among adolescents with respect to how completely they undertake a reassessment of their lives and their values. The developmental event that sets the process off is the transition, described by Jean Piaget in his stage theory of cognitive development, from concrete operational thinking to formal operation thinking. This advance is an explosion in the mind. The child is freed from the concrete and the here and now; the adolescent becomes able to imagine all of the possibilities in a situation. He or she becomes – cognitively speaking – a true scientist. The implications of this change for intellectual development are immense, and teachers know it. In junior high they begin to introduce curricula which involve a great deal more experimentation, generating alternative hypotheses, and imagining oneself in unfamiliar situations, because many children are now cognitively able to master such tasks. In the end, not all adolescents become formal operational thinkers; many will remain concrete thinkers, and the intellectual gap between the two groups will widen during the adolescent years.

What is the emotional impact of these cognitive changes? The adolescent suddenly realizes that life is an "experiment" that is in her or his own hands. He or she could have been a different person, born to different parents who believed different things. No parental value is fixed and immutable; there are no absolutes. This is traditionally the time when children call their parents' most cherished values into question or go against them in a reactive way. Adolescents from devout homes often start to question or even reject their parents' religious beliefs. Many adolescents consciously try to fashion a life different from their parents' values, like Cher's daughter in the movie *Mermaids* who reacts to her mother's outrageous and promiscuous behavior by setting up an altar in her room and praying to the Virgin Mary every day.

Adolescents become morbid and dwell on their own deaths. I once gave out a questionnaire at a boarding school, asking whether the students had ever thought of suicide. Forty-five percent responded that they had. I do not believe that forty-five percent had been suicidal; my understanding is that when kids feel that their lives are in their hands, they also feel death is in their hands. Paradoxically, adolescents also act as if they were immortal and – to their parents' horror – as if they are capable of surviving extraordinary risks. That exciting and reckless state of denial alternates with a lonely contemplation of death, the limitations of one's abilities and family. An adolescent may wish he or she had been born in a more idealistic time. Parents tell their children that things were rougher when they were children and that they were better prepared for life than they now observe their own children to be, and often children believe this timeworn parental motivation technique. Kids really wonder, "Do I have it? Am I spoiled? How can I ever be as hardworking or successful as my parents when I can hardly get myself to sit down and do homework for ten minutes?"

The task of designing a life is now in the adolescent's hands. As exciting as that is at moments, it is also terrifying, because adolescents do not know all that much and are aware – despite their angry denials – of their inadequate life experience. Adolescents worry constantly about whether they will amount to anything. They can feel, with some justice, that their worst life experiences, including psychological or sexual abuse, have left them damaged. The size of the challenges facing them can, at times, make them feel overwhelmed. Adolescents can be episodically moody or depressed in a way that psychologists consider developmentally normal, as long as it is not chronic. Those with the worst life experiences, such as continual school failure or abuse, can become clinically depressed.

An adolescent who is searching for a set of values to guide her, and is simultaneously full of self-doubt, can be caught up in a group that promises personal strength and a comprehensive and righteous vision of the good. Any insecure adolescent is prey for a mass movement or cult. The collective search for values can become a wonderful or a dangerous force, always powerful because it is fueled by the adolescent necessity to find an identity.

Then the adolescent is out in the world. In the slice of society that I serve, adventuring out into the world means going to college. The adolescent has to take everything he or she has ever been or done, put it on a piece of paper and send it away to a bunch of strangers with the implicit question, "Am I worthwhile?" Always there is the possibility of being rejected, and of feeling, however wrongly, that because College A did not accept you, you are not a promising person. The developmental challenge of this stage is truly to leave childhood and to embark upon young adulthood, a task that must be undertaken and mastered whether an adolescent drops out of high school or goes to Yale. No matter how poorly educated or highly prepared, there are some adolescents who do not feel ready to take the risk of growing up. Many enter a period of prolonged adolescence, which can last throughout their twenties. Erik Erikson called this period a "moratorium" in which individuals can resolve their "identity crises" and ultimately find themselves. Some people never find themselves, because doing so involves so much work. As Thomas Szaz says, "People often say that this or that person has not found himself. But the self is not something one finds, it is something one creates."

Adolescence is really a time of creation, creation that takes work. Think of the words that I have used throughout this essay to describe the tasks of adolescence: adapting, separating, finding, integrating, forming...all active verbs describing strenuous psychological work. What emerges at the end of adolescence is a person who knows who she or he is, a person with some sense of place in society and in history, a person with a clear moral code. A late adolescent must be able to make a commitment to friendship and to sexual intimacy, and an equally strong commitment to work. Finally, and above all, a late adolescent must have a solid identity which permits her to accept and love herself: to love that which came from family, friends, and school, and to treasure that which is unique to her.

None of us ever achieves a level of perfect self-acceptance either in adolescence or in adulthood. However, to strive for self-understanding, self-acceptance and self-love is the driving psychological force in all development, and it is what the adolescent must try to do in order to become a full person in adulthood.

From Lost to Found:
Finding the Child's Right Place

by Edward M. Hallowell

Author's note: This essay was originally written for an audience of specialists in school placement, particularly the placement of children who have a hard time fitting in. The "you" addressed in the essay is this audience of school placement experts, but it can include anyone who has wrestled with the question of finding the right place for a child.

Once upon a time there was a good and strong school, attended by good and strong boys and girls, boasting a faculty of good and strong men and women, presided over by a good and strong headmaster, and supported and protected by good and strong parents, alumni, and trustees. Founded long ago and destined to continue well into what the trustees called perpetuity, the school had a name comparable to its values and standards: it was called The Upright School. Since it was founded so very long ago, legend had obscured the origin of its name, but all agreed that, whatever the founding principles of the institution had been, they had all been conceived upright and straight and had remained so through centuries of buffeting by sideways winds. The great threat to Upright had always been, and no one doubt would always be, the forces of sideways thought and behavior, which the school had resisted through the proper management of torque and gravitational temptation.

Over the centuries the Upright School had indeed lived upright, graduating batches of scholars and statesmen every year, each one guaranteed to preserve upright what had been taught and to avoid at all costs any new thought. It was well known that new thoughts came into the world sideways, and, like infants, took time to gain upright stature.

As a measure of their devotion to upright thought and deed, all who attended or taught at Upright remained, while there, erect, that is to say, upright, on their own two feet. Taking the task of education seriously, one simply never sat, nor did one recline or crawl or kneel or, for that matter, cartwheel or supine oneself in any way at all. Running was allowed, of course, as was jogging or brisk walking. Brisk walking, in fact, was the hallmark means of self-transport at Upright. A passerby could not help but notice all the Uprights, as the school people were called, briskly walking about the campus like so many busy couriers. Some classes, even, were taught while at a brisk walk. Beadle

Beemaster, of Classics, particularly favored what he called the Conjugation Cadence produced by brisk walking in cold weather.

One conducted all activities of daily life upright. Rather than eat from a table one ate from a shelf like a mantelpiece that spiraled its way through the great dining hall. One learned to sleep upright in contraptions made of iron bars and leather straps attached to the sleeping room walls. Not only were they great space-savers and character builders, they obviated the need for such indulgences as linen, pillows, and mattresses. Some outsiders wondered how faculty who had been upright at Upright for years could still be mentally competent given the severely compromised circulation to the brain their posture imposed. Little did those outsiders understand that the character one built through maintaining an upright stance more than compensated for any loss of mental functioning.

Indeed, these senior faculty were responsible for teaching the core course at Upright: Upright Thought and Behavior in Everyday Life. Experienced faculty also took on the more challenging courses such as Resisting the Temptation to Lie (Down) and Shunning Innovation: A History of Upright Behavior. Newer faculty had to be responsible for the modern high-tech courses such as How to Swim while Upright and Defining What Is Upright in Zero Gravitational Fields. One year, it may have been last or it may have been this, or it may even be next, the records aren't clear, a new student was admitted to Upright. His name was Peter Pipedream. A seventh grader, he wore a yellow hat and he whistled many tunes. "I have gone to other schools," Peter told his advisor, Mr. Toethemark, "but I had to leave them because I didn't fit in. Do you think I will fit in here?"

"It's all a question of attitude and altitude," replied Mr. Toethemark, who had arrows painted on his trousers pointing up. "If you maintain the proper altitude and hold the proper attitude, you can't go wrong. Or is that if you hold the proper altitude and maintain the proper attitude? I'll have to look that one up," he said, being careful not to look down.

Peter felt puzzled. He looked down at his feet, one of which he tucked behind the other. "Oh, don't look down," gasped Toethemark, cupping Peter's chin in his hand and lifting it up. "Always upright, that's our way," he chimed. Peter scratched his nose. "I speak my mind, and I have too many ideas," he said, reciting what he had been told at other schools.

"I–d–e–a–s?" groaned Toethemark, drawing the word out, letting it wrap around Peter like a rope. "You say you have too many i–d–e–a–s, and you speak your mind, eh? The purpose of an education is to help you curb such dangerous tendencies. We should be up to the task as long as you and your ideas don't go sideways." He gave the sibilance of sideways the emphasis of a full hiss. "If you go sideways, you hit the highways, young man. You might begin by removing that yellow hat. It looks like an outgrowth of sideways philosophy."

Peter blinked. His yellow hat was his lucky charm, given to him by his grandfather, who always had told him to question everybody and everything. He didn't want his hat taken away, so he took it off. He would try his best to fit in.

He went to classes and he listened. He walked as erect as he could and he practiced getting to know all the stairs so he could descend them without looking down. One day, however, he tripped, as he thought there was one more step than there was, and he fell down. A teacher walking by snapped, "Get upright, Peter Pipedream."

"Wouldn't it be easier," Peter pleaded as he stood up, "to look down every now and then?"

The eyes of the teacher narrowed. "Easier? Easier did you say? Young man, you have definite sideways tendencies." The word sideways once again hissed its serpentine way through the man's lips.

Try as he might Peter couldn't stop himself from going sideways. He asked questions in class, he whistled, he laughed, he wore a yellow hat, all evidence, he was told, of sideways tendencies. Try as he might, though, he just didn't understand about sidewaysness. He didn't even really know what it meant. "I don't even know what it means to go sideways," he protested to Toethemark.

"Aha!" snapped Toethemark. "You don't know what it means. In that case, we will send you to a specialist, a Measuring Man."

Peter presented himself to the specialist. The sign on the door read, "Dr. Felix Findfault, Doctor of Angles and Measurements." When Peter went into the office, he found the doctor hanging from a horizontal bar. "Come in, young man," said Findfault. "Join me on this bar."

Findfault interviewed Peter as they both hung upright. Peter felt silly, but he answered as best he could all the same. Findfault asked him about all the measurements, distances, and angles in his life. Then he got off the bar and measured him with an imposing array of instruments. He concluded the session by saying to Peter, "If you're not careful, young man, you may go sideways for the rest of your life. There is a distinct genetic angulation from your grandfather's side. So, straighten up."

Peter, however, continued to tilt. He was called into the office of the Director of Studies, Mr. Tryharder, who reviewed with him the tests Findfault had done. "In the Dullard Normalcy Scale you were thirty-seven degrees off the perpendicular, Mr. Pipedream. What's going on in that head of yours? In the Boringbody Assessment of Uprightness you displayed thirty-seven instances of slant initiative, an appallingly bad score, the sort of score you'd expect from criminals or poets, not a student at Upright. However, on the Upright Quotient, a measure of your innate ability, you scored eighty-nine degrees, thirty-seven minutes, an almost perpendicular, truly gifted score. The top line, my friend, is that if you straighten up you could lead this school, but if you don't..."

At the word don't, Stanley Stretch, Headmaster, strode into the room, his bronze neck collar all aglitter in the noonday sun. "If you don't, Mr. Peter Pipedream, you will be cast out sideways from this school and you will perish in horizontal gloom," Stretch bellowed, his eyeballs looming out of their sockets downward at Peter while his bronzed neck remained perfectly erect. "You don't want that, do you, son?" Stretch whispered, rolling his eyes back into their capacious sockets.

Peter was terrified and trembling, so terrified and trembling that his true nature burst through, and he spoke his mind. "Yes, yes, please, ooh, yes, yes, cast me out into horizontal balloons!"

"GLOOM!" screamed Stretch, not accustomed to being misunderstood.

"Gloom, I'm sorry, sir, quite right, or upright, or whatever, just let me save you the trouble of all the good work you are going to waste on me and please send me out to the world of desks and chairs and beds and sit-down toilets and all the other bad things I'm too rotten to deserve more than."

Had Peter not, at that very moment, been wearing his yellow hat he probably would have been sent flying off the end of Stretch's long boot into the sideways gloom beyond the school, there to live a life of perpetual tilt, but, as it happened, he was wearing his yellow hat, which caught the eye of a passerby, a passerby from the world outside who knew about yellow hats and what it means to be different.

A colossal man, twice the size of Stretch, he lumbered into the headmaster's office and, much to the astonishment of Stretch and Tryharder, picked up Peter and put him under his left arm like a package.

"Who are you?" gasped Tryharder, who had never seen a man so large.

"You've turned the boy sideways," barked Stanley Stretch.

At that, the man extended his right arm, picked Stanley up by his neck collar, and drew his face close to his own. Stanley's feet kicked and squirmed, but his head held still in the strong grip of the very large man. "Let me introduce myself," the man said. "My name is Mansion. I am your imagination. You sent me away many years ago because you were afraid of me. Banishing me, you told me I would perish in the land of horizontal gloom. Instead, look at me. I have grown and grown until I am now twice your size and many times stronger. I wouldn't come back to you if you begged me. The only reason I am here now is that I knew by this boy's hat he was a friend of an old man who helped me when you sent me away."

"Put me down!" sputtered Stretch.

Mansion let him drop like unwanted debris. As Tryharder frantically helped him upright, Mansion left, Peter still under his arm.

Over the next decade Peter lived and studied with Mansion and learned everything he could about everything slanted and straight, reasonable and unreasonable, true and false, upright and sideways, real and imaginary. "Everything real was once imaginary," Mansion often told him. "Believe as hard as you can."

Peter, who was a good believer, soon became a master tradesman at make-believe. He grew big and strong and happy and playful, but there was a sadness in his heart.

One day he said to Mansion, "There is a sadness in my heart."

"I know," said Mansion.

"How do you know I have this sadness?" asked Peter.

"Because, like your grandfather, you feel for those you left behind, even though they would have hurt you."

"I'm going to go back," said Peter.

Peter went back to Upright and gave the school the rest of his life, drawing upon what he learned from Mansion for strength and inspiration. Although he never succeeded in turning the school completely sideways, he did manage to convince the administration of the desirability of sleeping flat, on soft, downy beds, rather than upright in chains, and he did convince them that certain eccentricities could make for a stronger, happier community. In fact, he did so well that by the time he died, a yellow jockey's cap was made part of the school uniform, to be worn on days of celebration and good cheer.

How many of you have known Peter Pipedream or have some part of him in you? How many of you have returned to schools or to working with schools out of a desire to repair some hurt of your own, heal some inner wound, or give others some chance you never had? Or, how many of you knew a Mr. Mansion of imagination who gave you so much you returned to schools to give some back?

The motivation to do the kind of work we are discussing today – finding the right place for the child who doesn't fit – must be special, for the work itself is often risky, not well mapped-out, and full of chances to screw up. There's not a lot of money or glory in it, and on bad days the work is full of angry people: exasperated, up-in-arms teachers; frustrated, hostile parents; impatient, solution-demanding school heads, and hurting, help-rejecting kids.

On those days it is hard to keep in mind that every child is a potential Peter Pipedream. But the work of helping a lost child find the right place to grow, difficult as it is, carries with it the possibility of changing an entire life. So as you turn in circles, looking up for some answer that doesn't come, wondering how in the world you got stuck playing guide when you don't even know the directions yourself, and everyone you ask just talks gobbledygook, take heart. If you persist and grope along and don't give up, you'll find experts you didn't know about who can actually help, schools you've never heard of that are made to order, little tricks your fairy godmother will teach you, and, like as not, with any luck, you'll find a way. And what a pleasure that is, and what a reward.

Let me offer some observations on the process, from lost to found. First of all, let me underscore that finding the right place for the child challenges one's imagination and ingenuity in the extreme. You need to know so much; no one person knows enough. There is no cookbook, no right way. The solutions often begin in a daydream with our saying things to ourselves like, "If only...," or, "I wish...," or, "This may sound off-the-wall but..." Our solutions for these kids often begin in off-the-wall places, in imagination.

In the fable of Peter Pipedream, it may seem that I ducked writing the hardest part of the story – namely, just exactly what did Mr. Mansion do with Peter? After he whisked him away out of Upright, he was still left with a funny-looking kid with a yellow beanie who hadn't fit in at three different schools. It may be fine for the storyteller poetically to slide over the nuts and bolts of how Peter changed, but for those of us who live in real life rather than fairy tales the nuts and bolts are what matter most.

I left them out on purpose. There is no one set of nuts and bolts that works. I meant to imply that in the hands of Mr. Mansion, in the hands of imagination, the solution evolves naturally and organically. But you must not, as you encounter your Peter Pipedreams, automatically reach for the child-owner's manual and furiously flip through pages for a diagram that isn't there or a set of instructions you will not find. Rather, you must be prepared to do the most natural thing in the world: Think for yourself. Let your mind roam. Let yourself empathize with young Peter, put yourself in his shoes and then think, What do

I need in order to fit in?

The answers to the question of what the Peter Pipedreams need can vary as much as the kids themselves. But to find workable solutions you need to be able to engage with the kids as they really are, not as you wish they were. Get in touch with the part of you that didn't fit, be guided by the part of you that doesn't fit yet, and suspend your disapproval for a little while.

Beware of Felix Findfaults. There is something about children who are different, and adults who are different, too, that activates the critic in us all. "I don't know what it is about Sammy. He's just so weird." Or, "Why does Jane talk with that accent? Doesn't she know how odd it is?" Or, "Can you believe the clothes she wears? Doesn't she know how it makes her stand out?" This carping tendency, taken one or two levels of sophistication higher, often comprises the psychological reports we read on many children or the so-called "evaluations" that are done in a few hours in some clinic. I am not dismissing all psychological reports. Far from it. The good, thoughtful ones, performed by clinicians who know their limits, can illuminate dark corners remarkably well. But the careless reports, not informed by a close knowledge of the child, can amount to little more than a high-sounding, jargon-laden indictment, full of angles and measurements that, in the manner of Felix Findfault, miss the essence of the child altogether.

There are Felix Findfaults everywhere, not only in my profession, but all over the place. Heaven knows they are among teachers, school administrators, and school boards, but they are also on every Main Street and in every P.T.A. If we can only condemn these children roundly enough and with the right rhetorical flourish, they seem to say, then we need not feel guilty when we spurn them or avoid them or deny them the resources they need or scapegoat them, or taunt them, or, ultimately, break them. If the truth be told, Felix Findfault, Doctor of Angles and Measurements, lives a little bit in us all. An important step in working with children who don't fit in is controlling the Felix Findfault within.

A child hurts when he or she doesn't fit. While Upright is a mythical school, for kids who don't fit in every school feels like Upright. Our starting point in helping these kids is to know the pain they feel and to anticipate the anger, frustration, and even fear they can engender in others.

I once treated a little boy, let's call him Leonard, who, by the time he was twelve had seen more than many people do in a lifetime. He had lived on four continents, experienced his father's death and his stepfather's disappearance, attended concerts with countesses, and learned history at the base of the pyramids. He would come to my office twice a week and carry on fascinating conversations about his travels and music and the differences between schools here and abroad. He would also tell me, with some effort, about the fights he got into at school, the bad names the other kids made up for him, and the nightmares he had at night of being chased. Leonard was a really nice kid. His problem was that he'd never had the chance to begin to fit in anywhere. The other kids at school disliked him because his worldliness posed a threat to them, and no one had taught Leonard how not to be too worldly around his peers.

I once treated a little girl, let's call her Sarah, who couldn't pay attention in class. Although her daydreaming took her to all kinds of magical places, seldom did it take her to the classroom. This was particularly galling to her teachers because she had a measured IQ of 154. Sarah was in a school for gifted children where teachers watched over each student like master chefs over special bubbling pots. When Sarah didn't respond to all the attention and special instruction she received, when instead she stared away blankly or worse, responded to questions with preposterous non sequiturs that only proved she hadn't been listening, teachers felt hurt and inadequate, and as they felt hurt and inadequate, they became angry, and as they became angry they let Sarah know she was not a good girl, that indeed she had tendencies toward what at Upright would have been called sideways behavior. Because her IQ was so high, no one considered that Sarah could have any sort of learning problem.

It was not until we were able to diagnose that Sarah had a neurological problem, namely Attention Deficit Disorder, that she got the treatment she needed and began to find a comfortable place for herself at school.

Or I think of another boy, Eugene, a tenth grader who wore a three-piece suit to his public high school every day and talked to his friends about the virtue of being an English gentleman. Since he was, as he put it, a pretty fair pugilist, he was able to get through school without being killed, but never was he accepted.

He would come to my office, remove his jacket, carefully fold it and lay it on the couch, then sit down and say to me, "I don't understand why the boys are so cruel."

"Because you wear a three-piece suit, Eugene, and you talk about being an English gentleman," I would say.

"And what's the matter with that?" he would respond. "One could do a lot worse than read Trollope to stay out of trouble."

Now what do we say to Eugene? Wise up, wear jeans? Or do we acknowledge and protect his individuality by trying to find or create an environment where he can fit in?

If we agree that not all children who are different should have their differentness trained, beaten, or psychotherapized out of them, then our question becomes how best to help these kids live with who they are.

To be who you are: That is hard. Alice Miller has written poignantly about how we adults train our children, especially our brightest, most sensitive children, to be adult-pleasers, thus hiding who they truly are from the world and even from themselves, often forever. It can be at great emotional cost that children do what we want them to. If we could only learn to celebrate what is different and, instead of being threatened by it, to take delight in what is new, if we could learn to join in rather than jeer when we feel uncertain, and if we could let ourselves play at least once a day, then maybe we could show our children that it is OK to be real.

Instead, too often, we urge them to be false. We want them to do what we want. Indeed, even when they are doing what we don't want them to, sometimes they are doing what we want. Let me explain with an example.

C.J. was a tough guy, an eleventh grader at a small New England boarding school, let's call it Foxfield. C.J. came from a family of Slavic extraction who lived on the wrong side of the tracks in Pittsburgh. C.J. was very smart. On scholarship at Foxfield, he played football hard and studied hard and did both very well. However, after he'd been at school a few months he began to get into trouble mainly having to do with beating up on certain students from very well-to-do families. On the face of it, it looked as if C.J. was simply taking out his envy and resentment of the rich by beating up their snotty kids. But as I got to know C.J. I discovered that he didn't hate the rich particularly much nor did he even dislike the kids he was beating up on. What he did feel was a tremendous need for a father figure, having lost his own when he was four. He found one at Foxfield in Blake Ransil, his dorm master, football coach, and math teacher. He and Blake quickly became close, C.J. staying up late into the night in Blake's apartment talking about football, school, and life. C.J. idolized Blake as the father he'd never had.

What C.J. didn't know about Blake, Blake barely knew about himself. After seventeen years of teaching, coaching, and raising the children of the rich, Blake had come to hate them and their parents. Year after year, they took all he had to give and they moved on, and they forgot him, never even saying thank you. So, without really meaning to, Blake subtly but deftly encouraged his surrogate son, C.J., to beat the crap out of all the privileged young men at Foxfield. C.J. had to be held responsible, but he was really only doing his coach's bidding.

If we look closely at the stories of children who don't fit in, we often find a Blake Ransil, a figure whom the child is trying to please through his or her puzzling behavior. While neither Ransil nor the child is consciously aware of what is going on, the child unconsciously is acting out the wishes of the adult figure. The adult figure may be a parent or teacher or sometimes a group of adults representing some great cause, such as universal thinness, for which the child is ready to sacrifice all.

If I sound as if I have been urging tolerance, imagination, and perspective in dealing with these children, well, I have. But I don't mean to imply that all these kids are innocent victims. Some are bullies, victimizing others. Some are leaders who in their chic nonconformity create factions and gangs that can endanger a school community. More and more we are seeing children from families whose parents are often absent, who have no idea how to control themselves, and so are perpetually out of control, waiting for someone to take over. The imaginative solution for some of these kids is to tell them to shut up. Some of these kids you need to hit with a two-by-four just to get their attention.

Sometimes the reverse is true. Sometimes these kids need to hit you with a two-by-four to get your attention. I think of Maria, a tenth grader at a private day school in the Boston area. Maria was a friend to everyone in her class and good company for most of her teachers as well. Generous to a fault, she never seemed to be too hurried to find time to talk or too busy to notice when someone else looked sad. Warm-hearted and generous, she was the student who always looked out for the one who was left out, or she was the one to see to it that a card got sent to the kid who'd been sick, or she was the one who thought to ask after a newcomer to the school who was having trouble. Maria brought warmth to the school every day and her dark brown eyes glowed behind her soft and gentle smile.

When she stopped smiling, people didn't want to notice. When she began to hint things weren't going well for her, people thought they didn't hear her right, and they went on talking about themselves as Maria nodded. When she began to be absent frequently people just assumed someone else would be looking in to see if everything was all right. It wasn't until Maria collapsed from exhaustion in the school cafeteria that people found out Maria had been depressed and feeling overwhelmed by school and family pressures for months. Maria's radiance and warmth had been covering the fact that she had been academically overmatched by the school ever since she got there. People thought of her as so happy they weren't prepared to see her pain. It is good to remember that most of the time these kids are trying to tell us something if we can just listen.

There are many reasons not to fit in. A physical problem, such as an undiagnosed hearing impairment, can cast a child out of the mainstream and lead to a host of abuses. Learning disabilities or attention deficit disorder can dramatically disrupt a child's life and if not properly diagnosed and treated can permanently disable not only the child but the family as well. The all-encompassing "problems at home" can preoccupy a child in the extreme. Simply the genetic luck of the draw can create a child who doesn't step to the same beat as the others.

There are various creative solutions to the problem posed by the child who isn't fitting in. There are various alternative placements that can help a child find a way. But I would like to end by focusing not on where these children might be sent, but on what happens when they get there.

Suppose for a moment there were no alternative placements. Suppose for a moment that for every kid you had your school was it. There were no hospitals, no special schools, no tutoring camps, no other places for any of your students. Any alternative had to be of your own invention, as if you were the only alternative place. As bleak as the situation would be, I would like to suggest that you could do a lot better than you may think. There is such a tendency in these days of specialization to rely on specialty fix-it places for whatever is wrong. We often don't look rationally at what goes on in those places. Instead we endow them with magical qualities. "Oh, Fred has a drug problem? Well, let's send him to a drug rehab hospital." "We've come to the end of our rope with Alice? Let's send her to the End-of-the-Rope School." "Harry just threatened the life of the president? It's nice to know the FBI will have an alternative placement for Harry." "Jennifer says she is going to quit school and study in Afghanistan? Well..."

Although I can't speak for Afghanistan or the FBI, I can tell you that as valuable as these special placements are–and they are truly indispensable–they don't practice magic. Much of what they do, you could do, if you had to.

This is where your imagination and intuition come in. If you get in a receptive mood, the kind of mood, say, where you want to go fishing for an afternoon, and you can forget for a little while the pressures and concerns of the immediate present, you might be ready to make the radical leap we call empathy. This can be very hard to do. Who wants to empathize with a weirdo or a drug user or an anorectic or a sullen, withdrawn fifteen-year-old who says "piss off" when you say "wanna talk?" Who wants to empathize with a little genius who tries to stick you with a pencil when you put out your hand or a scary seventeen-year-old who wants to kill his stepfather or a poetic fourteen-year-old who wants to kill herself or any of the troubled kids we know for whom we might like to find another place?

But if you're willing to swallow back your fear and pride, and if you're willing to horse around a bit and laugh a little and put aside the judgments and condemnations you've heard, above all if you're willing to play, you may find that you start to click.

You have to be willing to be surprised. If you are surprised, if your eyes light up and you step back and your mouth opens and you say, "Gee, what was that?" the child will sense the presence of an attentive player and will begin to open up and explain.

The child will tell you in camouflaged words what he needs. One will say that what he needs is to be told what to do, as in the sixteen-year-old boy who told me the other day, "Look, I'm just an asshole looking to have a good time." That means, please doc, make me wise up. Or the child will tell you that what she needs is someone to talk to, as in the fifteen-year-old girl who said, "No one listens to me." Or that what is needed is silence, as in the boy who had to holler at me for half an hour, or that what is needed is labor negotiations as in the girl who went on a sit-down strike and did not study for a year. The words may not say it straight out, but you will know the meaning between the lines by the push and pull of things as you ask this and that.

What you will find, between the lines, almost invariably, if you listen well and listen hard, is that most of all what the child wants, right then and there, is you. He wants a person who can play with him and not be on his case, who can hear him without being too full of advice, who can explore with him without telling him where to go, who can offer guidance without minding if it's heeded right away. Basically he wants a person, a connection. In this disconnected world, that can be hard to come by. For these disconnected kids, all the fancy plans and all the fancy places and all the fancy tests return inevitably to the need for a human connection with a good person. If you can find a way to offer that and have it accepted, you have found the lost child.

I imagine this is what Mr. Mansion offered Peter Pipedream as he whisked him away like a package under his arm to the land beyond Upright where imagination holds sway.

College Admission as a Failed Rite of Passage

by Michael G. Thompson

As a psychologist, I sometimes look at college admission and its impact on children, parents, and schools, and I think the gods must be crazy to have invented the process. College has achieved a symbolic importance so out of proportion to its actual meaning, and the admission process has evolved into such a Byzantine ritual, that it can make normal people act nutty, and nutty people act quite crazy.

I want to step back from the college admission process and ask two questions. First, what is it about the transition to college that is so difficult for so many children and families? Second, what is it about the college admission process that promotes or inflames these difficulties?

Each year I speak at the college weekend for parents of juniors at a nearby boarding school. The school, which has a hard time getting parents to participate consistently in any aspect of school life over four years, gets a 100% turnout for this weekend. Everybody has track shoes on, primed for the race. In the auditorium, the sense that the meeting is the beginning of the *big something* is palpable. Most people believe that the *big something* is helping your child get into a good college. From a psychologist's point of view, college admission is infected by irrational forces exactly proportional to the extent that the participants believe the issue is only getting into a "good college."

What is really going on is the most important and most difficult transition in all of life: the end of childhood and the late-adolescent separation and individuation from parents. Of all the normal separations in life in our culture, departure from home is the most traumatic. For a certain group of late-adolescent children in our society, the transition to college is the most dramatic and stressful point in the long process of becoming their own person, becoming more self-reliant and being able to operate outside their families – what is called "separation and individuation."

To separate after a profoundly close relationship of eighteen years' duration is a significant loss for both parent and child. The loss may not be permanent; college may turn out to be only a temporary interruption in a close lifelong relationship between parents and children. In fact, most people in the world live in the same place as their parents all their lives and do not experience the degree of separation in late adolescence that certain classes in American society do.

However, for middle- and upper-class children who aspire to maintain or improve their family's socio-economic position, the first step is begun, and neither party, in the years leading up to that separation, can predict how close or how distant the relationship between them will be after the transition to college or after college is finished. There is a feeling in both parties, often unarticulated or denied, that *this could be it. This could be the end.*

The launching of a child stirs up everyone in the family. For the parents it is the culmination of their child-rearing, the end of the parental curriculum. From now on if they act as parents for a college-age or older child, it will be by invitation only.

What is the main testing ground of fears about incomplete or inadequate child rearing? The college admission process.

If you are afraid you don't discipline your children enough – too much Doctor Spock – the incriminating evidence of parental failure is right there in front of everyone. The child is not filling out her college applications!

If you are afraid that you have allowed your children to watch too much television and settle for low grades, the chickens all come home to roost – painfully and publicly – during the meeting with the college counselor at the end of junior year.

If, on the eve of departure, a parent decides that a child needs more self-discipline, then surely the way to drum it in is through an SAT review course or with parental pressure about applications.

The frantic involvement of many parents in the process is, from my perspective, a cover for this profound parental anxiety: Did I do a good job with this child? Did I do everything I needed to do for this child? Is this child prepared? Is this child going to have a good life? I have seen many laissez-faire parents, not much in evidence in the tenth and eleventh grade years, swoop back into their children's lives at college admission time, trying to stuff all their wisdom and discipline into their children at the last moment.

Parents may need to be reassured, as their fledglings leave the nest, that they really have taught them how to fly. Since it is impossible to assess the quality of what parents have done for their children at this point, what is the next best thing? What comes closest to getting graded as parents? The status of the college to which the child is admitted.

From the standpoint of an anxious parent, an Ivy League college child is proof of better child-rearing than a small college child. Our human and common sense react against this notion: No one would actually come out and claim such a thing. But the uncertainties of separation can so infect anxious parents that they begin to operate on this concrete and terrible logic.

I once sat with a talented, emaciated senior girl and her brilliant, well-meaning parents. She, they, and the school had to decide whether she should remain in school or go into a hospital. In light of her anorexia, the result of a perfectionistic personality style run amok, and to ease the stress on the girl, the school recommended in the strongest terms that she not file her early decision application to Princeton. Upon hearing this, the girl looked at the adults in the room and said, "If I can't apply early to Princeton, I'll die." The parents of this young woman were not far behind her in their need to have her get into Princeton. Why did they all need this so desperately?

Because, in this case, something was askew in the family. Due to some flaw in her upbringing, this child was not happy or self-confident. Yet she was eighteen, the culture required her to leave home, and so her parents had to hide from themselves, and she had to hide from herself, the painful truth about what she had not gotten from her parents and probably never would get. The psychological solution for them all was the reassuring vision of *a great college.* Somehow going there would make her life fine and vindicate her parents' child-rearing.

Such fears about letting go of an unfinished child exist in all families. How can we let go of a child who is still so young in so many ways? With the greatest difficulty. It is painful and has no cure except time and hope. For parents looking for an analgesic, the college admission process is an action arena where they can work out their anxieties. What I do, as a clinician, is try to reach into the interior of the family and touch the fear and sadness. If the fear and sadness can be made conscious, a lot of the nuttiness goes out of the action.

The separation process for parents has many rough facets. Along with the ending of their roles as parents, other psychological stresses may be at work. The departure of a child means that they have to face – and this is always true when the last child leaves home – the viability of their marriage. Perhaps the children have been the pillars that propped up their marriage. They may be lonely. Perhaps their careers are not so fulfilling and the day-to-day responsibility for children has been what has given meaning to their lives.

The departure for college precipitates the "empty nest" syndrome. The separation of late-adolescent children from their parents may have almost the impact of divorce or death without anyone ever articulating the loss and grief that all are feeling. Two women were talking about dropping their children off for freshman year at college. Each had been quickly dismissed by her child at the dormitory door. One mother asked the other, "Did you cry when you got back to your hotel room?" The other replied, "Oh – you waited that long?"

Some children may be aware of what their departure means to their parents. I have had young people say to me that they are afraid their parents' marriage will fall apart after they leave or that one or the other parent will be terribly lonely. As one girl said, "Mom never went bird-watching with Dad; I was the only one in the family who would come along."

Children, even in the midst of their excitement about leaving, may feel they are abandoning the family. This can lead to considerable guilt. They can even feel that they have to make reparation to their family for their leaving. What is the best possible gift a child can make in these circumstances? Admission to a good college. A child may think, "If I can get into a good college – especially the same college my parents went to or wish they could have gone to – I will have gotten my parents an A in child-rearing and reassured them that I – and they – are going to be okay. And I can distract myself from being sad by competing ferociously to get into college, and wait until later to feel happy or sad by making it into that school or not making it."

Underneath the action connected with the admission process lie all the issues of self-esteem that inevitably arise in students who are applying to college: *Am I good enough? Have my parents and my school been telling me the truth about myself? If I put down on this application everything I am, everything I have done, all of my good points and faults, will somebody–anybody–want me?*

Applying to college is a pretty scary and courageous thing to do. After all, what if no one likes the fundamental you? Every student seen by a college counselor has fears about self-esteem as the admission process begins. Many naturally look to the quality of a college as a grade on their self-worth; who can blame them? The "best" colleges seem to want the "best" students. Everyone knows that the best students are not always the best human beings, but that complex human understanding may not come easily for high school juniors and seniors.

We are talking about a moment of maximum personal and family stress, one that the prominent family therapist Jay Haley believes is the most difficult transition in all of life. What is a family supposed to do? Does every family have to find its own way through this maze of feelings and pressures? Most do, in consultation with friends and family who have experienced the same developmental challenge. But those who cannot manage the separation-individuation process either hold on to their children too long or fling them out too abruptly.

In studies of children and parents who were separating, Helm Stierlin and his colleagues documented two types – centripetal and centrifugal – and three dysfunctional separation styles. Though Stierlin was working with troubled families, the concepts illuminate normal family separation styles as well.

Centripetal families exert pressure to keep a child from leaving. The completely successful centripetal family is the *binding* family which keeps drawing the child back as if it possessed a powerful invisible magnet. Children from such families may be simply unable to overcome this force and make the transition to college – or leave home for a job. They stay home, only to resent their parents' inability to let them leave and experience their parents' resentment of their inappropriate dependence.

Centrifugal families, according to Stierlin, are families that cannot tolerate the slow withdrawal and separation of the child and resort to abrupt separations. The *expelling* family simply flings the child out early, without reference to the particular child's needs. Boarding schools often have "expelled" children in their populations, but the expulsion may be justified by an educational rationale, so that these children feel thrown out without really being able to say that they have been. The parents of these children may not be able to tolerate the pain of their growing up and leaving them slowly, and so they send them away early in an attempt to avoid pain by means of a short, sharp separation.

When both centripetal and centrifugal forces are at work in a family, the result can be the *delegating* family. The delegating family sends a child out, and the child believes that she is free and independent, but in fact she is on a mission for her parents that must be fulfilled. What appears on the outside to be a truly independent child is someone who is not psychologically individuated and pursuing her own goals. Often the child from such a family is delegated to live out some dream that a parent or parents were unable to fulfill in their own lives, such as attending a high-status college.

Most college counselors and teachers will immediately recognize these categories. Families inevitably manifest one of the styles of separating that have been perfected over generations. Most healthy families are slightly centripetal or slightly centrifugal but able to adjust in a flexible way for different children and circumstances, alternating between impulses to hold a child in or spin a child out.

Rites of Passage

It is the job of a culture to provide a ritual framework that enables people in families to sustain the psychological stress of an important life transition. Many such rituals are religious, but not all. They create a series of prescribed steps that mark developmental transition. Weddings, christenings, Bar Mitzvahs, getting a driver's license, and registering to vote are all examples of cultural signposts that ease our way along the path.

Rituals marking the transition from childhood to adulthood are known as "rites of passage." A rite of passage formalizes and institutionalizes personal and family changes into a series of forms that symbolize and celebrate the importance of developmental changes. In American society, the end of childhood is marked by the end of high school. For those who do not go on to college, the end of childhood is marked by high school graduation and the events that surround it. For those who do go on to college, it seems that getting into college is a more significant ritual than graduating from high school; it certainly occupies more time, attention, and family preparation and anxiety. The major transitional step for these young people is the departure for college, and the series of rituals preparing for that step is the college admission process. How does this process measure up as a rite of passage?

Anthropologists studying traditional rites of passage to adulthood describe them as a three-part process. The first stage is physical separation from the community at large; children are taken away from their families in the company of others their own age.

The second stage, called the "liminal phase," is one in which the child is between classifications – neither child nor adult. In this phase, children and their age-mates become social comrades. They are challenged, made to suffer, and, in some societies, may be beaten, circumcised, or ritually scarred in some way. It is important to note that during this phase there is no hierarchy among age-mates. Children suffer their torments individually, but no distinctions are made among them; they are all treated the same. At the end of the liminal phase, young people are reborn as adults. During this phase they may wear clothes of death, symbolizing the death of the childhood self.

In the final phase, the group of age-mates is reintegrated into the community and the adults rejoice. Whatever trials and tortures may be used by different cultures, all put a time limit on the liminal phase and culminate in reunion with the adult community.

It is the strength and power of these rituals, and the community's agreement upon them, that permit all members of the community to share their anxiety about the important developmental moment, be they the parents who give their children over to the ritual or the children who fear the pain of the test.

The college admission process looks like a rite of passage, comes at the right time for a rite of passage, has some elements of a rite of passage, but *does not work* as a rite of passage to bring children through the separation-individuation phase of late adolescence. Getting into college makes everyone anxious, in the manner of a classic rite of passage, but it does not provide the climax, or the catharsis, that psychologically supports the age-mates and other members of the community. Instead, it too often leaves everyone more anxious, exhausted, and feeling bad about themselves, not less anxious, energized, and proud of themselves for having survived.

There are at least six reasons why the college admission process fails to function as a helpful rite of passage.

Children are not separated from adults during the college admission process. They have to go through their trials and tests in front of their parents, who cannot help being affected but who have no formal role – or do they? This leads to the possibility of shame for children, should they fail in front of their parents. It also leads to intense confusion in parents. Because of their love for their children, they either share the pain or choose not to share the pain, even when other parents are helping their children through the "torture." Better that all children should be in the hands of adults chosen by the community to see them through the ritual – but that leads to the second difficulty.

No consensus exists about exactly how important getting into college is in the life of the community. Each family, depending on its history and socio-economic aspirations, has to decide how excited or how upset to become, depending on its vision of how important getting into college – or into a certain kind of college – is in the life of the family and the child.

These varying views on importance result in uncertain criteria for success. If a child gets into college C instead of college A, has she failed to become adult? Has she done a terrible job of becoming adult? Will she be forever scarred, her future blighted by this failure, or isn't it really a failure at all? Many students who get into perfectly credible colleges where they have every chance of having a wonderful experience feel as if they have failed in life because they did not get their first choice. I have met adults who, years later, are still mourning the college they wanted but did not get into.

The worst thing about uncertain criteria for success, competition, and confusion is that they tear age-mates apart. In a classical rite of passage, children go through the experience together, become adults together, and have lifetime camaraderie. Here we have the destructive effects of different outcomes for different children. They begin to watch others, fear others' success, and ultimately wish others ill. I talked to a student last year who got into her first-choice college but was upset because another girl, her "enemy," had also been accepted by that college. High school seniors do not get "reborn" together; many get split apart.

The college admission process has no time limits. It has no clear starting point – in many schools it seems to be starting earlier and earlier – and it seems to go on forever. Early admission is fiendish in this regard because it offers two chances to fail. One of the saddest, most destructive aspects of early admission is to watch bright students go through the anxiety of applying early, fail to get in, and then have to repeat the process. Although they may end up being accepted, they spend most of their senior year in emotional turmoil.

Finally, because of our mobile society, there is no promise that children will be reintegrated into the community. They may return in some sense, but in other ways they do not. Perhaps most painful for parents and children is this great unanswered question in the separation/individuation process.

Having roundly criticized the college admission process by comparing it to classical rites of passage, I open myself to two easy criticisms. First, whoever said that getting into college should be a community ritual filled with meaning, especially in our pluralistic society? The life stories of Americans who go to college are so varied that no rite of passage around college admission could ever be designed to meet the psychological needs of everyone involved.

The second criticism asks, "Where have you been? Are you naive?" After all, getting into college is not a group or age-mate experience. It is a competitive sorting process that is tough and cold, but utterly essential for the economic and intellectual health of our society as it is presently constituted.

As for the first criticism, no one has said that college admission should carry the burden of being a community rite of passage. But it looks like a rite of passage, and it has the attention of the adult community. In my opinion, it should be made to function better as a rite of passage because so many adolescents break down at this time of life and are admitted to psychiatric hospitals.

So many depressed college freshmen and depressed young college graduates return home after college for emotional as well as economic reasons. For them, the separation/individuation process has been incomplete, and they return to try it again. Our society sends many late adolescents off too soon or not in the right way. Some more psychologically supportive ritual is needed; our society is paying too high a price in casualties among its late adolescents.

As for the second criticism, the reply must be, "Yes, of course this is a competitive society, and we do need a method for deciding which children should go to which colleges." However, the sorting aspect can be quicker and cleaner. It may be possible to sort age-mates by level of ability, yet retain the feeling of camaraderie.

It seems a tragedy to take the best and brightest young people in our society and put them through an ordeal that ends with them losing their families, their age-mates and, for far too many, their self-esteem. If we take the best-educated children in our society, the ones of whom we are going to ask the most, and deprive them of psychological support even as we subject them to stress, psychological casualties will be the inevitable result. If we put people through too tough a test for too little reason and with too little support, many of those who appear to thrive and survive will eventually take out their anger at society by doing whatever they please with their educations on Wall Street, in Washington, or wherever else they may work and live.

My mother always said that it is easy to tear things down, but so very hard to build them up. Having criticized the college admission process from a psychological point of view, I want to offer some ideas, in the form of questions.

Can we – through attitude, through deliberate education, through greater consciousness – talk with parents and children about the profound psychological process that underlies the transition from high school to college, from childhood to adulthood, from family interdependence to being on one's own?

College counselors, teachers, and school administrators see the hardship and pain of this transition more than anyone else. They see anxious parents and frightened students. Do school people address these issues? Or do they talk only about admission test scores, advanced placement courses, and the "right" extracurricular activities? People in every school should be listening for, and talking with families about, the grief of separation and the loss of childhood.

Can we better define the role of parents and other adults in the community in the college admission process so that parents do not end up in a free-for-all, with some children being hounded to death and others neglected?

I have heard of some good parent-child college visiting experiences, but wouldn't it work better to let thirty students go out on a college-visiting bus and let them rate the colleges? Can parents be assigned specific, limited tasks and be kept out – firmly, if necessary – of others?

Can we keep the senior year intact, to prevent it from getting cut to pieces by the college admission process?

One school I know has, more or less, simply given up on spring of the senior year. Two weeks before college admission letters are in the mail, the seniors go out on "senior project," scattered to the winds and reunited only for a few days before graduation. This saves the school problems of senior class-cutting and boredom during spring term, but it also splits up the seniors and robs them of being able to say extended good-byes to one another. Group sadness and separation anxiety go unacknowledged. This is only one manifestation of a tendency in many schools to give up on the senior year and allow it to be completely dominated by the college admission process.

Can we better sustain these age-mates as they go through their common ordeal, before they end up in different colleges and different places? Could students work on their admission essays in study groups, just as business school and law students do, instead of going off to work with educational consultants?

As a former Outward Bound instructor, I know that it is possible to form a strong group of young people of widely differing abilities and prospects in life. If you orient a group to facing a common challenge, they are bound together. Isn't it possible to introduce some group outlook and cooperation into the business of getting into college? Is the process inherently so competitive that such efforts are doomed, or do we just see it as being that way and not try to make it cooperative?

Finally, can we have more ritual around college admission in our schools and communities? Jack Wright, a college counselor at Franklin High School in Los Angeles who works with disadvantaged students whose families may know little about college, has a map on the wall with pins marking the colleges to which students have applied. When someone gets into a college, he uses a different-colored pin as a visible sign of success. In so doing, he emphasizes the common challenge and the success of individuals within a group and minimizes the chances for individual shame. Every student who walks into that counseling office looks at the map, is inspired by it, and feels the history of it.

If adults do not provide such occasions for ritual, students themselves will try to bind their wounds with their own rituals. Students hold "rejection letter" parties after April 15 that only those with rejection letters in hand may attend. This is clearly an attempt by the age-mate group to heal the wounded self-esteem of individuals. Shouldn't adults be helping too?

If it seems that all of these suggestions depend on group or community solutions, they do. The reason? Simple: the stress our society and the college admission process put on the individual and on individual achievement. The individual self is fragile. The self in isolation is not strong and can break down relatively easily, particularly a young self. The self supported by the love of family and by the ideals and rituals of the school and community, nourished by a rigorous education, and strengthened by the challenge it has faced – such a self, inhabiting the body and mind of a healthy young man or woman, can leave home and go on to one of the many colleges that are a good "match" for him or her and have a wonderful and productive experience there.

Chapter Two

Disorders and Traumas

The Waiting Room

by Edward M. Hallowell

Author's note: This essay was written for an audience of doctors. Its intent was to give some feeling of what it may be like to be waiting for help.

It was 4:45 in the afternoon and the waiting room was full. Serving a group practice in child and family mental health on the outskirts of the city, this waiting room had held its breath over many hopes and fears as it waited to see how things would turn out. From the framed prints on the wall to the couch and easy chairs around the room to the Oriental rug on the floor, the room took in much, but could only listen back.

So it was this afternoon, as the couch and chairs were filled and the floor was strewn with books and games and children of different ages and one Nerf basketball, its accompanying hoop suction-cupped onto the door.

Sally Marshall sat nervously picking up an old *New Yorker* and putting it back down again as she watched her son, Robin, play with dominoes and hoped he wouldn't throw them around the room. She felt so many things she was pushing away just to be able to sit in this room and keep her composure. This was, what, their third doctor, fourth if you counted the school psychologist? The first referral had led to another referral for testing, which had led to the first referral's saying she thought someone else would be better, sending Robin on to this new doctor, this new waiting room. Sally felt angry and guilty and ashamed and afraid. What had she done wrong? So many things. But damn it, she had tried, and she couldn't be both a mother and a father without losing something in the translation. Would this new doctor understand? Would he get the picture, or would he take notes? God, why do they sit there and take notes? Don't they understand that what you want is a person to talk to, a human being who will listen, not some stenographer? Do they ever put themselves in your shoes and imagine what it's like to walk in with your hat in your hand, looking for help for the person you love most in the world, all the while feeling ashamed for having to be there in the first place? And then to get some stiff who takes notes the whole time? C'mon, Sally, don't take it out on the doctors. They do the best they can. It's just that I hope so badly, I need so much, for someone, somewhere to get the point, to put his hand out to me and say, "I know Robin. I've seen Robin before. I can help you." Is that impossible? Will there just be more tests, more runaround? Robin, honey, I'm sorry to put you through all this. I don't know where else to turn. She looked down the hall at the new doctor's door and wondered and prayed over what would happen when it opened. Will he know how much this matters? Will he be able to see it in my eyes, how much we need him?

Ernie Kaposian, sitting in a chair next to Sally, was putting together a speech in his mind. He was about to be interviewed as part of a custody evaluation involving his two sons. What chance do I have? Lawyer says we've got a good case. But who knows? It's a crap shoot any way you look at it. How can I tell this woman what I know, that I love these kids and their mother doesn't? How can I say that and make her believe it? All I ask is fairness. But how can she be fair? How can she get to know us well enough to see past the facades? I'm not a good talker. She'll think I'm just a dumb Armenian from a shoe town. He turned his hat through his fingers as he sat and thought, oblivious to anyone else in the room, waiting for the tension to be broken somehow. I've got no chance. But I know I'm the one who should have those kids. And for their sakes I've got to go through with this. He stared at the closed door down the hall and continued to wait.

Albert Packer, age four, sat on the floor next to his mother scanning the room for something to get into. He had already pulled his water pistol from his back pocket, his mother intercepting the toy deftly just as it emerged from its hiding place. Now there was boredom, an intolerable state by itself made worse by its being boredom in this stupid room. It would only be a matter of time. . .

Lucille Newman had come for this, her second visit, without her son or her husband because she wanted a session alone. There were some things she needed to get off her chest. But she was now wondering if she'd be able to say them. As she waited, she was feeling more and more ashamed and defensive. How had it come to this, to be sitting in a psychiatrist's waiting room? My God, the very term sent shivers through her. Absently she brushed back her hair and stood up to get a magazine in hopes of distracting herself. Without luck. As soon as she sat back down she thought, Alex is only six. And we need professional help. He's biting other children and no other parents want their kids within miles of him, and Dick and I are attacking and blaming each other and we're ready to split up over it, and here I am reading *People* magazine in this so-nice-looking waiting room waiting to see this man who's supposed to understand. Last session he was so solemn. Can he at least crack a smile? Maybe even a laugh? Something, anything to make me feel this isn't malignant cancer we're dealing with here? Or maybe it is. What if it is? What if Alex is just going to be impossible forever? Please don't let that be. It can't be. Please, God, give that man in the next room the tools to help us. Please, God, give him the tools to give us our child, to help us fix our child. Please, God, give him the tools to fix me and Dick so we can be the parents we want to be. She closed the magazine and reached into her purse for a tissue. Life goes on, she thought, dabbing her eyes. It has to. We'll find a way. We have to. Maybe here. Maybe now...

Logan McMaster paced in the corridor outside the waiting room, refusing to sit down because he was angry to be there in the first place. What right had the school to require that he seek professional help? "For your son," as the principal had put it, "and, frankly, for you, Mr. McMaster. Things are getting out of hand." What gall! Who did he think he was, to recommend psychiatric help and then to insist upon it as a condition for Josh's returning to school?

And who is this, this shrink I'm going to see? He winced at the thought. He had taken the school's referral rather than find a therapist of his own because to his way of thinking they were all of the same quality – poor – so he might as well get blessed by someone the school recommended so the school would have to take what was said without any guff. I mean, the whole thing is ridiculous. Josh has a hard time for a while and they're all over him – and me – like we're crazy or something. And now I have to go submit to an interview with this little speck of humanity with a lot of diplomas on his wall in order to get my son back into school. What is he going to ask me? Just let him try and outsmart me. I'll talk circles around him. Just because he has diplomas, well, I have experience in the world. I have built more in a year than he will in a lifetime. He sits in the cheap seats of life while I've got a front row box. So let him try and outsmart me. Just once. Logan's eyes fixed on the psychiatrist's door and waited for it to open.

Tommy Lovalle, eleven, sat on the floor near the door drawing circles on the rug with his forefinger. C'mon, dude, he thought to himself, I'm ready to roll. He and his doctor called each other "dude," a practice begun early in their second session when Tommy had read from a comic strip the line, "Are you ready to roll, dudes?" It had cracked him up. Ever since they began each session by saying, "Hey dude, ready to roll?" and ended it with, "Later, dude." Even though "dude" was not really a part of the doctor's everyday vocabulary, it became part of their private arsenal of words. Of which they had many. Words for everybody. Words for everything. Lots of secrets. It's so righteous in there, Tommy thought. I can say what I want. The guy listens. He cares. I can get him mad – he doesn't know I know it but I do – and he doesn't kick me out. He doesn't lose it or anything. I wouldn't mind if he did. Couldn't blame him. Once in a while. Dude's got a right to get pissed. But instead he just stands up and goes over to his window and looks out for a minute. Doesn't see me laughing behind his back. Why couldn't he be my Pop? Ask him and he says cause that's not what he is. But he might just as well be 'cause he's better than my Pop, but that's just 'cause, I don't know anyway. I do know he better not go away anywhere anytime soon.

Tommy went from clockwise in his drawing to counterclockwise back to clockwise and his circles grew a little as he continued to wait for his time. His eye picked up on a crumpled ball of paper that had missed the wicker trash basket. He got up and threw it away, thinking, gotta keep this place straightened up, gotta do that for sure.

Molly Stone, seventeen, sat against the wall in what seemed like an extra chair. Or something, she thought. It's so uncomfortable. Gawd, this is awful. Harriet told me I would just walk right in. She didn't say anything about this line-up outside. It's embarrassing! What if I knew any of these people? Can you imagine? Just think of Lesley Carvin, no, even worse, just think if Bobby Cassidy were sitting in that chair where that woman is now. To die, absolutely for sure to die! Molly shifted position in her chair so there could be no eye contact with the woman across from her. Oh boy, this is just great, she went on in her thoughts. I mean, I'm willing to see this shrink, Harriet says she's so-o-o-o-o nice, but is it really necessary? I'm certainly not going to talk about anything that matters to me. I mean, how could I? I've never even met this Brenda Hansen, Ph.D. Wonder who she looks like, maybe Brenda Starr? Maybe she's a geek. She couldn't be if Harriet likes her. Although you never know with Harriet. She liked Eddie Bimpole. So what, you say, Hi, Doc, where's the pills, I'm losing my mind? No, I'll just sit down like she's one of my mother's friends at a cocktail party and make this *really* impressive, *really* intellectual, *really* phony conversation, and snow the hell out of her and she'll say, clearing her throat the way they all do when they give you a verdict, she'll say, "Miss Stone," or maybe she'll call me, "Molly," but I certainly hope not, I'm not her friend or anything yet, but maybe she'll say, "Molly, you are a perfectly delightful young woman, but I don't think you are in need of someone like me," and I'll think, right on, sister, and bop out of there faster than Jimmy McDonald in his Mazda. But what if she asks me to stay? What if she asks me about all that other stuff? Harriet said I should bring it up. But I can't. And if I can't, and she won't because she doesn't know anything about it, then everything should be safe. OK, shrink lady, it's show time!

Brandon Molloy sat in his usual spot in the waiting room, on the floor in the corner next to the large plant whose leaves he knew so well. He sat with his arms wrapped around his knees which he pulled up to his chest. Now sixteen, he had been coming to this waiting room for four years, longer than anyone else in the room. His man was Max, and his door would open for their appointment when Brandon wanted it to, not a moment sooner, not a moment later. Of course, that wasn't true. But he liked to think it was. It was a game he sometimes played while he waited, and wait he always did, since he came about a half-hour early. In the game he imagined he could signal Max through the wall about what was going on in his life. He'd give him a thumbs up sign if things were going well, thumbs down if not, and Max would signal back with a high sign, and they'd basically do most of the session while Brandon was sitting waiting on the floor, so that by the time he got into the room with Max he wouldn't have to do much of the thing he didn't like to do, which was talk, or *relate* as Mr. Bramble, his English teacher, put it. "Can't you relate to me?" he would ask. "Or, if not to me, to the others in the class? Can't you relate to them? Do you live in another world?" He wrote well, though, Bramble had to hand him that. "You write well, though. I have to hand you that," he said to him. "You write the best in the class. In fact, you write better than any student I've ever had. But why can't you *relate?*" Max said they would work on that, on relating, but he also said he imagined Mr. Bramble had some trouble on that score as well, which had given Brandon a big chuckle to hear. And he would make a friend one of these days. He would. He almost had it down as to how he would do it. "Would you like to get a hamburger?" he was going to say to Joey Bonomo. Joey was a nice guy. Brandon couldn't decide if hamburger was the right word. He'd talk it over with Max. He would give it a try. As soon as Max gave him the high sign.

But for now he looked toward the door. And waited.

How to Distinguish Normal from Abnormal Behavior

by Michael G. Thompson

The question I am most frequently asked in my school consultation work is, "Is this behavior normal?" What teachers want to know is whether the symptoms they are seeing are transient or whether they are more permanent and therefore more worrisome. Teachers imagine that I am going to teach them how to tell the difference between normal and abnormal behavior. I do not have to. They already know.

Teachers are good diagnosticians. Having worked with them for over a decade, I can say that some experienced teachers are master diagnosticians. They really know children, they accurately observe what is going on with children, they almost always see when something is wrong. What they lack are the psychiatric terms in which to frame their observations and the confidence in their judgment. As a consultant, I provide them with both, while they make my job easy to do, because they have such a complete grasp of what is normal for a child the age of children in their particular class, in their particular slice of the American demographic pie. A teacher carries an internal yardstick that allows him or her to make diagnostic judgments: "He's too angry." "He's a space shot." "I don't like the way she eats at lunch."

Though teachers don't think in statistical terms, when they speak that way I understand them to be speaking of statistical norms, roughly placing a child on the bell-shaped curve of normal behavior. Translated, they are saying, "This boy has more than average anger for a boy his age," or, "This boy is two standard deviations away from the mean in his capacity to pay attention," or, "I see normal children eat every day, and the way this girl is eating is abnormal." Virtually every eating disordered child I have come across in a school environment has been spotted and diagnosed by a teacher. All I have to do is put my stamp of approval on a teacher's diagnostic judgment.

I would go farther and say that most people are good diagnosticians of others, because we are all so attuned to human behavior. People can train themselves not to watch others, or can choose not to judge, but we all register when something is wrong with another human being's behavior. The greatest diagnostic tools are common sense and life experience. Indeed, I think that people in general and teachers in particular arrive at diagnostic judgments in much the same way mental health professionals do. You reflexively use the same criteria as we do. What may be different between the way you decide a case and the way a mental health professional decides is that we may work more systematically and less from intuition than you do. However, the underlying process is the same.

Perhaps you are not convinced by my argument; perhaps you think I am flattering teachers and my readers. The best way to convince you is to give you a test of your diagnostic abilities. What follows is a set of cases drawn from my school consultation work. I have fictionalized the cases to protect the identities of the original children, but they are essentially as presented to me. In your mind, please rate the cases on a four-point scale. Rate a case as "1" if you think the child is completely normal, that no adult intervention is needed and all that is required is for time to pass and the apparent problem will evaporate. In other words, this is perfectly normal behavior for a child this age. Rate a case as a "2" if you think the behavior is normal, but that it requires some change in child-rearing or school routine. For example, what would be required is a phone call from middle-school director to the parents suggesting some change at home. Rate a child as a "3" if you think he needs to see a mental health professional. For the sake of this brief quiz, "abnormal" is going to be operationally defined as needing to see a psychologist or psychiatrist. Finally, if you cannot come to any judgment at all and need more information, rate the case a "4." But remember that all these cases are abbreviated; anyone might want to know more about each child. So if you rate the case a "4," force yourself to say what one piece of information you might need in order to rate the case as a "1," "2," or "3." Here are the cases:

Case #1

Tori, a seventh-grade girl, born in Japan, who wants to be a professional violinist, finds herself – after several major family moves – a student in an American independent school. Her English is superb and she is quite bright. She practices the violin four hours a day and has begun to play concertos with small amateur orchestras. Her mother, who is a professional violinist, is her teacher. She supervises Tori's playing, her practicing, her homework and her social life. Tori has virtually no friends in school; other children often don't even make the effort to be anything but superficially friendly to her, though they don't tease her either. She is just left out of things. When asked, Tori says that she is not lonely, that she doesn't have time for friends, that she is dedicating herself to music.

Case #2

Katherine, a fifth-grade girl, exhibits an extremely strong will toward other children and toward adult teachers. She is a subtle bully. The boys in her class uniformly fear and despise her, though she is very pretty. The girls find her intimidating and vacillate between admiration and avoidance. Katherine uses shocking words within hearing distance of teachers all the while pretending she does not want to be heard. She has indicated that she has a rocky relationship with one of her parents; this does not surprise teachers who often experience her as challenging their authority.

Case #3

Cecilia is a newly-arrived seventh-grade girl who reads and stays by herself during the school day. She reports not being close to children at school or close to her family, but says she is close to friends in a youth group at church. She confides in a teacher that she fantasizes for hours a week, alone in her room. The teacher finds her shy and likable.

Case #4

Andy is a sixth-grade boy who is constantly using themes of violence and death in his art work and in his creative writing. He doodles in school, drawing pictures of severed heads and gouged-out eyes. He is a big fan of horror films and of Stephen King's novels. He often tries to shock other children – unsuccessfully – with his recitations of gory events from movies and books. He has never been violent. He is a brilliant but erratic student.

Case #5

José, a tenth-grade boy, is a gifted actor and singer. He has been in every school play since elementary school and has already starred in high school productions. In the spring of his tenth-grade year he begins to spend time talking with teachers, bringing them into his confidence and telling them how unhappy he is at school, how different he is from other kids. Since he is from a poor family which is ethnically different from the rest of the school population, teachers are sympathetic to his dilemma. Eventually, the teachers begin to trade notes and realize that he is talking to all of them at great length and taking an enormous amount of their time.

José joins the Drama Society and becomes a member of a highly alienated group of boys. Despite this affiliation, he continues to talk to teachers constantly and they are all baffled by the storm of conversation that leads nowhere but is apparently essential to José. His dress begins to change as well and he wears increasingly flamboyant, eccentric and "arty" clothes.

Case #6
Jill, a ninth-grade girl, tells her teacher that her older brother is coming home on leave from the Navy. She hasn't seen him in over a year and she is extremely nervous about his return home. In the past, she says, he did things to her that she has never told anyone about. Once she tried to hint to her parents that she was afraid of her brother, but they did not respond to her clues. The teacher sees that the girl is obviously deeply frightened.

Case #7
Tony, a second-grade boy, is afraid of the bottle of glue and the bottles of paint in the classroom. He believes there are dangerous germs in them. He will not change desks with anyone because he believes there are germs on other desks. In good weather, he will not eat outside with other children because he says that germs "may fall on his food." One day he left his coat at home and refused to wear a spare coat from the "lost and found" because it might have germs on it.

Case #8
Tanya, an African-American girl, was a class leader in eighth grade in a predominantly black neighborhood school. When she moved from her old school to a new, largely white school, things seemed to change. Her racial and socioeconomic status suddenly seemed more and more important to her. She had to help get her three brothers off to school before taking a long bus ride to her new school. She was often late and envied kids whose parents drove them or who had cars. She began to cut afternoon activities and sports because that was the only time she could see her friends from her neighborhood. Tanya, the former student leader, began to get into a lot of trouble with the administration of her new school.

Before we discuss these case examples, I would like to say a word about behavior and symptoms. We are all communicating messages to others through our behavior at every moment. We say a great deal about our personal state of mind, our reactions to events, our intentions toward others, our strengths and weaknesses, by our every gesture, word, and action. A symptom isn't anything very special. It is nothing more than an ordinary behavior that is repeated frequently enough, or with enough intensity, to acquire a signaling value. Any behavior, no matter how ordinary, can become a symptom. Take the classical obsessional symptom of hand-washing. We all wash our hands one or two, perhaps five or six times a day. Surgeons and ceramics teachers probably wash their hands a lot more often than that. But if you should ever happen to see someone wash their hands twenty-five times in immediate succession, you are alerted to something extraordinary going on inside them. Even three or four times might be enough to signal their symptomatology and allow you to diagnose them as having obsessive-compulsive disorder. Though this is a classic symptom, any behavior can become a symptom if it is repeated too often, with too much intensity, or in the wrong place. Very few human behaviors are only and unmistakably symptoms. Self-mutilation is one of those intrinsically symptomatic behaviors, though anthropologists and tattoo enthusiasts might argue even about that.

A symptom is many things in a condensed package. First, it is a distress call. This distress call comes out of people unbidden and beyond their control. Depressions are like that. Depressed people see that their behavior is slowed down and depressed, they do not wish it to be so, and they struggle constantly against the manifestations of depression, yet the depression persists. The sufferers usually hold themselves responsible; they don't want to recognize the signal value of symptoms any more than the target audience does. As a heroic and very sad girl said to me, "But, I don't want to be depressed!" It was perfectly evident to me that she did not want to be depressed and blamed herself for being so immobilized. It was also clear to me that she could not stop being depressed until her parents got the message of the symptom and helped change the conditions of her life. She had simply gone on strike inside and was letting everyone know it through the symptoms of depression.

Second, symptoms are a protest against some overwhelming or unlivable situation in the outside world or the inside world of a person. When I am asked to evaluate a child, I first look at the child's outside world, particularly the youngster's family relationships and social situation. After that, I try to think about the child's inner world and relationship with him- or herself. In the example of the depressed girl mentioned above, both were intolerable. Her mother had been hospitalized for a serious depression and was not getting well. The girl had taken it upon herself to "save" her mother and be surrogate housekeeper and wife to her father without being sexual and without being disloyal to her mother. At the same time she was keeping up the academic and social life required of her by a demanding school. The result of this external situation and her internal demands upon herself was a depression.

A number of children in the diagnostic quiz are manifesting symptoms as a distress call and a protest. Tanya, in case #8, is protesting the loss of her security in her old neighborhood school and the amount of change and adaptation required of her to go to a predominantly white, upper-middle-class school a long distance from home. Through his dress and his incessant conversation, José is signaling that something – we don't know whether it is inside or outside of him – is causing him pain.

I once had a boy return to boarding school after a Christmas vacation in which he had learned the family secret that had been so long kept from him – that his mother had committed suicide when he was five. Upon his return to school he immediately began stealing valueless things that he did not need. It was his only way to let people know that he could not bear his psychic burdens alone. His symptomatic actions got him the response he needed: a referral to therapy so he could talk about what he had learned.

Third and finally, in addition to being a distress call and a protest, a symptom is an adaptation. It is the best that a person can do at a given time. Everyone is always struggling to be the most competent person he or she can be on any given day, in the face of life's obstacles. I imagine that even burglars get up intending to do their best burglary that day. Since we all struggle to be our best selves, when someone becomes symptomatic, you can safely conclude that they are exhausted from so much expenditure of energy adapting to a difficult situation. Again, in the example of the depressed girl, she had the emotional choices of being angry with her mother and abandoning her father to his life and just being a high school student, which would have been to abandon her standards for herself. What she "chose" – and by that I mean an unconscious choice – was to become depressed herself rather than willfully fail the people in her life. Symptoms very often function to allow people to maintain their integrity in their own eyes. They would rather become mentally ill – to the extent they have a choice – than be weak or disloyal.

The first thing that one pays attention to in a symptom is the manifest content. In the case of Tony, the second-grader who is afraid of germs everywhere, the content of his symptom is intrinsically worrisome. He experiences danger everywhere. His frank fear of being surrounded by invisible dangerous germs reveals that he is radically unsafe in his world. Jill, who reports her fear of her older brother to her teacher, is implying that she was sexually abused by him in the past. For any teacher, such a report should trigger a mandatory report to the appropriate state child protective agency. The manifest content of the symptoms of these two children signal dangers in their lives. For Tony the danger may be inside and completely imagined; it is nonetheless overwhelming. For Jill the danger is outside and very real. Both should be rated "3;" both need to talk with a mental health professional in addition to other interventions which need to be made on their behalf.

After paying attention to the content of a symptom, you need to examine the duration and intensity of the symptom. A teacher of mine at Michael Reese Hospital in Chicago said that the most important diagnostic question you can ask is simply, "How long has this been going on?" If a child is scared of a bug for a short time, you let it pass. If a child is deeply frightened of bugs in all situations, and has been for a long time, it is symptomatic. Such a fear is too intense and lasts too long. Or, by contrast, if a symptom has just popped out recently, the "How long..." question can get you right to the precipitating event.

Though the content of Tony's worries in case #7 are troubling, so is the intensity of his reaction and the duration of it. Tony has been too scared for too long. On the other hand, Jill, in case #6, has just become frightened as her brother's return home becomes imminent, so it is the short duration of her fear that leads you to the important scary person in her life.

Duration and intensity can also be mitigating factors, if they are part of the base-line data that one has about the functioning of a child. One does not take notice of a behavior that has always been there in a child, or in a child who tends as a style to be shy, or to be hotheaded and intense. We all adapt our standards and expectations to the individual child. Thus you react differently to the same behaviors manifested by two different children. If your ordinarily quiet, reflective child seems somewhat withdrawn you may be mildly concerned; if your highly active three-and-a-half-year-old boy is withdrawn, you are immediately concerned. What teachers develop naturally and inevitably is a tremendous capacity to recognize, respect and adjust to individual variation and changes in developmentally appropriate behavior.

Along with duration and intensity, developmental appropriateness is the most significant criterion by which children's behavior must be evaluated to determine whether it is normal or abnormal. Any major deviation or arrest in the expectable developmental sequence is a cause for alarm. Parenthetically, I want to say that I hate the word "appropriate." It is, along with "share" and "relate," among the most noxious words of the new psycho-babble. However, in relation to development there isn't a better word than appropriate. Please understand that I am not using it in the moral sense, as it is so often used in the smarmy question, "I don't think that behavior is appropriate, do you?" I am using it in the sense of what is usual and expectable among a majority of children at a certain age. My underlying assumption is that normality can be judged by what is average. I imagine that the criterion of developmental appropriateness was the criterion on which you relied in making your judgments in cases #3, Cecilia, and case #4, Andy.

When I have presented Cecilia and Andy to teachers, there is always a woman teacher who says, "Oh, when I was in seventh grade I spent hours daydreaming!" And an experienced middle-school teacher always says about Andy, "I have three kids like this in my classroom." Gory drawings and stories of horror are a staple in grades six to eight. They have ordinarily disappeared by tenth grade; they are unknown in second grade. In middle school, they are developmentally appropriate. After all, Stephen King does have a large audience; it begins in middle school. Andy was sent to me by a worried teacher and in our first interview he asked, "Have you ever read a Stephen King novel?" I replied, "No," and he said, "You can't understand me until you have," and he assigned me *Firestarter*, a classic story of an angry child with an impact on adults. Junior high is the time when children start feeling their power and anticipating being adults. Stephen King gives them an artistic expression for their normal, if antisocial, impulses. Every age has its characteristic sunny and dark sides; teachers know this.

I rate Andy a "1" as long as he does not act out his violent thoughts and fantasies. Women sometimes disagree with that judgment, citing the abnormality of such violent fantasies, but their criticism is an indictment of our society, not of Andy. Men teachers almost universally vote Andy a "1," and I agree with them.

Thinking about developmental appropriateness reminds me of a visit I once paid to the office of Gordon Harper, a child psychiatrist at Children's Hospital in Boston. On the wall he had many drawings by children. There was one piece of paper that had on it all the letters of the alphabet, but hopelessly mixed-up, reversed and upside down. It was a mess. He asked me what I thought about the child who did it and after an initial hesitation I asked, "How old is the child?" I am glad I did because the alphabet had been done by his son. It turned out to be the precocious alphabet of a preschool child. It could have been the very developmentally disabled work of a seven-year-old. There are many similar examples: vandalism committed by a six-year-old or a nineteen- year-old has different meaning than vandalism committed by fourteen-year-old boys in groups. Most of the vandalism in the United States is caused by boys of this age. It is – regrettably speaking – developmentally expectable.

The fourth criterion that I think we all automatically use in evaluating behavior is the personal suffering of the child who is manifesting the symptom. What is confusing about Cecilia is the absence of personal suffering. It would be a much easier case to classify if the girl were miserable; that is what we initially expect to be the case. The lack of personal suffering suggests either that there isn't anything wrong, and this girl is satisfied with her friendships with the church youth group, or that there is something very serious going on here – that this girl is heavily defended and detached – schizoid is the diagnostic term – or that she is depressed. What is needed is more information, so I rate case #3, Cecilia, as a "4," more information needed, because in most children social isolation is ominous and would be a cause for much suffering on the part of the child.

As sensitive as we are to the suffering of children, we tend to overlook a certain subtle kind of suffering that goes on in talented, bright children. It is too often the acting-out and angry children who get the psychological attention in schools, and not the overly conscientious, precociously mature, and quietly depressed kids. What I want to know about Cecilia is whether she really does have friends in her church youth group. If she has, we can relax and give her time to make friends in her new school; she is simply shy and takes her time in warming up to a new social environment. That turned out to be the case with Cecilia, and so she really was a "1."

The suffering of peers is an important criterion in diagnosing the difficulties of children. In case #2, what is disturbing about the behavior of Katherine, the girl bully, is that other children react so strongly to it, avoiding her or admiring her in a fearful way. If children consistently suffer at the hands of another child, something is wrong with that child. Katherine was too intimidating, too angry. Kids have all had to work so hard to suppress and socialize their own angry, greedy and cruel impulses that they react immediately to behavior on the part of their peers that is too cruel, too angry, too...symptomatic. Adults can rely on this diagnostic information from other kids with considerable confidence. In this case I thought Katherine was going to need therapy, but before I could get her to a therapist I worked with all the teachers to stand up to her and limit her ferocious behavior. She immediately settled down. It became evident that she was simply trying out her personal strength. She was having an early puberty, was larger than many kids and was experimenting with challenging adults. The moment the adult world set limits on her, she became a child again. Her parents were encouraged to do the same and Katherine became an effective social leader in school, not a tyrant. What I thought was a "3" was in fact a "2." Schools make "therapeutic" interventions like that all the time, without thinking of them as therapeutic.

When teachers and families suffer at the hands of a child, it is also a sign that the child is symptomatic, and perhaps quite disturbed. There is a type of conduct-disordered child who may be headed for the adult diagnosis of "character disorder." These children do not suffer personally in the way a depressed child does – rather, everyone else suffers from their behavior. Most of these kids get picked up by a school's disciplinary system and get to mental health help by that route. Other, more subtly disturbed, children make their families or teachers suffer in less overt ways. I believe teachers need to take their own suffering seriously or they are losing a diagnostic tool. The teacher who repeatedly forgave or ignored the provocations of a disturbed girl until he found tacks in his coffee is an example. This girl pushed the teacher to the personal limit in order to have her symptomatic behavior recognized.

I believe that families are more resilient, accepting, and altogether better adapted to adjust to symptomatic behavior than peers or the school. It is obvious why: many children are symptomatic in the same ways their parents are, or in ways their parents were as children. Or the children are reacting to internal conflicts of the parents. The children are trying to "solve" these problems for their parents, but they are overwhelmed in the process. I do a lot of family therapy and I am struck, time and again, by the family's capacity to absorb and digest strong feelings, even verbal and physical assault, that would – in another context – be outrageous and terrifying for others. I used to see a family whose every therapy meeting began with an angry outburst on the part of the late adolescent daughter toward the mother. It was a furious shouting attack during which the mother sat, listened, cried and knit. The mother, though hurt every time, was able to accept this level of attack because she knew that this was a multi-generational family problem. She knew that she had treated her daughter in some of the hateful ways her mother had treated her, and she would have liked to have been able to say to her mother exactly what her daughter was yelling at her. Many parents, unconsciously recognizing the ways in which they burden their children, are guilty and therefore accepting, or – as in this case – identified with both sides of the family battle.

All children in all families, families without the level of trouble I have described, develop transient symptoms throughout childhood. Parents become accustomed to working around these "phases." Let me give you an example. Many children who are wrestling with the issue of autonomy in the years four to six want to change their name. They suddenly become allergic to the family's nickname for them. So the parents give up calling the child Teddy, call him Ted, change to Edward or Ed, then – with considerable difficulty – accede to his request and call him by James (his middle name) for a period of days or weeks and finally are allowed to return to Teddy again.

Because of this resiliency on the part of the family, when the family does complain to the school about a child's behavior at home, someone better listen. It doesn't always mean that something is wrong with the child; often the child is expressing through his symptoms something seriously wrong with the parent. However, families tend to be so proud and private that when others complain about their child's behavior at home to outsiders, it is often a serious call for attention.

Incidentally, in my private practice I almost always make a recommendation for therapy for a child under twelve without seeing the child at all. I see the parents first, listen to their complaints and make a recommendation for therapy on the basis of their words alone; only then do I see the child. If the child appears healthy, I can always retract, but if I fail to make my recommendation before I see the child, and then have to come back to the parents and say, "I saw your child and he needs therapy," parents almost always react defensively. They cannot help feeling exposed and criticized. If I make a recommendation from their words alone, that effect is much reduced. Unfortunately, schools are always in a position of dealing with parents who are on the defensive. What saves the situation is that the vast majority of parents – unfortunately not all parents – respect the time that teachers have spent with their children and pay attention to teachers' observations.

A frequent difficulty between parents and schools occurs when there is a cultural barrier between them. A parent may be culturally so different from the school that a gulf exists between them that they have to bridge. A private school teacher in a conference with some Islamic parents finally realized that they were asking her and the school to help them protect their daughter's virginity from what they saw as a highly sexualized American adolescent culture. The school administrator had to finally explain – much to the parents' dismay – that she could not guarantee their daughter's virginity.

The socio-cultural context of behavior is an important criterion for assessing symptoms. In case #1, Tori, the Japanese girl, and in case #8, Tanya, the African-American girl, are displaying behavior that is symptomatic not of mental illness but of cultural difference. Tori is being raised as her mother had been in Japan, where the mother had gone to a music school for children. She is raising Tori exactly as she was raised, and in a way very different from the American children. It makes Tori look "abnormal," but one must hesitate before calling it that. Tori is simply marching to a different drummer, and it is the life her mother has chosen for her. Still, I had some concerns, but in talking with Tori's mother I established that the mother also had some worries about Tori's lack of friendships, so I helped the mother change things so that Tori could become integrated into school a bit more. Both Tori and Tanya should be rated a "2;" they need the environment to help them and their cultural adjustment, so that they can act normally. It is increasingly the challenge for schools to respond to a greater variety of children. The Los Angeles Public Schools are educating children in eighty different languages.

My next criterion for assessing normality-versus-abnormality is the issue of public-versus-private action. Some behaviors are perfectly normal and appropriate in private and quite symptomatic in public. Masturbation is the classic example. In private it is absolutely normal and not symptomatic of anything. In small children, occasional public masturbation is equally harmless. Public masturbation in older children or adults is, however, a cause for serious worry. How does the issue of public-versus-private relate to my cases? Consider the case of José, who seems to be trying to signal something publicly through his obvious identification with a group of alienated boys and his flamboyant dress. What is his public message? I asked the drama teacher at the school about him and he said matter-of-factly, "I think José is trying to decide whether or not he is gay. Don't worry about him; he's in a group with other boys who are trying to decide the same thing. He isn't ready to talk about it yet, but he's in the right support group." What a sophisticated diagnostic formulation by a teacher! Here was a case where a boy seemed to be asking for therapy and was receiving it informally from a school drama group. On the criterion of intensity, José appears to be a "3;" his behavior is also increasingly public. However, his symptoms are quite controlled and he has found the help he needs to struggle with an issue which affects a significant minority of kids in adolescence, deciding whether they are straight or gay. Since homosexuality is not a mental illness, he doesn't require a psychologist. Yet many kids going through this discovery process are at risk for depression and suicide. If he had not had such good support in the school, I would have recommended it for him.

When I consult to a school I don't start with the children. I don't cruise around the school looking for odd behavior on the part of students. I talk to teachers first and foremost, because teachers are such good diagnosticians. Unless we are talking about a very brittle and inflexible teacher, most teachers can deal with everything that is normal within a wide range. So I wait for teachers to start feeling overwhelmed, frightened, and worried; that is my diagnostic jumping-off point. I diagnose using their observations and reactions.

The best of families and the best of schools are places of emotional turmoil. They are topsy-turvy places full of love, full of hate, full of crisis, as well as creativity, confusion, and law and order...all by turns. Why should this be? Why can't much of what we see in schools that is symptomatic be left at home? D.W. Winnicott, an English pediatrician-turned-psychoanalyst, explains it in the following way:

What is the normal child like? Does he just eat and grow and smile sweetly? No, that is not what he is like. A normal child, if he has confidence in mother and father, pulls out all the stops. In the course of time he tries out his powers to disrupt, to destroy, to frighten, to wear down, to waste, to wangle and to appropriate. Everything that takes people to the courts (or the asylums for that matter) has its normal equivalent in infancy and childhood, in the relation of the child to his own home...

The child whose home fails to give a feeling of security looks outside his home for the four walls; he still has hope, and he looks to grandparents, uncles and aunts, friends of the family, and school. Often a child gets from relations and school what he missed in his own actual home. In my experience, all children, even those from the best and most loving homes, need to test the outside world as they have tested their parents. I did it to my teachers in my schools and I am sure you did it to yours.

Maturation is hard on kids, and they develop strong impulses and feelings. They need help so that they can learn in time to control, modulate, and channel these impulses. The challenge for us is to distinguish between these necessary and inevitable developmental assaults, if you will, and symptomatic behavior which signals some more profound worry or disturbance which the child is not going to outgrow. These are difficult distinctions which we all struggle to make, you with your students and we in our work. I believe we all use the same data and the same criteria to make our judgments: the content, duration and intensity of behavior; the developmental appropriateness of behavior; the suffering of the individual, family, and school; and the public-versus-private nature of behavior. We take into account the socio-cultural context of behavior before attributing "odd" behavior to a child's mental disturbance.

Finally, we have to rely on our common sense and our instincts. There are some child behaviors that are always upsetting: blank-staring, flapping and rocking behavior, repeated feces-smearing, self-hitting, failure to be toilet trained at late ages, and repeated lying and stealing. There are also behaviors that I characterize as having a creepiness factor in them: fire-setting or torturing and killing small mammals, for example. You never need to worry that you don't have the expertise to diagnose something really crazy and that a mental health professional is needed. You may want a psychiatrist or psychologist to affirm and refine your judgment, but some behaviors are so creepy and weird that they broadcast psychopathology. I have heard clinicians report that they diagnose schizophrenia by whether the hair stands up on the back of their neck when they first interview the patient. It is not a foolproof diagnostic tool; it is, however, a useful sign.

I have a friend who is a psychologist and lawyer on the faculty of the University of Pennsylvania Law School. He has argued that expert psychiatric witnesses should be thrown out of the courtroom. His premise is that if someone is truly crazy, a jury of lay people can easily see that. If the defendant is not clearly crazy, mental health professionals will disagree inconclusively, so throw them out of the process.

I am not encouraging schools to throw out mental health professionals. I do think psychologists and psychiatrists have an important role to play in schools. At the same time, I do want people in general and teachers in particular to trust their instincts. Over the years, I have given many versions of my diagnostic quiz, and I have been mightily impressed by the intuition and good diagnostic sense of teachers and administrators, people who do not think of themselves as diagnosticians, but who really can distinguish between normal and abnormal behavior in children.

Unheard Melodies

by Edward M. Hallowell

Author's note: The following was presented as the keynote address at the New York Orton Dyslexia Society, March 1993.

When I was in high school – and that was 1968, not so very long ago – one of my classmates asked our math teacher what a learning disability was. "There are two kinds of learning disabilities," the teacher responded, "one treatable, the other not. The treatable one is laziness, the untreatable one is stupidity." I like to think we've come a long way since then, but in the minds of a stubborn few I'm afraid we have not. The Orton Dyslexia Society has been one of the major reasons the views of that old teacher are on the retreat.

My message to you today is about connectedness and disconnectedness. The pain of a learning disorder resides not only in the strain one feels to function, but in the disconnections one can suffer: a disconnection from language and from thought, from expression and from creativity, from books and from words, and from people and from feelings.

I also believe that one of the pleasures of the various problems we are here today to discuss is the fanciful variations they bring up. While the dyslexic child may stammer, stumble and reverse, while he may disconnect from the word or the page or the person, he may also soar, he may connect in new and unexpected ways, he may, in his stumbling, stumble onto something new and great. It is therefore of great urgency that we keep the windows of these children's minds clean, we keep them free of the smudge and grease of shame, criticism, defeatism, and devaluation. It matters that we keep their sight lines clear so they may see around the corners and underneath the logs to the unusual frogs they are able to find.

Let me tell you a story. There was once a little boy who was pronounced writing-phobic. This pronouncement was made by a psychologist. The report read:

Karl is writing-phobic. I reach this conclusion based upon psychometric testing as well as projective testing which reveals a partial inability to retrieve certain words under stress as well as an incomplete release of the preverbal memory structures as initiated by image recall and impromptu stimulation. This leads to a relative inhibition of the capacity to form written expressives, that is to say a tendency to avoid external prompts or stressors related to the act of writing. These neurological factors are complicated, on a psychodynamic level, by the fact that Karl has a precocious awareness of his parents' own internal conflicts. For a boy of eight, he displays an unusual understanding of his mother's unfulfilled literary ambitions as well as his father's shame-slash-pride over certain verbal successes vis-a-vis his own career, namely that he is a successful writer for what are commonly referred to as television sitcoms. Thus, the neurological and the psychodynamic combine to create in Karl an intense ambivalence as to whether or not he wants to write, whether or not he should write, whether or not he can write, and what, exactly it means to write. Until these issues are resolved he will remain writing-phobic. It is my advice not to tamper with this delicate balance, but rather to respect Karl's defensive structure and wait for the issues to resolve. Failing this, resource room time might prove invaluable.

My friend Priscilla Vail, the renowned author and educator, read this report and laughed out loud. "What does this mean?" she asked herself. Not quite believing the report, Priscilla decided to take a different tack from the one the psychologist had recommended. She told Karl that as much as he might want to write, he would have to constrain all his written output within the bounds of one 3 x 5 note card per day. She then began to work with him on all sorts of fun projects that involved writing – games, puzzles, mazes, wish-lists, fan letters. In no time Karl was asking for a bigger note card. "I don't know about that," Priscilla said, stoking her chin. "That's an awful lot of space you'd have to fill."

"Oh, please, Mrs. Vail!" Karl pleaded.

"Well, if you think you can handle it..."

"Handle it?" Karl interrupted. "I can handle much more than that!" he said proudly.

Soon Karl's written output exceeded that of most professional writers. The "writing phobia" and the resource room were forgotten as Karl eagerly got busy with words without knowing that he wasn't supposed to be able to.

I think people come to words much as lovers get together. They stumble onto each other, at the oddest of times, in the strangest of places. They will meet in an empty laundromat on a rainy Sunday afternoon, or they will catch each other's eyes across a ballroom dance floor in the middle of a wedding waltz. They will meet without appointment and strike up a relationship without an agenda. They will meet on street corners or in airplanes or in old hotels in Paris in the middle of the night while no one is stirring, not even a mouse. They will meet at work or at the beach or at a train stop or while singing a hymn. There may be a long courtship or a whirlwind romance. There may be protracted avoidance, even what looks like a phobia, as it did in Karl's case, or there may be an instant avidity, what amounts to love at first sight. Some carry on a kind of epistolary relationship with words, attenuating their feelings through the formal prose of elegant notes, while others jump at words and bark them out at the world in the immediate poetry of certain street corner vendors. Some slap their words up on posters on telephone poles, while others keep them in reserve, like a pistol concealed in a pocket book. Some read haltingly, like the nervous lover, hat in hand, while others are born to speechify or to orate. We all woo language differently, and language grants us her favors in different ways. Sometimes the relationship takes off, although rarely is a ride without bumps. Language is willful, disobedient, independent, and unpredictable. Language waits for no one, and changes without warning. While utterly beautiful, endlessly varied, and thoroughly transfixing, language is also frustrating, confusing, exasperating, and unforgiving. Language goes to bed with us all, but makes love with but a few. The relationship language offers is seldom without conflict.

Priscilla Vail, one of the great couples counsellors we have for troubled language relationships, knew intuitively and from great experience how to bring Karl together with words. She knew how to coax him from the periphery and onto the dance floor. She knew if she played the right music and showed him a few simple steps, the allure of the dance would overcome Karl's shy way with words.

Priscilla knew what all of you in this society know: that language is not an inert tool that you take down from the shelf like a hammer. Rather, it is a living companion, a strong but sometimes vulnerable friend, whose company you keep for most of your waking life. For most people, language is the friend they never knew they had until she went away, or the friend they never knew they needed until they asked him for a favor. For many people, language is a best friend they take for granted.

For some others, though, language never comes easily. The company of words is always an effort to keep. These people, and I count myself (as one who is dyslexic) among these people, never know quite what to expect from words.

Theirs – ours – is not a straightforward relationship with words. It lacks the solidity of the well-made play or the smooth contours of classical sculpture. It is a relationship rooted in unpredictability. One moment we are Abraham Lincoln composing a Gettysburg Address, and the next moment we are as clumsy with words as a boy on his first date.

Let me tell you another story.

"Separate me from my language and you separate me from my self," the patient said. "Words comprise my awareness. Without words I don't know what I am." The patient looked slightly past the doctor as he spoke, as if he were speaking to an audience of more than one, an audience that included the many people who never have understood. "Words are like my rope bridge that keeps me from falling into a chasm of insensate experience. Because I have words I can conjure up the unnameable and give it a word. Do you know the line from Keats, 'Heard melodies are sweet, but those unheard are sweeter still?' When we read, we read in what appears to be total silence, but in fact there is great volume and melody in the act of reading, volume at a special pitch, and melody of a special timbre. Those unheard melodies played by words, those silent sonatas we compose as we read, amplify whatever beauty our other senses may perceive. It is a special sense all its own that words set stirring. Do you think I'm foolish when I say I love them all, all the words, all those dauntless, little smudges of life set down in chiseled stillness?"

"I don't think you're foolish," the doctor said.

"But, doctor," the patient went on to ask, "how can it be that I am in love with language and a language-cripple at the same time?"

"You are not a language cripple," the doctor answered. "In fact you have a great facility with words."

"You know what I mean. Despite all your reassurances, I do still have dyslexia, and I do still have attention deficit disorder, and the last time I checked, those problems qualified me for special considerations under the Americans with Disabilities Act, so that means I'm a cripple, no matter how you might want to slice it."

"George, I don't want to argue with you," the doctor said. "All I'm saying is that you use language well."

"And all I'm saying is that it hurts me every day to know, no, to *feel* how distant I am from words sometimes. Does that sound absurd to you? That it hurts me to feel distant from words? Does it make sense that I love language as if it were my close friend? It's just that sometimes, like all friends, it isn't there, and when that happens I feel sad and scared."

"I do understand that, I think," the doctor said. "But tell me more just what you mean."

" 'Just what I mean.' That's the problem. And what if one turning should say, 'No, that is not what I meant at all.' It is not a matter of niceties. It is a matter of fundamental importance to me. I'm not talking about a tiresome search for the *bon mot* or the *mot juste*. I'm talking about my being in a cloud half the time when I'm trying to read or speak or write. But then, on the other hand, I'll have these moments of lucidity. In these moments, when I can speak clearly, or more importantly, when I can write clearly, I feel as if I have conquered something hard as rock. I feel as if I have been given the gift of flight for just a moment before I come crashing back to earth. It's quite a way to live, flying one minute, crashing the next.

"Sentences are for me like golf swings for a weekend golfer. Ninety percent feel just awful. They rattle my arms and make my shoulders shake. But the ten percent that are good, oh those ten percent keep me coming back. Those ten percent, the good swings, they feel absolutely effortless. It is as if the ball isn't even there. You just swing right through it. And, whoosh, you look up, and there is that little white rock soaring into a ring of sunlight where it gets lost for a moment before it arcs down smoothly and drops down, sure as a gull grabbing onto a buoy, right next to the hole. A good sentence will do that. It will take cumbersome, homely, old reality and, whoosh, send it flying in a beautiful arc, and make it land foursquare on that clear, well-trimmed green of the imagination where none but the most beautiful, roundest words of all can roll."

"Why do you think you care so much, George?" the doctor asked.

"I don't know. Maybe it's because I've had to struggle with language all my life. Did you know that Joseph Conrad and Samuel Beckett both wrote some of their great works in a foreign tongue? And they were master stylists. Maybe because they had to think about every word, they couldn't just paint it on the way you can with your native language. I often feel as if English is not my native language. But then, that means I don't have a native language because English is the only language I know, aside from my own language of associations and images. What does it feel like to have a native language?"

"Well, I don't know," the doctor said. "I mean I do know, because I have one, but I don't know that I could explain to you how it feels."

"Would you try?" George asked, leaning forward.

"Well, it's just such a disarming question," the doctor went on, somewhat flustered. "It would be much easier to tell you what it feels like to have a foreign language, as I do speak a bit of French and a bit of German. That I could tell you.

But what does it feel like to have a native language? It just feels natural, I guess. It is just the way things have been for as long as I can remember."

"But you haven't always had words," George said. "None of us has. Still, it must be pleasant to feel as if you always have. I feel as if I always have not."

"How can that be, George," the doctor asked, "when you use words so well?"

"That is just my point. I don't know. Where does the ability to use words well come from? I can't turn it on and off. One minute it will be there and the next minute it won't. It is like dancing with a ghost. One minute you're flying around the room with a beautiful partner, turning pirouettes on tiptoe, and the next minute you're stumbling over your own feet, looking foolish like you're dancing with a wash bucket and mop."

"Who is this beautiful partner?" the doctor asked.

"I don't know," George said. "I had hoped you might. She is – what can I tell you? – she is a fairy goddess who comes and goes on wings we can't control, who takes up our hearts in her hands and strokes them till they sing, and then she puts our hearts down and flies away, and the singing stops."

"You make it sound so poetical," the doctor said. "Isn't there a more practical way of putting it?"

"I'm afraid not," George said. "Oh, I suppose there is, but it wouldn't get to the truth of the matter in my opinion. You who know all about the brain still can't tell me how to call the goddess or how to make her stay. Poets have been talking of muses longer even than you doctors have been talking of cures. We must know something, don't you think?"

"I didn't mean to imply you didn't know anything," the doctor said, straightening himself up in his chair.

"No, I know you didn't," George said. "I'm just touchy. And I don't mean to make it sound like fairyland. Believe me, if I knew of a way to make my relationship with words more steady and predictable, I wouldn't care a bit how prosaic it was. It's just that it does feel like magic, and rather out of my control. So I use terms like muses and goddesses. I could also use terms like demons and devils for the pain my frustration causes me. Why am I wired up in such a screwball way? Can you tell me that?"

"No, I can't," the doctor replied. "I'm sorry, but I can't. Can you tell me what is the worst of your pain?"

"Yes, I can tell you that," George said after a moment's reflection. "It is the sea gull's problem."

The doctor stared back at George.

"No, I can see you are not familiar with the sea gull's problem," George went on. "You must think me a very difficult man, the way I speak to you in all these metaphorical ways. I'm sorry."

"No, not at all," the doctor said. "But, please, do tell me what the sea gull's problem is."

"I'd be glad to," George answered. "You couldn't know what the sea gull's problem is because it comes from a story from my childhood. You see, one day I was out fishing with my father. I was very young, maybe five or six. We were fishing off a bridge, an old wooden bridge I remember well. When cars went over it, the bridge made a wonderfully resonant sound, almost like a giant wind instrument, as the vibration of the thick planks would bounce off the water below like a contra-bassoon. It would have made a wonderful addition to the bass array of a symphonic orchestra. Some people said the sound scared the fish away, but my father said it called them to us. I don't know. We always caught a lot of fish." George looked at the doctor, who looked back faithfully. "Don't worry, doctor, I'll get to the point. We were fishing one day, fishing for flounder if you'd like to know, when a sea gull swooped down and grabbed my bait just as I was lowering it into the water. The gull took the bait, as they say, hook, line, and sinker. You have no idea what a racket a caught sea gull can make. Believe me, this was not symphonic music. It was terrifying to me. I felt as if I had the very devil by the tail, and the devil was mad as hell. My father must have seen my terror, because he quickly grabbed the fishing rod from my hands.

"'Well, what have we here?' he said in reassuring fatherly tones, as if he caught sea gulls all the time. Gradually he reeled the gull in. I crouched down behind his back, just about trying to crawl up under his sweater, as that screaming bird got closer. When I thought the gull was going to pick me up and fly me away, my father reached out and grabbed it. I don't know how he did it, but he steadied it within one arm while he used the other to free the hook. For a few horrifying moments, the gull and I stared at each other, my human eye taking in its bulging, red-black gull's eye. It was like a look from the other side of the grave. We both seemed to be saying to each other, underneath our fear, 'What the hell are you doing here?' The longer I looked into the gull's eye, the larger it bulged, as my father pushed on the belly of the gull. But I didn't know why the eye was bulging. I just saw this awful looking bruise of an eye growing buggier and buggier, turning white and yellow and red and green and black and blue, poking out at me like it was about to go splat, all over my face. Finally my father got the gull to cough up the hook and he set the bird free, sending it squawking off into the morning sky. 'Hope you catch a big fish,' my dad called after the gull.

"Well, since I was very young, I was still quite scared as the gull flapped off into the distance. 'Where have you gone to, Georgie?' my father asked, pulling me off the back of his sweater like a large insect. He lifted me over his shoulder and into his lap. 'Are you frightened, Georgie? Never seen a gull up close, hey?' he said. 'What'dja think of her?'

"I was quiet for a minute as I let the comfort of my father's lap and his steady breathing calm my rattled nerves. 'I looked her in the eye,' I said boldly, not inquiring as to how my father knew the gull's sex, which I also did wonder about and to this day don't know.

"'You looked her in the eye, did you, Georgie?' my father said, ruffling up my hair. 'And what did you see there, son?'

"'I saw that she's got a big problem,' " I said, giving an answer that would become part of my family's mythology.

"'You did!' my dad answered, astonished. 'And what might that sea gull's problem be?' he asked, credulously.

"'She can see, but she can't talk, and the words are popping out of her eyes,' I said, in dead earnest.

"Well, did my father ever laugh to hear that. And so did many others as the story got told again and again. I laugh at it, too, particularly when I envision what a sight we must have been, that old sea gull and me, eye to eye, behind my father's back. But, you know, I was onto something, even then. And when you ask me what is my greatest pain, it is that: when I can see but I cannot talk. When I can see so much, but I can't get to it. When I can't read right, I can't write right, I can't speak right, I can't even listen right. I'm like that dumb sea gull, flying everywhere, seeing everything. What a view! But half the time I have no more words than the gull."

"But what about the other half of the time?" the doctor asked.

"That can be good," George said. "That can be very good, very nice, very nice."

While George's relationship with words was inconstant and strained, it brought him much pleasure as well as pain. It is this way often with dyslexia, and with other disorders: There is a "good" side to it.

But much of the pain lies in disconnection. Listen to this from a man who spent the first forty-nine years of his life with undiagnosed, untreated attention deficit disorder. He wrote this piece shortly after the diagnosis was made and treatment was begun:

Words cannot describe how I feel now. I sometimes feel sad that I have missed so much in my life up to this point. I am experiencing feelings and sensations I have never known in my life before. The relationship I have with my wife is so different today. We have always been very close, but as I progressed in age with this disorder, I became more and more out of control. My wife used to complain of this 'other' person that used to come out in me that she hated. I used to get so defensive about things all the time it really had become a problem for me. But since treatment began, my wife hasn't seen a sign of 'my other me.' It is still easy for me to get off track, but I don't get the anxiety that I used to, so I can quickly get back on. Since finding out about ADD I have noticed some friends who I think have it, too. I guess that we like each other's company or something.

Untreated ADD was an exhausting disorder for me. As I got older, it became harder to deal with it, although I didn't know what it was I was dealing with. I was like the short kid who couldn't see over the fence unless he jumped up as high as he could and even then he would only catch a glimpse of what was on the other side. The peek is all he gets. I only had a peek at this life and instead of me getting taller so I could see over to the other side, the fence got taller or I got shorter. I'm not sure which. It was a lonely life.

Since treatment, I have realized that there is a different life that other people have enjoyed that I missed out on. The fence is lowering or I am growing. I'm not sure of which yet. I know now that I am not alone.

Often the problem is less apparent than in the last example. For many adults, dyslexia or ADD or other peculiarities of cognitive style are a subtle but definite part of who they are, like a red thread sewn into a pinstripe suit, changing its look but only visible upon close inspection. The red thread may be a thread of distractibility, or of impulsivity, or of disorganization, sewn into a stripe of creativity or gregariousness or industry. And the treatment may not be to remove the red thread but rather to change its hue only slightly so that it enhances rather than clashes with its surroundings.

One woman, for example, found that she needed help only with technical writing. Since that was a major part of her job, it was important that she do it well. Prior to her discovering she had ADD, it was an excruciating chore for her. She could not focus on it, and the more she tried to focus, the more anxious she became, thus becoming further distracted. She tried tranquilizers but they only sedated her. Coffee helped some but it made her jangly. Once the diagnosis of ADD was made, she tried stimulant medication. It helped her focus quite definitely, and it had no side effects. She found that taking medication a half hour prior to writing made things go much more smoothly for her. She didn't need the medication for anything else.

To give another short example, a man was having problems getting along with other people. It was nothing blatant, but he could sense that people pulled away from him. He could feel it even as it happened, as he was talking to someone and the conversation went bland. Although he felt it happening, he was not aware of what specifically he was doing. It turned out that he had mild ADD, the most problematic manifestation of which was an inability to observe his own behavior and to gauge correctly the responses of other people. This made him appear quite self-centered or indifferent. In fact, his problem was in paying attention, in noticing the subtle cues social fluency depends upon and in regulating his own responses.

Before leaping into the psychodynamic realm to explain such "self-centered" behavior, it is worthwhile to check at the doorway of attention. Are the lights on? Is the individual neurologically able to notice the particulars of human interaction, from voice tone to body language, to timing, to irony, and so forth? In this man's case, he needed some coaching and role playing to learn how to tune into what he was missing. In treating this hidden ADD, his interpersonal life improved greatly. The treatment reconnected him to other people.

These are a few of the kinds of places mild ADD or dyslexia may interfere with an adult's life: achieving at one's ability level; reading one's interpersonal world accurately; getting started on or finishing a creative project; staying with emotions long enough to work them out; getting organized; getting rid of perseverative, negative thinking; slowing down; finding the time to do what you've always wanted to do; or getting a handle on certain compulsive types of behavior.

Taking stock of yourself in terms of attention or cognitive style is not the drift of most adult introspection. We are more geared to think in terms of who likes who, or who dislikes who else, or why our families did this or that, or how we can deal with this fear or that. We introspect in terms of stories and we quickly jump into the plot. But learning disorders precede the plot. They adjust the lighting and set the stage. If the lighting is too low or significant props are missing from the stage, the story cannot be fully comprehended. Before getting the story going, before developing the plot lines of one's ongoing narrative of introspection, it is worthwhile to have a lighting specialist and prop expert check things out.

Finding out that you have ADD or dyslexia or other learning disabilities in adulthood is a bit startling. These kinds of things, one imagines, are supposed to be sorted out during childhood. After that, you make do with the brain you have, with the lighting you've been wired with. You don't expect at, say, age forty, to be told you have a learning disorder or that you have ADD. You don't expect to get therapy to help you read and study better, to learn your way around stage. But there are millions of adults out there who could benefit greatly from realizing they have such a problem.

Consider Sarah, a woman who was told from an early age by her father that she "had no more sense than a jaybird," and that her main problem was that she was "lazy." Although a part of her bristled at these remarks, knowing they were untrue, another part of her accepted them, took them in, and incorporated them into her self-image. At fifty, married with grown children, Sarah had a career as a potter. She came in from out of town to see me for a consultation because her husband had discovered he had adult ADD, and Sarah thought many of her symptoms might be understood in light of that syndrome.

She and her husband, Jeff, arrived, sat down, and Sarah smiled back tears. "I don't want to cry. I told myself I wouldn't cry," she said.

"It's OK to cry in here," I said. "Maybe you can try to tell me what the tears are about?"

"It's just that it's been so many years living like this," she said, letting the tears come, "thinking I'm stupid, but knowing I'm not. I brought along this list we wrote last night. I just wrote down everything I could so you might read it." She handed me some papers bunched up like a scarf.

The first item on the list referred to a cough drop. As I read it I asked her about it.

"Oh," she answered, "that is about a cough drop someone left on the dashboard of our car. The other day I got into the car and saw the cough drop and thought, I'll have to throw that away. When I got to my first stop, I forgot to take the cough drop to a trash can. When I got back into the car, I saw it and thought, I'll throw it away at the gas station. The gas station came and went, and I hadn't thrown it away. Well, the whole day went like that, the cough drop still sitting on the dashboard. When I got home, I noticed the cough drop on the dashboard and thought, I'll take it inside with me and throw it out. In the time it took me to open the car door I forgot about the cough drop. It was there to greet me when I got in the car the next morning. Jeff was with me. I looked at the cough drop and burst into tears. Jeff asked me why I was crying and I told him it was because of the cough drop. He thought I was losing my mind. 'But you don't understand,' I said, 'my whole life is like that. I see something that I mean to do and then I don't do it. It's not only trivial things like the cough drop, it's big things, too. That's what made me cry.'"

It was such a classic story I've named it the "cough drop sign" when a person habitually has trouble following through on plans, on a minute-to-minute, even second-to-second basis. This is not due to procrastination as much as it is due to the busy-ness of the moment interrupting or interfering with one's memory circuits. You can get up from your chair, go into the kitchen to get a glass of water, and then in the kitchen forget your reason for being there. Or, on a larger scale, the most important item on your agenda for a given day might be to make a certain telephone call, a call that, say, has crucial business consequences. You mean to do it, you want to do it, you are not afraid of doing it, indeed you are eager to make the call and feel confident about doing it. And yet, as the day progresses you never get around to making the call. An invisible shield of procrastination seems to separate you from the task. You sharpen your pencil instead, talk to an associate, pay some bills, have lunch, get interrupted by a minor problem, return some other calls to clear your decks so you can make the important call, only to find that the end of the day has come, and the call still has not been made. Or, on an interpersonal level, you may mean to bring home flowers to your spouse, have it in mind to do it all day, really want to do it, in fact on the subway home envision just which florist shop you will stop at, only to find yourself standing in front of your spouse, saying, "Hi, honey," with no flowers in hand. Sometimes, this is due to unconsciously not wanting to buy the flowers. But sometimes, far more often than most people realize, it is due to a cognitive problem such as ADD.

Our disconnections in everyday life, so often ascribed to unconscious motivation or complexities of our past histories, may, more often than most of us realize, derive from neurology, from the anatomy and biochemistry of our brains, rather than our lived experience.

Let me tell you another story. When I was growing up on Cape Cod there used to be an old man who sat by the side of the road on nice days and read the Bible. I remember him well. He had a white and gray beard, which smelled of garlic because he ate garlic regularly for, as he put it, "its medicinal properties." Because I liked this man, I liked the smell of garlic, and to this day think of him whenever I detect the aroma of that pungent bulb. His name was Ezra, the only Ezra I knew growing up, the only Ezra, for that matter, I've ever known. He lived in a house made of cinder blocks, which was really an old garage left standing next to a house that had been torn down. Ezra would sit in an old wicker chair with his Bible in his lap and he would read. I passed him every morning on my way to school. He often offered encouraging words about school. If you stopped to talk he would give you a few sentences from the Bible before he let you go. And he would ask about you. No matter what your age, he would want to know what you'd been doing, how things were going. He would nod at all you said, take it in, into his beard I imagined, where the words would find a place.

He was the town philosopher. Adults sometimes asked his advice. Whether it was due to his beard or his Bible, people trusted him. I think it might have been due to his enunciation. He spoke each word as if it were a note, chosen and then percussed with a purpose. We children loved to hear his stories about the town, and his stories of high adventure from his years as a seaman. I can remember him well, sitting there next to the honeysuckle bushes that crowded around the old garage. Those bushes gave off a sweet smell in summer. Honeysuckle, garlic, Ezra, and the Bible.

What I didn't learn until I was a grown-up was that Ezra didn't know how to read. He sat with his Bible, which gave people the impression he was reading, but in fact he couldn't read a word. He had the Bible memorized, or pretty nearly, so he could quote long passages as if he were reading, but he had no reading in him. How life must have been for Ezra! He loved words. To listen to him recite the Bible was to hear those rotund verses from the King James as I have never heard them since. A man by the side of the road, in love with words, who could not read.

Ezra is at the heart of what I want to say today because out of his pain he spun a song. He sang to us children with his words each morning on our way to school. Seeing Ezra by the side of the road made our world the more secure. He sang to us in words he could not read, a philosopher on Cape Cod. There he sat, an old man, and he spoke his song of words with what I imagine must have been tears inside as he watched us children trip off to school to get the knowledge and skill he had never been able to get but dearly loved. I imagine the words he turned over in his mind became all the more carefully turned as he felt what he did not have, and as he watched us go off to find what he would never get, the knowledge to read and to write. If he had tears inside, those tears watered the growth of many words.

While we talk of the disabilities of learning, the disorders, the impediments, we should also talk of the beauty spun out of the pain. How much more do we love a thing we have to struggle to acquire? How much more do we respect and care for a gift we know we can lose so easily? How much more do we treasure what we fear we cannot have? "Heard melodies are sweet, but those unheard are sweeter still."

The struggle to hear what we cannot hear, to feel what we cannot feel, to read what we cannot read, to speak what we cannot say, to see what we cannot see – these are the struggles of the dyslexias and of ADD and of all idiosyncrasies of learning. Just as the poet struggles to fashion out of words a new way of seeing an everyday object or event, so we with our various learning disorders struggle to connect with the world in a comprehensible fashion. The struggles are not dissimilar. For neither the poet nor the dyslexic is the way at first clear. He, or she, must clear a path.

For me, reading a novel can be a little like hacking my way through thick woods and underbrush. At the start of a book, after a few gloriously easy pages, pages relatively free of woods and brush, the pages with just the title or the copyright history or the dedication, pages numbered with small case Roman numerals, then I hit the first real page of text and there they sit, the words, the sentences, starting usually about halfway down that first page. It is like hitting the timber line. The trees begin. And there are so many of them! Not one, or two, but row upon row!

The words sequence into sentences which fold into paragraphs which comprise pages which turn into chapters which bind into books. I may stride into the first sentence with determination to go on, but then I drift off, turned away by the density of what is to come. In order to push on I need a spirited guide, a pretty piper of a writer whose story cuts me a path I can't resist.

If that happens, something wonderful happens in my brain. The unheard melody takes over and beckons me on, the anticipation of what is to come. It is like what happened in Karl's brain when Priscilla Vail distracted him from his fear of writing and activated within his mind the hope of activities to come, the engagement with what is behind the words: the plot, the suspense, the puzzle, the fun. Then the impulse to connect, that powerful urge to join in, overcame Karl's phobia or disability or call-it-what-you-will.

While we must be able to see or hear or feel in order to apprehend words, words do not depend primarily on any one sense for their main appreciation, not in the way that art depends on sight or music upon hearing or movies upon both. Words enter our brains through one sense or another, but once they are there they do their real work by activating the imagination in a way no other art form does. As we take in the word, we make a picture of our own, see a scene of our own, hear a song of our own. With other art forms, the beauty is usually already out there, external; that is, the beauty resides outside the mind, in the painting hanging on the wall, or on the film projected on the screen, or in the sound made by the instruments. But, leaving aside the tonal beauty of words, the beauty they create is entirely internal. We never speak of a beautiful poem and mean that it looks beautiful on the page. We mean that the images it induces us to create in our own brains are beautiful. Words connect us to the dormant creator within us all. In a true sense, as we read a novel we write it ourselves, we create it for ourselves, image by image, character by character, melody by melody.

Let me make up a sentence at random for an instance of what I mean. Let me think of something I would like to do, but have never done, and take you there with me with words. "Sipping my second martini, I listened to Bobby Short at the piano in the bar at the Hotel Carlyle." If that sentence were a photograph or a painting, you would see me now. If it were a recording you would have the great good luck not of seeing me, but of hearing Mr. Short. But since it is a sentence, you all have different views of the scene right now. Some of you are looking at me, others at Bobby Short, still others at a smoke ring caught in the light from the door. You are looking at your own scene. Am I in a corner or out front? Am I alone or with someone? Is Mr. Short visible, or hidden behind the crowd? And how does he sound? What is his song?

Without taking away anything from Bobby Short, I suggest that the unheard melody the sentence conjures up within your mind is a sweeter melody than anything Bobby Short has ever played. As words activate our imaginations, they connect us to a special part of ourselves, a part made out of memory, hope, and experience, a part of ourselves that is hard to reach more effectively by any route other than the route of words. The words, those blasted little puzzles lined up across page after page, may frustrate us, but they also connect us miraculously to ideas, to beauty, to each other, and to inner parts of ourselves.

This will to build a bridge from concrete reality into the imagination, into the ineffable, into the unspoken and unheard, lies at the center, I think, of what both troubles and propels the learning-disabled. Moreover, it lies at the center of the will to communicate in most people. But especially in those of us for whom that act is in some way blocked, the will to bridge the gap between what is outside and what is inside is particularly strong. It is what George saw pulsating behind the bulging eye of the sea gull – she could see, but she could not talk.

At the beginning of my training in psychiatry, I treated a man named Joey. He was schizophrenic; his greatest problem was that he had everything locked up inside, unable to get out except through psychotic delusions or violent acts. One day he missed his meeting with me, so I went looking for him. When I found him sitting in the day room watching TV, I asked him why he had missed his appointment. I have never forgotten his answer. "It's personal," he said to me. "It's so personal even I don't know why."

In trying to express what we cannot express, to hear what we cannot hear, to connect with that from which we feel disconnected, we feel some of Joey's pain, the pain of understanding or expressing what is so personal even we do not know of it.

We may shy away from the task, disappointed once too often by words, and so remain that much more disconnected, within ourselves. Or we may choose to have at it. We may choose to push on into the novel, or break beyond the bounds of the 3 x 5 index card, or memorize the whole Bible and tell stories to the little children in the hope that they will take the next step. We may choose to come face to face with an old and ordinary image and call it by its wrong name, some new name, something amazing. We may see waves and call them, "blue-lunged combers, lumbering toward the kill," or we may state our age by calling it, "that time of year thou may'st in me behold when yellow leaves, or few, or none do hang," or we may describe our fear at seeing a snake slide through the grass as, "a tighter breathing and Zero at the Bone." Zero at the Bone? The words have no meaning, we might protest, yet no words say it better.

As we reach to connect with what is lived, which is always receding before us, we begin to make answers to a question Ian Litten, a little boy with attention deficit disorder and dyslexia, asked his mother upon waking up one morning in Iowa: "When you wake up, where do your dreams go?"

Just as the dream begins to recede the minute we wake up and try to hold onto it, so does experience disappear before our very eyes. Where does it go? Ian asks. It goes into an invisible world, I would answer, a world words can take you to. Dyslexia, far from being the crippled passenger on that voyage, may be the most adept guide. "I sang in my chains like the sea," Dylan Thomas said in "Fern Hill." So do many of us sing; so do many of you.

What Is It Like to Have Attention Deficit Disorder? *by Edward M. Hallowell*

Attention deficit disorder. First of all I resent the term. As far as I'm concerned, most people have attention surplus disorder. I mean, life being what it is, who can pay attention to anything for very long? Is it really a sign of mental health to be able to balance your checkbook, sit still in your chair, and never speak out of turn? As far as I can see, many people who don't have ADD are charter members of the Society for the Congenitally Boring.

But anyway, be that as it may, there is this syndrome called ADD or ADHD – attention deficit hyperactivity disorder – depending on what book you read. So what's it like to have ADD? Some people say the so-called syndrome doesn't even exist, but believe me, it does. Many metaphors come to mind to describe it. It's like driving in the rain with bad windshield wipers. Everything is smudged and blurred and you're speeding along, and it's reeeeally frustrating not being able to see very well. Or it's like listening to a radio station with a lot of static, and you have to strain to hear what's going on. Or, it's like trying to build a house of cards in a sandstorm. You have to build a structure to protect yourself from the wind before you can even start on the cards.

In other ways it's like being super-charged all the time. You get one idea and you have to act on it, and then, what do you know, you've got another idea before you've finished up with the first one, and so you go for that one, but of course a third idea intercepts the second, and you just have to follow that one, and pretty soon people are calling you disorganized and impulsive and all sorts of impolite words that miss the point completely. Because you're trying really hard. It's just that you have all these invisible vectors puling you this way and that, which makes it really hard to stay on task.

Plus which, you're spilling over all the time. You're drumming your fingers, tapping your feet, humming a song, whistling, looking here, looking there, scratching, stretching, doodling, and people think you're not paying attention or that you're not interested, but all you're doing is spilling over so that you can pay attention. I can pay a lot better attention when I'm taking a walk or listening to music or even when I'm in a crowded noisy room than when I'm still and surrounded by silence. God save me from reading rooms. Have you ever been into the one in Widener Library? The only thing that saves it is that so many of the people who use it have ADD that there's a constant, soothing bustle.

What is it like to have ADD? Buzzing. Being here and there and everywhere. Someone once said, "Time is the thing that keeps everything from happening all at once." Time parcels moments out into separate bits so that we can do one thing at a time. In ADD, this does not happen. In ADD, time collapses. Time becomes a black hole. To the person with ADD it feels as if everything is happening all at once. This creates a sense of inner turmoil or even panic. The individual loses perspective and the ability to prioritize. He or she is always on the go, trying to keep the world from caving in on top.

Museums. (Have you noticed how I skip around? That's part of the deal. I change channels a lot. And radio stations. Drives my wife nuts. Can't we listen to just one song all the way through?) Anyway, museums. The way I go through a museum is the way some people go through Filene's Basement. Some of this, some of that, oh, this one looks nice, but what about that rack over there? Gotta hurry, gotta run. It's not that I don't like art. I love art. But my way of loving it makes most people think I'm a real Philistine. On the other hand, sometimes I can sit and look at one painting for a long while. I'll get into the world of the painting and buzz around in there until I forget about everything else. In these moments I, like most people with ADD, can hyperfocus, which gives the lie to the notion that we can never pay attention. Sometimes we have turbo-charged focusing abilities. It just depends upon the situation.

Lines. I'm almost incapable of waiting in lines. I just can't wait, you see. That's the hell of it. Impulse leads to action. I'm very short on what you might call the intermediate reflective step between impulse and action. That's why I, like so many people with ADD, lack tact. Tact is entirely dependent on the ability to consider one's words before uttering them. We ADD types don't do this so well. I remember in the fifth grade I noticed my math teacher's hair in a new style and I blurted out, "Mr. Cook, is that a toupé you're wearing?" I got kicked out of class. I've since learned how to say these inappropriate things in such a way or at such a time that they can in fact be helpful. But it has taken time. That's the thing about ADD. It takes a lot of adapting to get on in life. But it certainly can be done, and be done very well.

As you might imagine, intimacy can be a problem if you've got to be constantly changing the subject, pacing, scratching and blurting out tactless remarks. My wife has learned not to take my tuning out personally, and she says that when I'm there, I'm really there. At first, when we met, she thought I was some kind of a nut, as I would bolt out of restaurants at the end of meals or disappear to another planet during a conversation. Now she has grown accustomed to my sudden comings and goings.

Many of us with ADD crave high-stimulus situations. In my case, I love the racetrack. And I love the high-intensity crucible of doing psychotherapy. And I love having lots of people around. Obviously this tendency can get you into trouble, which is why ADD is high among criminals and self-destructive risk-takers. It is also high among so-called Type A personalities, the more recently classified Type T or thrill-seeker personalities, as well as among manic-depressives, sociopaths and criminals, violent people, drug abusers, and alcoholics. But it is also high among creative and intuitive people in all fields, and among highly energetic, highly productive people.

Which is to say there is a positive side to all this. Usually the positive doesn't get mentioned when people speak about ADD because there is a natural tendency to focus on what goes wrong, or at least on what has to be somehow controlled. But often once the ADD has been diagnosed, and the child or the adult, with the help of teachers and parents or spouses, friends, and colleagues, has learned how to cope with it, an untapped realm of the brain swims into view. Suddenly the radio station is tuned in, the windshield is clear, the sandstorm has died down. And the child or adult who had been such a problem, such a nudge, such a general pain in the neck to himself and everybody else, that person starts doing things he'd never been able to do before. He surprises everyone around him, and he surprises himself. I use the male pronoun, but it could just as easily be she, as we are seeing more and more ADD among females as we are looking for it.

Often these people are highly imaginative and intuitive. They have a "feel" for things, a way of seeing right into the heart of matters while others have to reason their way along methodically. This is the person who can't explain how he thought of the solution, or where the idea for the story came from, or why suddenly he produced such a painting, or how he knew the short cut to the answer, but all he can say is he just knew it, he could feel it. This is the man or woman who dreams up million dollar deals during a catnap and pulls them off the next day. This is the child who, having been reprimanded for blurting something out, is then praised for having blurted out something brilliant. These are the people who learn and know and do and go by touch and feel.

These people can feel a lot. In places where most of us are blind, they can, if not see the light, at least feel the light, and they can produce answers apparently out of the dark. It is important for others to be sensitive to this "sixth sense" many ADD people have, and to nurture it. If the environment insists on rational, linear thinking and "good" behavior from these people all the time, then they may never develop their intuitive style to the point where they can use it profitably. It can be exasperating to listen to these people talk. They can sound so vague or rambling. But if you take them seriously and grope along with them, often you will find they are on the brink of startling conclusions or surprising solutions.

What I am saying is that their cognitive style is qualitatively different from most people's, and what at first may seem impaired, with patience and encouragement may become gifted.

The thing to remember is that if the diagnosis can be made, then most of the bad stuff associated with ADD can be avoided or contained. The diagnosis can be liberating, particularly for people who have been stuck with labels like "lazy," "stubborn," "willful," "disruptive," "impossible," "tyrannical," "a spaceshot," "brain-damaged," "stupid," or just plain "bad." Making the diagnosis of ADD can take the case from the court of moral judgment to the clinic of neuropsychiatric treatment.

What is the treatment all about? Anything that turns down the noise. Just making the diagnosis helps turn down the noise of guilt and self-recrimination. Building certain kinds of structure into one's life can help a lot. Working in small spurts rather than long hauls. Breaking tasks down into smaller tasks. Getting help where you need it, whether it's having a secretary, or an accountant, or an automatic bank teller, or a good filing system, or a home computer. Maybe applying external limits on your impulses. Or, in the opposite direction, getting enough exercise to work off some of the noise inside. Medication can help, too, but it is far from the whole solution.

Let me leave you by telling you that we need your help and understanding. We may make mess-piles wherever we go, but with your help, those mess-piles can be turned into realms of reason and art. So, if you know someone like me who's acting up and daydreaming and forgetting this or that and just not getting with the program, consider ADD before he starts believing all the bad things people are saying about him, and it's too late.

The Emotional Experience of ADD
by Edward M. Hallowell

When it comes to attention deficit disorder, I am a radical moderate. That is to say, I am passionate about trying to preserve a balanced view of this disorder. It disturbs me that the diagnosis of ADD has become a kind of fad, with ardent proponents and equally ardent opponents. I am sometimes asked if I believe in Ritalin as if it were a religious tenet or if I believe in ADD as if it were a magical incantation. I can only tell you that I am neither an opponent nor a proponent but an investigator who, like all of you, is trying to understand children and use whatever tools are at hand to help them.

My radical moderation does not, however, leave me emotionally neutral on the topic. Having grown up with ADD myself in the days when it was called everything from dyslexia to minimal brain dysfunction, and having struggled within various schools to sit still and pay attention, I feel very strongly about the importance of diagnosing ADD and understanding the emotional experience of having it.

That last is what I intend to focus on. But before proceeding, let me give a quick definition. If you think in terms of two words, you will have a good feel for ADD: distractible and impulsive. The syndrome is characterized by difficulty in paying attention, sitting still, sustaining attention through the completion of a task, following directions of more than a few steps, waiting one's turn, tolerating frustration, and containing energy.

Boys have the syndrome more than girls, but girls do have it. Onset is before age seven. It may go away during adolescence or persist late into adulthood. We don't know what causes it, but it seems clear there is a genetic factor.

The keys to treatment are as follows: first, make the diagnosis. No diagnosis, no treatment. Second, educate the people involved. In teaching the child, family, and school about ADD, one lifts a tremendous burden from them. This alone brings relief and helps avert the usual secondary problems with self-esteem. Third, look for specific strategies that might help. A careful history from child, parents, and teachers will often reveal various tricks each has discovered that will aid in treatment. Fourth, structure. These kids do best in an environment that structures externally what they have trouble arranging internally. Fifth, consider medication: most commonly Ritalin, but there are several others.

Medication alone is not adequate treatment.

Psychotherapy may or may not be necessary. When it is, there are primary uses for it. First, a therapist may help the child, family, and school to understand what is going on with this particular child and what can help. Second, psychotherapy can deal with the secondary problems of poor self-esteem and impaired social relationships. Just as a child with undiagnosed myopia may perform poorly and be called stupid and so develop a poor self-image secondary to the primary problem of nearsightedness, a child with ADD may develop a host of psychological problems secondary to the primary neurological problem of ADD.

With that as introduction, let me take you now into the world of Maxwell McCarthy, a fictional character, a boy whom I have made up, a composite of the hundreds of ADD kids I have known or treated.

When Maxwell was born, his mother held him in her arms and cried tears of joy. He was the most adorable baby she had ever seen. He was the son Sylvia and Patrick McCarthy had wished for after their two daughters. Maxwell stared up at his mom as his dad leaned across the pillows and drew little circles with his forefinger on Maxwell's wrinkled forehead.

"I'm so happy," Sylvia said.

"He looks like my father," Patrick said.

"You can't tell this soon, silly."

"I just have a feeling," Patrick replied. His father, Maxwell McCarthy, after whom this new Maxwell was named, had been a prominent Boston lawyer, the rod and staff of Patrick's life, his hero and his guide. The values of intellectual achievement and rock-solid integrity combined with a hard-drinking, convivial bonhomie made the senior Maxwell an almost legendary figure. As Patrick looked down at his son now, he saw some of his old man in him. The large head size, he concluded, meant brains. The twinkle in the baby's eyes meant joie-de-vivre. And the integrity would come from a disciplined upbringing. A gurgling, swaddled package now, Maxwell McCarthy was destined for great things.

Sylvia's fantasies drifted more toward the simple but boundless joy of holding this little baby. Oh, she had thought about his future before he was born, she hoped for him what she hoped for her other children, that he could have the advantages she hadn't had when she was growing up. Her family had been torn apart by mental illness, depression, and alcoholism. She had worked her way through law school, where she met Patrick, and she was now juggling part-time legal work with being a mother of, as of now, three. In the process, she'd lost all contact with her family, and she was never far from the sadness of that, an undertow tugging at her ankles in the sand. As she looked down at Maxwell she thought, We will be good to you, beautiful one.

As an infant and toddler Max never liked to be left alone. He was gregarious and active. When he learned how to walk, it was almost impossible to childproof the house, Max was so fast. Cute as he was, it was exhausting to take care of him. As one of his babysitters said, somewhat vengefully after a long night with Max, "You have a very high-maintenance baby."

By the time he was four, young Max had a nickname, Mad Max. "How shall I put it to you?" said Max's day-care provider to Sylvia and Patrick. "He is very enthusiastic."

"You can be straight with us," Patrick said sternly, for the moment forgetting he was surrounded by teddy bears, little bunnies, and story books, not leather-bound tomes.

"Well, it's just that he likes to do so many things, he's all over the place. The minute he starts one thing he's into another. He's a bundle of joy, but he also can be very disruptive in the group."

In the car on the way home Patrick said, "What Miss Rebecca of Sunnybrook Farm was trying to tell us is that Max is a brat."

"She was not," said Sylvia. "He's just rambunctious, like you used to be."

"I was not. I had discipline. Standards. Max has no standards."

"He's only four, for crying out loud," Sylvia said. "Can't you let him be a little boy?"

"Sure. Just not a spoiled little boy."

"Oh. And I suppose his behavior is all my fault," said Sylvia.

"I didn't say that," Patrick replied.

"No, you didn't say that, but since I'm home twice as much as you, you've made it pretty clear to me who has primary responsibility for the kids. But, Pat, boys need dads."

"Oh, so it's my fault now. Clever way of turning it around." They drove on in silence.

At six, Max entered the first grade at Meadow Glen, a coed private school. Things went all right at first, but then one day, as the kids were on the floor doing projects in pairs, Max suddenly took his jar of paint, smashed it on the floor, kicked the project he and his partner were making across the room, and started punching himself in the face. His teacher took him outside to calm down while the co-teacher stayed with the other children. "What happened in there?" his teacher asked Max.

"Everything I make breaks," he said, tears beading down his cheeks.

"That's not true," his teacher said. "Your project was looking very good."

"It was not," Max said. "It sucked."

"Max, you know we can't talk like that here."

"I know," Max said sadly. "I need more discipline and better standards."

Later, at the request of the teacher, some testing was done on Max, but as it turned out it was only intelligence testing. Max had a full-scale IQ of 145, with a ten-point split between performance and verbal. "You see? He's plenty smart," Max's dad would say. "What he needs is to buckle down."

Through the early years, Max's grades were fine. The comments on his report cards, however, were upsetting, comments like, "Despite my best efforts I cannot persuade Max to pay attention consistently," or, "Although he doesn't mean to be, Max is a constant disruption in class," or "His social adjustment lags behind," or, "He is so obviously bright – but he is a born daydreamer."

As for Max himself, he felt confused. He tried to do what he was told, like sit still or pay attention or keep his hands to himself, but he found that in spite of his best efforts he couldn't do these things. So he kept getting into trouble. He hated his nickname at home, Mad Max, but whenever he complained about it, his sisters teased him, and when they teased him, he hit them, and when he hit them, he got in trouble. He didn't know what to do.

"I don't know what to do with you," his father said one day.

"Why don't you send me back to the dealership like you did with the Fiat? Maybe they have a lemon law for kids." He had learned about the lemon law through listening to many conversations between his parents.

"Oh, Max," his father said, trying to give him a hug, "we wouldn't trade you for anything. We love you."

"Then how come," Max asked, pulling away, "how come you said to Mom that all the problems in this family are because of me?"

"I never said that, Max."

"Yes, Dad, you did," Max said softly.

"Well, I didn't mean it if I did. It's just that we need a game plan for you, like when we watch the Patriots, and I tell you about the game plan. What kind of game plan can we come up with to keep you out of trouble?"

"Well, Dad, you say it's up to the coach to come up with a game plan that works, and if he can't do that they should fire the coach. You're the coach around here, aren't you Daddy, you and Mom?"

"Yes, Son, we are. But we can't be fired. And we need your help."

"I'll try harder," Max said. He was nine at the time. That night he wrote on a piece of paper, "I wish I was dead," then crumpled it up and threw it in the wastebasket.

His life, however, was not all gloom. For one thing, he was, as his second grade teacher put it, "chock full of spunk." And, as that same teacher said, he was cute as a button. He was smart, no doubt about that, and he did love to get into things. He could turn a telephone booth into a playground and a telephone book into a novel. His father thought Max was more creative than just about anyone he'd ever met; he just wished he could help Max contain it.

What Max couldn't do was behave. Conform. Sit still. Raise his hand. And he didn't know why he couldn't. Because there was no explanation, he began to believe the worst: that he was bad, a spaceshot, a dingbat, a functional retard, all names he'd been called. When he asked his mother what a functional retard mean, she asked him where he'd heard the term.

"I read it in a book," Max said, lying.

"What book?" his mother asked.

"Just a book. What does it matter what book? Do you think I keep records?"

"No, Max, I just wondered if maybe someone called you that and you don't want to tell me who." As soon as she said it, his mother realized her mistake, but the words were out and irretrievable. "Max, it doesn't mean anything," his mother hurried to add as she tried to hug him.

"Let me go," he said.

"Max, it means nothing. Whoever said it is stupid."

"Like Dad?" Max said, staring into his mother's eyes through tears.

By the sixth grade, Max's grades became erratic, ranging from the best in the class to barely passing. "How is it," one of his teachers asked him, "that one week you can be one of the best students I've ever had and the next week act as if you weren't even in the room?"

"I don't know," said Max glumly, by now getting used to this line of questioning. "I guess I've got a funny brain."

"You've got a very good brain," the teacher responded.

"A brain is only a brain," said Max philosophically, "but a good person is hard to find."

The teacher look astonished at this precocious remark, astonished and perplexed, which Max picked up on. "Don't try and figure me out," Max said with resignation in his voice. "I just need more discipline. I'll try harder."

Later, at a parent-teacher conference one of the teachers offered this description: "Watching Max sit at his desk in class is like watching a kind of ballet. A leg will come up, then an arm will arch around it, and then a foot will appear as the head disappears from sight. This is often followed by a crash. Then, often, a swear. You know, he's so hard on himself, it's hard for me to come down on him."

Max's parents listened, felt guilty, and sighed.

Although Max thought quite poorly of himself by now, his spunk and pride kept him from talking with anyone about it. However, he did have conversations with himself. Sometimes he would beat up on himself. "You're bad, bad, bad," he would say. "Why don't you change?" Then he would make a list of resolutions. "Study harder. Sit still. Get homework done on time. Don't do things that make Mom and Dad worry. Keep your hands to yourself."

Brought up Catholic, sometimes he talked to God. "Why did you make me so different?" he asked.

And other times, the best times, he would wander unperturbed with his thoughts, from one image or idea to the next, so that big chunks of time could pass without his even noticing it. Often this happened when he was reading a book. He would start on page one and by the time he was in the middle of page three he would be off in fantasy on a moon walk or winning a football game with a rushing touchdown in the last minute. The daydream could go on for a half hour or so as Max sat staring at page three. This was one of his greatest pleasures, but also a real obstacle to getting his homework in on time.

Although Max had friends, he at times annoyed them by what they took to be his selfishness. As he got older, he found it hard to follow the conversation in a group of friends, and so he stared off, blankly. "Hey, what's with you, McCarthy?" his friends said. "You on drugs or something?"

But because of his basically cheerful personality – he had learned how to put up a good front – and because his raw intelligence could carry him academically, Max avoided social or academic catastrophe.

By ninth grade his family had grown accustomed to him as Mad Max; instead of fighting back, he took the teasing and added to it by making fun of himself, tripping over his feet intentionally, or pointing to his head and saying, "crazy." His mother moved his room to the basement. "At least the mess can be contained in one place out of sight," she said. "Since you're constitutionally incapable of straightening your room, at least we can move you to the least offensive spot." That suited Max just fine.

In contrast to the time he drew circles on his son's forehead when he looked at him as a baby in the hospital, Max's father now just hoped and prayed that Max could survive in this cruel world, that he would find some niche for himself where his creativity and good nature were rewarded and his gargantuan carelessness and irresponsibility would not get him fired. When his mother looked at him now, she thought of him as her lovable genius-goof. At times she felt very guilty at not having been able to straighten Max out, but after three children and more professional compromises than she cared to think of, she was trying to learn to go easy on herself. Indeed, she felt relief that the family had not been destroyed by the problems Max had caused earlier on.

This period of relative calm and accommodation ended as Max encountered the greater stimulations the world of high school offered. He felt an internal restlessness that could only be soothed by engaging in some external situation of equally high energy.

He began to find release in athletics, becoming a fanatical long-distance runner and wrestler. He talked about "the pleasure in the pain of the long-distance run" and the mental relief, the feeling of "absolute psychic clarity" in the last half-mile. He was also an excellent wrestler. He was especially good at the move at the start of a period when you explode out of your opponent's grasp. Here at last was a place where he could legitimately go crazy, where, at last, he could release all the energy he had stored in his cells and slash through the bonds of good behavior as if escaping from a briar patch. In wrestling, Max could break free. He also loved the agony of getting down to the lowest weight for a meet. "I hate it, of course," he would say, "but I also love it. It focuses my mind on one thing, one goal."

But, as relatively adaptive as his sports were, he also began to flirt with danger. He began experimenting with drugs, particularly cocaine, which he noticed calmed him and helped him focus. He was always on the go. He had more girlfriends than he could keep straight. All this left him little time for studying. He continued to play a game he called "chicken," walking into exams totally unprepared and seeing if he could fake his way through. He began to discover that he couldn't do this as well as he had in grade school.

In a part of his being, he knew he was courting disaster. On his way out the door one day, he casually said to his mother, "You know, Mom, I'm a walking time bomb."

Thinking he was joking, she answered with a laugh, "At least you're not a dud." The family had learned long ago to turn Max's self-deprecatory remarks into jokes. They weren't unfeeling; they just didn't know what else to do.

What happened next could have happened in many different ways. Or, it could not have happened at all. There are many adult Maxes out there who have managed not to trip and fall. They simply live frenetic lives, a whirligig of high stimulation, and often high achievement, with an abiding sense that their world is on the brink of collapse.

But Max, fortunately, did trip and fall. It could have been academic failure or drugs or alcohol or some high-risk prank. In Max's case, though, it was the unusual route of wrestling. In an effort to make weight, he violated all the rules; he was found comatose and thoroughly dehydrated in his basement room. When he was hospitalized, his family doctor was sensitive enough to see this episode as a signal of some pretty serious psychological problems.

In the course of Max's evaluation, neuropsychological testing revealed, in addition to Max's already documented high IQ, a number of other issues. There was good evidence that he had attention deficit disorder. Second, projective testing revealed extremely low self-esteem as well as recurring depressive themes and images. In marked contrast to his cheerful exterior, Max's inner life was, in the words of the psychologist, "full of chaos and impulse surrounded by a fog of depression, heated by desperation."

At a parent-child meeting with the psychologist, Max's mother broke down in tears. "It's not your fault," Max said softly. His father cleared his throat defensively. "It's not your fault either, Dad."

"It's nobody's fault," the psychologist interrupted, and began to explain to Max and his parents what they had been living with for these many years.

"But if it's this attention deficit thing," his mother said, "why didn't we pick it up earlier? I feel so guilty."

"It often goes undiagnosed," the psychologist said, "particularly in bright children."

The more Max listened, the more things began to fit together and make sense to him. What he had known about himself, dimly, intuitively, for a long while, finally had a name. "Just giving it a name really helps," Max said.

"Better than calling you Mad Max," his father said. "I guess we all have some guilt to deal with."

"But the good news is that there are some corrective steps we can take now," the psychologist said. "It won't be an easy process, but life will be a lot better than it has been."

I will end my story of Max at this point, rather than take you through his treatment. Although he is a fictional character, he has a life, the way fictional characters do, and so you may be curious about how his story ends. Max's story and his family's, although bumpy, ends happily. In fact, Max becomes a high school English teacher, a wrestling coach, and an informal specialist in so-called difficult adolescents.

In addition to finding the right medication, his treatment consisted in large part of undoing, in therapy, many of the negative numbers he'd done on himself or had had done to him. In addition, he needed coaching on learning how to live with the brain he had, which we all have to do. It is worth noting that not all brains have the same style. Let us hope that we can begin to appreciate differences instead of punishing them.

While Max's story ends happily, many similar stories do not. I tell you his story, rather than giving you numbers and statistics, to try to impart a feel for this syndrome, and a sense of its impact over time.

There are a few points from Max's story that I'd like to highlight. First of all, he came from a relatively stable family. I want to dispel any notion that ADD is someone's fault. While inadequate parenting can exacerbate the situation, it does not cause it. We don't know what causes it – our best evidence says it's genetic – but we do know it is not the result of bad mothering or fathering.

Second, Max's high IQ delayed the diagnosis of ADD. When a child is obviously bright and gets good grades, one erroneously fails to consider ADD as a possibility. A corollary to this point is that the diagnosis of ADD should not carry with it an educational death sentence. After all the testing and psychiatric interviews children go through en route to the diagnosis, many a parent and child leave the consulting room where the diagnosis of ADD has just been pronounced thinking they have been told, in very fancy language, that the child is stupid. A frequent though hidden component of the emotional experience of ADD is the feeling of being defective or retarded. It is very important that parents and teachers reassure the child about this matter. While one doesn't rejoice at the diagnosis of ADD, neither need one despair.

Third is the crucial differentiation between the primary and secondary aspects of ADD that I alluded to earlier. The longer the diagnosis of ADD is delayed, the greater the secondary self-esteem problems may become. There are a great many adults out there in the world with undiagnosed ADD who think of themselves in all sorts of unneccessary negative terms. They may have fast-track hyperkinetic personalities, be impatient, restless, impulsive, often intuitive and creative but unable to follow through, frequently unable to linger long enough to develop a stable intimate relationship. Usually they have self-esteem problems that began in childhood. The earlier the diagnosis can be made, the better these secondary problems can be managed, the sooner one can begin the creative process of learning to live with one's brain without the obstacles of moralistic or taunting labels.

Fourth, I want Max's story to stress that ADD occurs within a developmental framework. That is to say, it evolves over time; just as the child's personality and cognitive ability evolve over time. It is not a stagnant phenomenon but a dynamic one, and its influence changes over time.

Fifth, although we tend to focus on the cognitive aspects of ADD, it is equally important to pay attention to how this disorder affects relations between people. Max's friends thought he was egocentric or on drugs as a way of explaining his spacing out or failing to connect with them; many adults also misinterpret the emotional style of the ADD child. People with ADD often do not pick up on the subtle social cues and messages that are crucial in getting along with others. These people may appear to be blasé or indifferent or self-centered or even hostile, when they are simply confused or unaware of what is going on around them. As they become more confused they may get angry or they may withdraw, both responses causing interpersonal damage. Bear in mind that just as the child may have trouble focusing on his math assignment, so he may also have a hard time listening to an account of what his friend did over the summer. These problems with people can be just as damaging to one's ability to get on in the world as the cognitive problems.

Sixth, the family problems I alluded to in Max's story can be severe indeed and contribute heavily to the painful experience of ADD. These kids are often the source of family squabbles or marital discord. Parents get so angry and frustrated that they lash out, not only at the child, but at each other. Soon, full-scale battles erupt, as the child becomes the scapegoat for everything that's wrong with the family. This same process can happen in the classroom. Two or three children with undiagnosed ADD can turn a happy classroom into a war zone and a kind and competent teacher into a burned-out wreck. In this way the emotional experience of ADD expands to take in whole families or entire classrooms.

The pain of the experience of ADD has been an unknown pain, until recently. These children – and adults – suffered without knowing the cause of their suffering. They were accused without being understood. They struggled and groped their way along tenaciously, but often without help or direction. They lived in a kind of fog, without knowing what to call it or how to get their bearings within it. They looked for beacon lights, but often only found darkness.

Now times have changed. Thankfully, we have the knowledge and science to help these children and adults. Let us work hard to keep our compassion and sensitivity on pace with our knowledge so that that these truly talented individuals may find their way to where they ought to be.

Child Sexual Abuse

by Michael G. Thompson
with Catalina Arboleda, Ph.D.

In the last few years, there has been a dramatic change in our society's understanding of and reaction to child abuse. The most closely protected secret in the lives of many people has become a matter for public discussion and the subject of a large and growing body of psychological research and legal activity. As more and more adults have talked about their childhood experiences to researchers and to one another, it has become clear that sexual abuse in childhood can produce harmful psychological effects that in many cases afflict the personalities of victims for many years or even for a lifetime.

The legal system of the United States has responded powerfully to the revelations and new understandings of the scope and harmfulness of child sexual abuse. All fifty states now have mandatory reporting laws requiring educators, physicians, mental health professionals, and anyone having caretaking responsibilities for children to report suspected abuse of children. Reporting and prosecution of child sexual abuse has increased by more than 1,000% across the nation in the last twenty years, and the annual increases in such reports continue to grow. In Massachusetts, for example, reporting increased 58% in 1984 and 78% in 1985. There is no immediate end in sight to the increase in awareness, reporting, and prosecution of child sexual abuse cases.

However, even with all of the news articles, the well-known cases like the McMartin day care center case in California and the Steinberg case in New York, and the numerous talk show discussions of sexual abuse, the subject is one of the most difficult topics for people to think about and especially to talk to children about. Parents warn their children against the vague dangers of strangers and kidnappers, but they cannot bring themselves to face the much more likely possibility that their child – even at a very young age – could be the victim of sexual abuse.

Why is there such reluctance to address the subject in thought or in conversation with children? The answer is that most children who are abused are abused by family members or by family friends. Only a minority of children are molested by people they do not know. Therefore, in order to warn children against sexual abuse, adults must face the reality that the abuser could be in the family, that the abuser could be someone that both the adult and the child love and trust. It is a profoundly disquieting thought for most people and one that most would prefer to deny. To face the reality of child sexual abuse is psychologically to strip away the belief that the adult world is able to protect children, because it is actually caretaking adults who are victimizing them.

Because of the double barriers of ignorance and psychological denial, many educators have not yet faced the possibility of child sexual abuse in their schools. Many have already ignored or overlooked cases. A study in New York revealed that 40% of teachers had not reported suspected cases of abuse. More than 50% of physicians in the Los Angeles area were found to be failing to report cases of venereal disease in children, a clear sign of sexual abuse. Because the psychological and institutional barriers to reporting child sexual abuse are sometimes so strong, the only remedy is education and psychological preparation.

I am certain that every school in the United States, public or private, has in it children who have been, are currently being, or will be sexually molested during their childhood. The majority of them will suffer from incest. Sexual abuse is not something that happens to other children in other schools; if teachers and administrators train themselves to see it, they will see it in their own schools.

Definition of Sexual Abuse

There are as many different definitions of sexual abuse as there are state laws and researchers on the subject. Some are narrow, and some are quite broad and include, for example, seeing an exhibitionist. Perhaps the most unequivocal definition is simply this: *any sexual contact between a young child and an adult, even in the absence of coercion or force, constitutes sexual abuse.*

Because of their relative emotional and cognitive immaturity and position of lesser power, children are unable truly to consent to such a relationship. They may submit, they may participate, they may believe that they are a "partner," but because of the inequality of the power relationship they cannot be considered to be a partner, psychologically or legally.

Most researchers agree that sexual contact is abusive if the child is sixteen or seventeen or younger; others argue that consent is possible by fourteen. There are cultural differences as well; ages of consent in Western Europe are lower than in the United States. Sexual contact between peers is also considered abusive if there is an age difference of five years or more between the victim and the perpetrator. Sexual contact between peers is a different phenomenon from sexual abuse. For children to experiment sexually with someone their own age does not usually have long-term harmful effects.

Prevalence of Sexual Abuse

Until the last ten years, no one had any idea how widespread child sexual abuse was in this country. We still have no definitive answer to the question of how much there is. Studies trying to estimate the number of adults who were molested during childhood report a wide range of results. Research has involved the use of many differing methodologies, and hence has defined sexual abuse in differing ways, so we have no clear answer to the question.

In a review of all epidemiological studies conducted to date, Stefanie Peters and her colleagues found that between 6 and 62% of all women, and between 3 and 31% of all men, were sexually abused in the course of their childhood. The two best studies, those of Diana Russell, in San Francisco, and David Finkelhor, in New England, indicate that slightly more than one in three girls (38%) and at least as many as one in ten boys (10%) were sexually molested as young children. The large majority of these incidents were never reported to child welfare agencies or to health professionals.

Who Is at Risk for Sexual Abuse?

Virtually all studies report higher rates of child sexual abuse for women than for men. By compiling the data from all the available studies, Finkelhor and Baron found that there were approximately 2.5 women victims for every male victim. But in fact sexual abuse of boys by men is likely to be much higher than is presently reported. It is underreported because it offends men's image of their masculinity and breaks the homosexual taboo. As more is learned about sexual abuse, it is likely that the number of known incidents of abuse of boys will greatly increase.

Children are more vulnerable to abuse during preadolescence than during adolescence or early childhood. The highest risk appears to be for children between eight and twelve, and especially between ten and twelve. This fact should guide education and prevention efforts aimed at children to make sure that the at-risk group receives the knowledge when it most needs it.

Child sexual abuse cuts across all class and socioeconomic categories. While more cases of child abuse among the poor are reported to clinics and child protective agencies, studies that have interviewed subjects at random reveal that abuse affects families of all levels of education and wealth.

Although socioeconomic status does not protect children or place them at additional risk, there are some clear risk factors: being an only or oldest daughter, living without one's natural father or with a stepfather, and having a mother who is emotionally absent or unavailable because of disability or illness.

Families in which there are psychological reasons why one of the parents may not fulfill his or her protective role are particularly at risk. Children who are abused sometimes come from homes in which the father surrogate uses alcohol, in which the mother has a prior history of sexual abuse, or in which the sexual relationship between the parents has broken down.

Who Are the Abusers?

Children know most of the people who abuse them. Abusers tend to have ready access to and legitimate power over the children they abuse. They tend to be relatives, caretakers, or in other positions of authority over the children they exploit. Family members, baby sitters, neighbors, friends, clergy, troop leaders, day care workers, and teachers have been found to be abusers. The large majority of abusers are male.

Many offenders who have entered child care professions may have considerable talent in working with children. These adults – particularly those who are psychologically regressed following disappointments in adult life – have an affinity for children that other adults do not. Children may experience these people as being more sympathetic and understanding than other adults. For these reasons, they may be harder to detect; adults may be more motivated to overlook and deny any signs of their sexual orientation, and children may protect the secret of the sexual abuse more closely than they might for a less appealing and generous character. For emotionally deprived children particularly, the nonsexual aspects of the relationship may represent the best contact with an adult that they have had. That, in addition to the spoken or unspoken message that children should not reveal, induces them to keep the secret.

The Nature of Sexual Abuse

Girls are most often abused inside the family, boys outside the family. In Diana Russell's study, almost half of the women who had been abused were victims of incest; the average period during which the abuse took place was four years. While the most common form of incest is probably between brothers and sisters, it is greatly under-reported. Father-daughter incest is the best documented form of incest, mother-daughter the rarest. Nicholas Groth, who has studied sexual offenders, has found that most pedophiles who abuse children outside their families prefer young males to females.

Sexual abuse within the family or in the context of a caretaking relationship is usually a series of repeated and progressive sexual acts, starting with incidents of exposure or self-masturbation and then proceeding to more intrusive forms of bodily contact, such as fondling, and finally penetration. Abuse by outsiders is usually of shorter duration and may be less severe. The betrayal inherent in incidents of incest by a trusted family member makes it more traumatic to the child than abuse by a stranger.

Initially, offenders may appeal to the child's need for attention and the specialness of their relationship or their "secret game." Soon, however, the offender may try to convince the child of the need to maintain the secret through threats or blackmail. Elements of force, pressure, or coercion, which are present in most cases of child sexual abuse, ensure that most children will keep the secret for months or years, and sometimes for life.

The Accommodation Syndrome

Roland Summit has described sexual abuse from the child's point of view in a paper titled "The Child Abuse Accommodation Syndrome." He said that, even when no direct coercion has been used, the secret nature of the activity leaves the child with a sense of badness and danger, a sense that everything will be all right if he or she doesn't tell. Soon, however, the child begins to feel quite helpless. The person who is supposed to be in a trusted position of authority is behaving in a more and more sexually intrusive way, leaving the child feeling more and more defenseless and overwhelmed.

Children caught in such a situation often try to distance themselves from the abuse, pretending that it is not happening, that their bodies are not responding. Because children are usually unable to make the activity stop or to find a way out, they try to find a way of accommodating to the situation to survive psychologically. Frequently children see themselves as the bad one who caused the abuse and come to believe that if only they were good enough the behavior would stop. Some children become model children at home and in school, hiding the anxiety and depression they feel behind "normal" faces. Others, especially adolescents, sometimes act out, expressing their anger in rebellious and self-destructive ways.

No matter how they have coped with the abuse, children are rarely believed when they disclose it. Compliant children are often not believed because they have been coping so well. Angry, rebellious ones, who often disclose their abuse impulsively, perhaps in the midst of a fight with their parents, are also rarely believed. Children are less likely to be believed if their family and the offender have good standing in the community.

Whether disclosure is made on purpose or is accidental, it tends to be extremely stressful for children. As part of the normal process of accommodating to abuse, children are likely to reverse whatever they have said about it. The retraction, Summit says, is more easily believed than the truth about sexual abuse. "It confirms adult expectations that children cannot be trusted. It restores the precarious equilibrium of the family."

Signs of Abuse

A few children show physical signs of abuse, such as sexually transmitted diseases, pregnancy, or trauma to vaginal or rectal areas. However, the majority of sexually abused children do not show such signs. Instead, they show adults by their behavior that they are suffering from acute or chronic distress, the result of having tried to adapt to the trauma in their lives.

The behavioral changes that we see in children who are being or have been abused are a signal or communication to us that they are emotionally distressed. Many of the symptoms we see – acting-out behaviors, depression, withdrawal, anxiety, sleeping or eating problems – are not direct indicators of child abuse. They can be symptoms of other psychological conditions, such as problems with parents, reaction to divorce, undiagnosed learning disabilities.

It is important, however, for teachers and mental health professionals to consider the possibility that any child who is sending out these kinds of distress signals is being or may have been sexually abused. Suzanne Sgroi and others have found that, when a child engages in excessive masturbation, promiscuity, or sexual abuse of others, one needs to consider much more strongly the possibility that the child is being or has been sexually abused.

Young children (ages two to seven), school-aged children (ages seven to twelve), and teenagers signal the distress that results from abuse in ways that are appropriate to their developmental level.

The youngest children may display the following signs of distress: stomach-aches, sleep disturbances (nightmares), inability to sleep alone, regression in their toilet training, separation anxiety, fearfulness, withdrawal from or avoidance of certain people or places, and hyperactivity or aggression. Again, these are also common symptoms of other types of disturbance. The important thing is to consider sexual abuse as *one possible source* of the distress. The sexualized behaviors that sexually abused preschool children tend to manifest include excessive masturbation, compulsive and inappropriate sexualized play with other children or dolls, atypical sexual knowledge, and a change in their level of modesty or exhibitionism.

School-aged children show some of the same psychosomatic complaints that young children do, such as eating and sleeping disturbances, constipation or bedwetting, and stomachaches. In addition, they may show erratic and unpredictable moods and reactions, inability to concentrate in school, a sudden drop in school performance or motivation, or sudden loss of interest in activities or peer relationships. Some of these children cope with their victimization and powerlessness by bullying or victimizing younger children. Sexualized peer relationships and exhibitionism or, on the other hand, excessive modesty and fear of males (in the case of girls abused by males) may also indicate abuse.

Adolescents manifest many of the same symptoms shown by sexually abused preadolescents, such as eating and sleeping disturbances, withdrawal, changes in school performance or motivation, nonparticipation in previously interesting activities, and psychosomatic complaints, such as constipation and abdominal pains. Other behavioral indicators include the classic symptomatic profile of adolescence. Anorexia or bulimia, suicidal feelings, substance abuse, aggressive behavior or delinquency, unexplained hostility toward parents, and defiance and lack of trust toward authority figures are more particular to adolescents who tend to act out their anxiety and rage.

Some sexually abused adolescents, especially daughters who take on the role of a substitute parent or even of a wife, sometimes become pseudo-mature, overly compliant, and so involved in their family life that they fail to participate in age-appropriate activities with their peers. In adolescent females, promiscuity, overly seductive behavior toward males or excessive fear of males, pregnancy, prostitution, and runaway behavior may signal a history of abuse. With males, sexual victimization of younger children almost always indicates abuse.

Long-Term Effects of Abuse
While not all adults show symptoms related to abuse in their childhood, a significant number show about twice as many symptoms as adults who were not sexually victimized as children. Browne and Finkelhor found that as many as one-fifth of abuse survivors manifest signs of serious psychopathology. High rates of abuse have been found among prostitutes, sex offenders, and psychiatric patients.

While not all survivors manifest long-term effects, many of them show symptoms years after the abuse has stopped. Emotional reactions such as depression, feelings of powerlessness and hopelessness, and self-destructive tendencies are quite common. The stigma associated with the abuse may also distort victims' self-perceptions and self-esteem. Many continue to blame themselves, feeling a marked sense of badness and shame as well as isolation and alienation from others. Some have difficulty relating to others, especially in areas of trust and intimacy. Their relationships with other men and women, with their parents, and even with their children are sometimes affected. Their sexual functioning may be poor, they may experience confusion around issues of sexuality, and they seem to be more vulnerable to sexual assault or abuse by spouses or partners.

The severity of the long-term effects of abuse appears to be related to several factors summarized by Browne and Finkelhor in a recent review. The worst outcomes center in those victims who suffer long-term and frequent abuse, penetration or genital contact, use of force and aggression, and victimization by fathers or stepfathers rather than teenagers, and by men rather than women. It is unclear whether children who suffer abuse at an earlier age suffer more damage than those who are older when abuse begins. The reactions of families and law enforcement and social service agencies also appears to affect the long-term impact of abuse.

Lack of support from family members or being separated from one's family of origin as a result of disclosure appear related to more serious aftereffects. A significant minority of both boys and girls do not suffer noticeable long-term effects from sexual abuse. This phenomenon is not yet understood completely. Effects must be assessed on an individual-case basis. Abuse in general must be considered high-risk; however, it is not invariably significantly harmful.

How and Why Does Abuse Occur?

In our society, laws prohibiting adult-child sexual contact as well as the incest taboo – the psychological barrier prohibiting sexual intimacy between family members – are so strong that it takes a complicated set of personality factors and life circumstances to push an adult over generational lines into a sexual relationship with a child.

It has been customary to think of sexual abusers as a special class of emotionally ill people. We call them pedophiles and define them by their behaviorally established and psychologically fixed sexual interest in children. But pedophiles are not the sole cause of the problem. A recent *Los Angeles Times* survey described by John Crewdson in his book *By Silence Betrayed* asked men anonymously over the telephone whether they had ever sexually abused a child. The results revealed that perhaps one man in fifteen or, after correction for every possible statistical error, at least one man in every twenty-five had sexually abused a child. If that study is an accurate estimate of the number of men involved, then the sexual crossing of generational lines is a relatively common phenomenon, which argues against all sexual abuse being perpetrated by a special class of emotionally ill people who are molesters. Psychological research is also beginning to reveal that more women than previously thought have molested children.

A more complicated answer than pedophilia is needed to explain the amount of sexual abuse in the United States. The model proposed by Finkelhor in his book *Child Sexual Abuse* is perhaps the most comprehensive theoretical explanation of all possible kinds of incest or molestation. Finkelhor argues that the two previous lines of explanation, focusing on either the psychodynamics of sexual abusers, or on the family-systems model of father-daughter incest, leave many cases unexplained and cannot account for abuse by siblings or baby sitters, nor for mother-son incest. What Finkelhor proposes is a list of four preconditions which are likely to result in abuse.

The first precondition: some motivation or life experience that propels an adult toward a sexual interest in children. Many adults who have a sexual interest in children were seriously deprived in childhood; for them, sex with a child can fill a powerful emotional need. Or the adult may be more than normally sexually aroused by children. Or, finally, other forms of sexual gratification may be unavailable or less gratifying to such a person. Any one of these factors, if it is particularly powerful, or some combination of them can predispose an adult to child abuse.

The second precondition: overcoming internal inhibitions. To do so involves a combination of factors in the individual and in the society. Alcohol use, impulse control problems, or outright psychosis may lower an adult's inhibitions and lead him or her to cross the social barrier. So may social toleration of sexual interest in children, two examples being child pornography or a cultural acceptance of patriarchal prerogatives for fathers.

If a person is motivated to have sex with children and can overcome internal inhibitions about this behavior, he or she will still encounter powerful external barriers to the behavior. Finkelhor's third cluster of factors are those that predispose a molester to overcome *external* inhibitors. These include mothers who are not close to or protective of their children, who are dominated and themselves abused, or who are ill or absent. Other, less personal factors are unusual opportunities for the molester to be alone with the child and unusual sleeping or rooming conditions.

However, even if all three of the above conditions exist, a child may still refuse the approach of an adult interested in sexual contact. The fourth and final precondition is overcoming the resistance on the part of the child. Many children do refuse and do immediately tell their parents. There are other factors that make it easier for some children to overcome their own internal resistance and to submit to a sexual act with an adult. The most obvious one is coercion, a factor that is present in the majority of cases. Sometimes, however, children are emotionally insecure or deprived, they lack information about sexual abuse, or unusual trust exists between the child and the offending adult. Such trust ordinarily occurs between family members, and it may exist between some teachers and students, particularly in a boarding school situation, where faculty members explicitly assume family-like roles.

Management of Cases by Schools

All child sexual abuse cases are inherently tragic and difficult for a school to manage. What every school must do, when faced with the suspicion of child sexual abuse – or any child abuse or neglect, for that matter – is to consult with and report to the appropriate state agency. The mandatory reporting laws were designed to protect children first and foremost, but they were also designed to protect caretakers who want to act to protect a child but are reluctant to act on vague suspicions or are afraid of retaliation by families.

Despite the fact that the law makes reporting mandatory, it has unfortunately not been easy for states to obtain the cooperation of all child care professionals in using the law. This has been true of educators and physicians, as well as mental health and law enforcement professionals.

People have not used the laws for several reasons.

First and most important is ignorance. Until recently, most teachers were not trained to use the reporting laws; in many independent schools, teachers are not even aware of them.

Second, respect for the privacy of family life has often prevailed over concerns about children.

Third, offenders are often known and respected by potential reporters, and that makes the decision to report intensely difficult; for example, a pediatrician might not report on a child in hopes of "not losing the child's trust" and being able to work with the family.

Fourth and finally, many reporters focus on the reality of the state system rather than on the law. Already hesitant to file, they may focus on the fact that the state agencies responsible for investigating child sexual abuse reports are close to being overwhelmed by the workload. These reporters fear that the tremendous increases in reporting have so burdened the system that cases are not always well handled nor handled consistently. Not knowing what to expect, they are reluctant to use the system. This problem is a significant political one and beyond the scope of any school to remedy.

Child sexual abuse is a vitally important issue. What every school must do is educate itself about the nature of the problem and plan how to manage it. Every school should take three simple steps to ensure that it will be able to respond to a suspected case of sexual abuse:

1. A school should formally teach its faculty to recognize symptoms of child abuse and inform them of the state's mandatory reporting laws.

2. A school should have a "reporting protocol" that provides an outline of actions to be taken by teachers and administrators as well as outside legal and mental health consultants in the event of alleged child sexual abuse.

3. A school should develop a relationship with the regional office of the state agency responsible for dealing with child sexual abuse. Having established such a connection, the school can call on the agency as a consultant and the two can work together if an incident occurs.

If, as we stated at the beginning of this article, the two major barriers to the recognition and proper handling of child sexual abuse are ignorance and psychological denial, both can be overcome with education and preparation. The difficulty is, obviously, that denial can prevent a school from taking the necessary educative steps.

Administrators and teachers in all schools face the same human and bureaucratic difficulties when confronted with child sexual abuse. Most independent schools want to think of themselves as a large family that honors its own children, parents, and faculty. Such schools try, whenever possible, to honor the requests of "their" families and to protect their faculty.

For a school to report one of its families to a state agency can be psychologically difficult; to expose a child within the school – which may be the inevitable result of the ensuing state investigation – can feel terrible and wrong to a school administrator. And for a school to report suspected abuse by a faculty member can be traumatic for the entire school community.

Just as a family may react with denial to the revelation of incest, so too may a school react with denial. Every family likes to think of itself as being protective and good; every school also wants to think of itself as a protective and caring place for children. The idea that one of "its" families or "its" faculty members has been sexually abusing children may be extremely painful.

Among other factors that predispose independent school educators to want to handle a situation privately are loss of control over the situation that results from a report to the state and possible adverse publicity for the school and, in the case of an abusive faculty member, the damage to that teacher's life and family that could be done through a false report.

Traditionally, private schools have handled abusive families and faculty members in three ways: by looking the other way; by helping the families or faculty members to leave the school in some innocent way, thereby solving the school's problem; or by arranging private treatment for the affected parties. Changes in our understanding of the problem of child sexual abuse now make such private handling illegal, unwise, and unacceptable.

There are no easy answers to some of the problems raised by sexual abuse cases. At this point there is still much that is not known about the true incidence of child sexual abuse and its long-term effects. Finkelhor writes that research is still needed in almost every area of the field. However, even if the phenomenon were completely understood by professionals, the barriers of ignorance and denial make it difficult to communicate the necessary message to the public.

People do not want to see sexual abuse or understand its effects. Even with strong reporting laws in place, the problems are formidable: many state systems are under-financed and overwhelmed and cannot respond adequately or consistently to cases. No universally effective methods yet exist for treating offenders; imprisonment does not solve society's or the offender's problem, for in most states effective treatment is unavailable for child sexual abuse offenders in the penal system.

Many experts on sexual abuse look to education of children as the major weapon against child abuse; certainly it is one. But, because of its intrinsically upsetting nature, there are barriers to getting schools to teach about sexual abuse. No parents want their children to be told that the adults around them, even in their family, may be dangerous to them.

For all these reasons, it will be many years before our society comes to a satisfactory solution for the education of children, the identification of victims, the treatment of victims, and the punishment and treatment of offenders. In the absence of good answers to these complex social, legal, and psychological problems, what every school must do – at least – is to educate its faculty, its children, and its families to the widespread nature and tragic consequences of child sexual abuse.

Chapter Three

To
Teachers
and
Other Adults

Finding the Heart of the Child: Working with Emotional Conflict

by Edward M. Hallowell

Let me begin with a story.

It is a winter night in New Hampshire. In a third-floor bedroom of a gabled, white clapboard house, a thirteen-year-old girl named Anna is falling asleep as the snow swirls around in moonlit darkness outside. Anna pulls her thick quilt snug under her chin and sinks deeply into her plump pillows.

When she is almost within the arms of a dream, a loud voice startles her. "Anna, wake up! Anna, come down her now! You have some work to do." She recognizes her father's voice. She knows his voice drunk better than she knows almost anything. She knows that she had better obey, and she knows that she and her mother will be up for a while. Beyond that, she doesn't know what to expect. Putting on her bathrobe, she closes the bedroom door so her cat, Begonia, will not become involved.

When she reaches the living room her mother grabs her and pulls her close. "Leave her alone," her father says, pacing in front of the fireplace. There is a tumbler of what Anna knows is Jack Daniels on the mantelpiece, and next to it there is an object that Anna thinks is a gun. "Hush, honey," her mother says. She is shaking and holding Anna too tight.

"It's OK, Mom," Anna says, wriggling free a bit.

Over the next few minutes she listens to her father give a speech, delivered mostly to the portrait of his own father above the mantelpiece, but now and then directed at Anna's mother. It is a string of scary words that Anna has learned how to tune out pretty much. But the end of it is too scary to ignore.

"And so, you see, it has come down to this," her father says, affecting an air of eloquence, "that you, Anna, must decide between your mother and me. With this remarkably reliable little weapon I have here I am going to shoot one of us, either your mother or me. Now before you quickly sentence me to death, remember that it will play strange tricks on your mind for years to come. Wouldn't you agree, sweetheart?" he asks his wife, then takes a long swallow from his glass. "I mean it, Anna," he goes on, now severely, "you must decide. If not, I'll shoot us both. I swear to God I will."

At that moment Anna feels more fright than she has ever known. She looks up to her mother's eyes, instinctively, as if that were all she could do.

Over the next hour Anna watches and listens as her mother, using all of her skill, tact, and experience keeps her father talking, of this and of that, into tirades and into weepings, bellowings, and threats, until, at last, mercifully, he passes out, falling asleep beneath the portrait of his father.

Anna didn't tell me this story until I had known her for two years. We were friends in college. One spring afternoon we were driving out to Crane's Beach together, and I mentioned that she never talked much about her parents. She offered that story as explanation. She told it in a tone of near indifference, almost successfully concealing the emotion pent up beneath. "There were so many incidents," she said. "That was just the most juicy. What do you think? Was he right? Has it played tricks on my mind ever since?"

What struck me was that it had not seemed to play such tricks on her, and I told her so. She was, in fact, the picture of sociability: lively, vivacious, a friend to many, funny, kind, and warm. She kept a certain distance about her, however, a distance I had been trying to bridge in asking about her past. But never would I have suspected the kind of trauma she recalled.

"That's the thing about us survivors," she said, taking a big bite out of a roast chicken leg she'd brought along as part of our picnic. "We don't look the part."

I asked her where her optimism and vitality came from. At first she disclaimed having any, as if out of modesty, but then, allowing as how she did have a way of looking on the bright side of things, she talked of schools, of teachers, and of friends. "The night with the gun, it was in my mother's eyes that I saw courage and hope, and that has stayed with me mainly because of schools. When my mother realized she couldn't deal with both my father and me, she sent me to boarding school. In the eighth grade. From then on, I made school my life, my world."

I've lost touch with Anna. The last I heard she was teaching English and modern dance at a prep school. A child of schools returning to a school.

Unfortunately, most children of such severely impaired families do not do as well as Anna. Such early chronic deprivation usually leads to serious complications in adult life.

Some of these children from severely disturbed families do very well, however. In one large study it was noted that ten percent of the children of psychotic parents were extremely successful in adult life, both in terms of rewarding careers and gratifying friendships. What remained missing in the successful ten percent was the ability to make a commitment to one person, resulting in a tendency to stay unmarried. As to what allowed for these kids' remarkable adaptation, one factor emerged as most statistically significant.

That one factor was the child's ability to reach out. Those children who, against all odds, managed still to trust enough to continue to reach out ultimately prevailed. Where did it come from, their resiliency, their continuing ability to reach out? We don't know. Why do some kids, after they've been knocked down six times, come back for a seventh? We don't know. Just as we don't know how to bottle and preserve the special enthusiasm of childhood, we don't know where the courage to hope and to try comes from in those who are traumatized in childhood.

But it is a safe bet that schools, in good ways and in bad, have a lot to do with it. I contend that the ability to reach out, as crucial as it is, can go to waste if the school cannot reach back, and that furthermore, if the school is very artful and persistent in its reaching out, some kids who wouldn't otherwise will reach back. At the heart of all this emphasis on reaching is the notion that human contact is worthwhile, indeed transforming, and that, whether they know it or not, whether they direct it or not, schools are a virtual bath of transforming human contact. In the case of the child from the troubled family, it is terribly important for all that human contact to be channeled in some constructive way. My hope here is to suggest how schools can and cannot intercede in the lives of these children.

First, let me give you a few assumptions that underlie what I have to say. I have alluded to one already – that it is essential to reach the child, to touch him or her.

Second, few families want to fail their children. In the main, the parents of troubled children are in pain themselves. It is best not to judge these people – they get enough judgment just about everywhere they turn. It is best, rather, to try to understand.

My third assumption goes against conventional psychiatric wisdom. I think in most of these cases it is better to take action than not to act. Children have weak voices, and their complaints too often receive dismissal rather than attention. There is too much at stake to put propriety first. Child advocacy is God's work, and no one is better equipped for it than schools.

My fourth assumption will make you smile. It is that it is good for the soul to tackle the impossible, to take in lost causes, to help the unhelpable. You can see that I am a Red Sox fan. But seriously, even if you think you do not stand a chance with a certain child or family situation, it is worth a try. I'm sure you've all had the experience of the angels coming in to help out at the last moment. Moreover, the most important work any of us can do is not necessarily the most practical, and heeding the cockeyed optimist within us can be more useful than heeding the voice of reason.

My fifth assumption is that you do not need to have a degree in some field of mental health to bring emotional assistance to children and families. Don't be timid. Stick with what you know is right and good and act upon it. If it seems foolish, persist in that folly, and you'll be amazed at how much good you'll do.

Sixth and last, I assume that a school is more than a place where you go to learn. I know of no school that would describe itself simply as a learning center. We should take it as a given that a child's emotional development is as much within the right and proper purview of a school as is intellectual growth.

Having said all that, the main contention of this essay is simply as follows: that a school can and should provide a safe haven for children from troubled families while that trouble works itself out; that a school can and should embrace a child while others can't, favor a child while others fret, love a child while love is missing. Further, that schools can and should trust their most basic instincts of wanting to help. No more than you would watch a child drown in the river while you got parental consent forms signed before diving in, would or should you let a child languish out of worry for the niceties of custom or politeness. We live in a time when, like it or not, more and more kids are in need. It is best to be ready to jump in and help.

If my message is such a simple one – try to save the child – where do the problems lie? If schools have the chance to do so much good, to save children and mend families, why is the process so often frustrating or ineffective?

Let me propose four areas of difficulty which I will label as follows: over-involvement, denial, parental resistance, and what I call "the weight of the world." I will take them up one at a time.

I am encouraging you to take up child advocacy with zeal. I am sure you do already, but I am urging it upon you with frenzy, with reckless, rule-breaking, down-home foot stomping impolite excess and razzmatazz. I am urging you as leaders of schools to go out and save. Not to stand on ceremony, but to stand on love and on principle. However, you cannot, and should not, do it all.

One should proceed with caution. The road to hell is paved with good intentions, and as an older teacher of mine once said, "No good deed goes unpunished." The first punishment is the punishment of over-involvement. Each July first, I used to receive a group of rookie first-year trainees in psychiatry, and I was given a year to introduce them to the joys and sorrows of treating the mentally ill. Usually the first and hardest lesson for them to learn arose when they became so devoted, caught up, and involved with a certain patient that they lost all critical judgment, started proposing treatment plans that included inviting the patient home with them, and became bitterly disappointed, angry and ready to go into another field when the patient did not miraculously get well.

As much as I urge that you attach yourselves to children, particularly those who aren't getting what they need at home, as much as I urge that you take them on full force, you must be careful to watch what you are doing. The best way to do that is to talk it over with someone whose opinion you value, someone who has been there before you. To return to the example of the child drowning in the river, it would be best to plan your entrance into the river and have a passer-by help you out, even call the fire department, before you dive in. We like to avoid double drownings.

It is not only your own over-involvement that needs to be watched out for, it is the child's as well. You don't want to get in the position of having offered more than you can deliver. As your relationship with the child develops, think about ways of reconstructing the family or finding other supports, and also consider just how much of your time you are willing to invest. It has been said that any child can be helped as long as he or she can find someone to idealize, look up to, emulate, follow. It doesn't really matter who the person is. If you are that person, you will know it, and you will feel it: eyes that won't let go of you, a presence that is always there, sometimes obnoxious, sometimes testing, sometimes driving you nuts. "What does this kid want from me, anyway?" you will ask. In starting to answer that question and in figuring out how much of it you can and cannot provide, you will begin the healing work.

For psychiatrists, modulating our involvement is relatively easy, for we have set appointment hours, and predictable frequency of sessions, as well as scheduled meetings with parents.

The teacher, however, is on the open prairie, grazing and galloping with everyone else, as ready to be devoured as not, to be sabotaged by a class, button-holed by an administrator, or set upon, with no thought of something as formal as an appointment, by a parent with great concerns. This is part of what makes school work invigorating as well as exhausting. If on that open prairie a particularly needy child should attack, one can feel quite unprotected. Now I don't mean to portray kids as monsters. But anyone who has worked with deprived children knows how monstrous their needs can feel. And the one-shot feeding – that is, a long, meaningful conversation with a child with no follow-up – is a disaster. As much as you, the teacher, have been warmed by the honesty of the conversation and touched by the pathos of the situation, another perhaps unconscious part of you has stared into the great unfed mouth of the ages and said, "Lemme outta here!" You haven't the time nor the energy to fix it all by yourself. Which is why you need to pick your spots, use a team approach, share the worry and the work, and temper your own involvement so that you can be effective.

Without a team approach, without backup from the school, without a well-fed support network for doing this kind of work, what often happens is the non-response of denial. Often a problem can be so large and so obvious and so seemingly dangerous that we all conspire to pretend it isn't there at all, as if we could literally ignore it to death. One of my teachers used to say in reference to such a problem, "There's an elephant in the room and no one is talking about it." Most schools have an elephant or two or three in their schoolyards. And many children from troubled families ride elephants to school – right into the classroom. It can make for rather close quarters as the teacher squeezes between elephants to try to do his or her teaching.

This is quite understandable. In my work at the Massachusetts Mental Health Center, a state hospital for the most severely mentally ill, I go about my business cheerfully every day, routinely denying the pain and agony surrounding me. We need to be able to look away in order to be there when it counts.

As necessary as some denial is, too much can be tragic. The one great preventable problem in schools' dealings with kids is ignoring a problem in the first place. "A drug problem? At Sunshine-by-the-Sea School? You must be joking." Or, "What do you mean Rachel has bruises and a black eye? She gets straight As." Or, "So Mrs. Big Donor walks through the school corridors carrying a crystal cocktail shaker full of martinis asking the kids who stole the olives. So she has a sense of humor. So what?" These are of course exaggerations, but, in subtler forms, they happen all the time. We ignore a problem either because it threatens us in some way and so we do not like to see it, or because we do not know what to do about it. "Betsy seems sad lately. Gee, she used to be such a happy kid. Must be the full moon." Or, "Frank is flunking all his courses, huh. Must be playing too much football."

Although some of this denial is inevitable, the best way for the school to minimize it is to create an atmosphere where following these matters up is encouraged, and where there are regular procedures for doing so, with easy access to additional resources to aid in intervention. I am not just saying that you should have a school psychiatrist, although I can hardly oppose such an idea, but rather that it is up to the entire school from head or principal on down to create both the administrative structure and the emotional permission and support for investigating and following up the signs of emotional distress the children may show. If instead the school wants to establish an ethic of self-reliance, a tone of sink-or-swim, then the major problems of many children will go hidden and unnoticed while preventable pain singes its way through the developing psyche of the child. The great thing about working with kids is that they are so malleable, so responsive to help, so able to get better. It is when their signs of distress go unheeded that the great, avoidable damage gets done.

Okay, so what happens when you identify the problem and plan a course of intervention, only to have parents give a ringing refusal to cooperate? I have three solutions to this predicament: persist, persist, and persist. The first "no" is usually the parents' own denial born out of guilt. The second "no" is usually an "ouch." The third "no" usually means, "I want to say yes if only you can show me how." So persist. Get support. Don't give up. And give yourself and the parents time. It takes most everybody a while to change their ways. Furthermore, if you get the parents' cooperation, don't expect their admiration. All you need is for them to work with you.

For three years I treated a little boy whose mother would bring a paper cup into our once-a-month meetings to use as a spittoon. From time to time – it seemed related to how aggressive I was being – she would rumble like a cement mixer as she cleared her nose and throat and lungs of everything she could summon, and then she would spit into her cup. She had no medical condition that warranted such expectoration. No, she was sending me a clear message: I spit on you for needing you. That was fine. All I needed was her cooperation. Admiration she could save for her son. The important thing was to make the connection and get the work done.

This can be very difficult. For you, the most realistic goal may be just getting professional help. We psychiatrists encounter resistance in parents as well, to be sure, but we have the time to deal with it, whereas often you do not. The situations can be most bizarre. I once treated a boy whose mother was psychotic. The crazy part of her thought her son was her husband, while the not-crazy part of her wanted to treat him like a son. She solved that dilemma by adopting me as her husband. She would come into our sessions all prettied up and tell marvelously vivid stories of the great time we had had at the theater last night, or the difficulty she had with me working such long hours, or what a wonderful dinner we would have that night. Some days she would be admiring of me physically and telling me what a great lover I was. Other days she would tell me I was shamefully neglectful of her and that she was sure I was having an affair. Now I hasten to add that none of her stories were true, but rather the psychotic productions of a very theatrical lady.

It was odd, to say the very least, for me to be winked at and complained at as if I were the lady's husband, but I let the game go on because it was serving a useful purpose. While she had me as her husband, she became the model mother to her son, and, guided by the saving instincts many crazy people have, never shared her delusion with him. I suppose if he ever had come into the office calling me "Dad" I would have had some backtracking to do. But that never happened. The boy progressed well. When I had to end my participation in the therapy, because I was moving from one program to another, I transferred the case, mother and son, to another psychiatrist. My meeting with the new therapist was rather strange, as I explained to him that he was about to get married. He resisted at first, as one might suppose, saying that it would be better to interpret away her delusions. But I prevailed upon him, saying that although his plan was most reasonable, it wouldn't work. Brave soul, he said he'd give it a try. The mother, simply, creatively, transferred her delusion onto him. I can tell you, not without some first husband's jealousy, that their marriage is going well and that the boy is fine.

I cite the story because with children whose parents are truly failing the child, the resistance can often be extreme and bizarre, and the solutions somewhat beyond the ken of the average Dear Abby column.

The fourth reason I cited for the failure of schools successfully to intervene with these kids I called "the weight of the world." It is a very heavy world, and teachers carry more than their share of the weight. Speaking personally, there are days I wonder why I do the work I do at all, and there are days that feeling makes me sad and blue and not very good at what I do. I imagine that happens in teaching as well.

Part of this is reality. We live in a peculiar time of social reorganization. There are so many dual-career parents, single parents, divorced parents, and overworking parents that it is often difficult for a child to find the safe haven in childhood that he or she needs. I sometimes wonder if childhood itself is disappearing. As parents achieve and achieve and pressure their children to do the same, the embryos of visions and dreams that grow in childhood and adolescence can get crushed, only to be replaced by a dismal parroting of adult plans quite lacking in vitality or spontaneity, and a bleary worriedness that inhibits free play.

We live in a time of worries to be sure, from drugs to AIDS to the national debt, to pollution, to hunger, and on. But part of the job of parents and of schools is to protect children from the worries and preoccupations of the adult world so that they may grow confident and creative enough to tackle them later on. I am not at all opposed to programs that educate children about the risks of the world. But I worry that the weight of the world is bearing down heavy upon childhood. Inundated with well-meaning programs on drugs and alcohol and hunger and nuclear war and divorce and everything else, what is happening to the world of the child? Has it all become too complex, too scary? In our efforts to prepare children, might we be asking them to bear too much?

We need to create a safe place for kids to play. Play is so important. It is the calisthenics of the imagination. We need to create safe spaces for kids to make friends and to make dreams. That is what childhood is all about. If parents have forgotten that, then it is up to schools abidingly to remind them and insistently to make the school environment one that favors and is built for childhood.

But even if you can do that, how can anyone cope with the current weight of the world? Particularly in dealing with those children whose needs are great and whose deprivation is extreme, one can get to feeling like Sisyphus: another day, another stone, another hill.

That's okay. The best advice I ever got about this came from a surgeon when I was considering a career in surgery. I asked him how he dealt with death, all the patients whom he fails. He said quite simply that he did his best and that in the main his patients were better off with him than without him.

The same can be said for teachers. If you simply try to be there for these kids and their troubled families, you can do a lot of good. You don't have to fix everything. Often the most effective interventions occur without your even realizing that you're doing anything at all. It is a paradoxical fact in this strange field of human interaction that our most directed efforts often yield the least results and our least directed efforts often succeed far beyond intention.

So do not feel that in order to attempt you must be able to prevail. If you try to bear the weight of the world you will surely fail. Rather, bear what you can accept and know that others will do their part as well.

See to it first of all that your own needs are being met. In this kind of work, we are all a little bit too giving. Believe me, you will do better work if you take care of yourself first.

Trust a little bit in magic, and, as I mentioned earlier, in the power of the angels. You often will not know how they're working with you. I saw a boy at a school last year who came from a totally disorganized family, a wealthy, aristocratic WASP family with the not uncommon WASP complications of alcoholism, mental illness, and politeness. This boy, a sixth grader – let's call him Jeffrey – had no idea on any given day who was in town or who was out of town, who would be drunk, who would be sober, who would be threatening divorce or wrapping themselves in an Updike novel and unavailable.

Mercifully sent to a boarding school, Jeffrey also started seeing me. But his real psychotherapy happened away from me. Jeffrey found a stable person. He watched one teacher – call him Mr. Jones – all year. Mr. Jones was his math teacher, a rather reserved and correct man, the sort of man who populated Jeffrey's family tree, minus the mental illness and alcoholism. Mr. Jones showed up on time for class. Mr. Jones was never drunk. Mr. Jones was in charge without being disdainful or rejecting. Mr. Jones dressed well; Jeffrey particularly admired his shoes. Mr. Jones was fair and could be counted on. All in all, Mr. Jones was a very nice man, and Jeffrey liked to watch him and be around him.

Now Mr. Jones hadn't the least idea that Jeffrey had adopted him as a father and Jeffrey never put it that way himself. But over the year Jeffrey changed dramatically, from shy, insecure, and afraid, to outgoing, confident, and bold. He also acquired more shoes than any of his friends.

At the end of the year he organized the math class to give Mr. Jones a standing ovation, which quite startled the unsuspecting Mr. Jones, who only thought he had been teaching adequate math.

There are many Jeffreys out there, and many Mr. Joneses. If you can trust in the magic, sometimes it will transpire. After all, plants do turn to the sunlight. Children do surely want to grow.

It is at the moments of connectedness that change and transformation occur. For a child from a troubled family the signs of connection may only be glimmers at first. But if you're ready for them you will pick them up.

I worked with a teacher all this year who formed a most intense and useful relationship with a boy mainly through short conversations in the corridors, eye glances at lunch, and little walks outdoors. You don't have to do four-times-a-week psychoanalysis to get under these kids' skins and be effective. Once you're in place, once you've been adopted, you'll fall into a kind of orbital, circling around the school, having your transforming effect even when you're quite out of sight. These kids are missing things, and like an atom short one electron, when they find another with an electron to donate, they bind.

And once they bind, if you've paid attention to some of the cautions I've suggested, the fun begins. I've worked with many teachers who, over three or four years, literally reclaimed children from the most horrific situations. It may not be ideal, but a substitute father or mother in the form of a teacher can be just enough to make the difference between an impaired child and a child who makes it. I have seen a teacher take a girl into her home while the girl's single mother got prolonged treatment for alcoholism. I have seen a teacher essentially do family therapy over two years, averting what would have been an unnecessary divorce. I have seen a teacher, by using imagination, intuition, and stick-to-itiveness, reach a child who had been incorrectly diagnosed schizophrenic. And then of course, there are the many times teachers intervene in the daily emotional crises that pepper each week. You know all these, and so many more.

Teachers, just as deftly and as definitely as my surgeon friend, do heal and fix and cure, particularly with children from troubled families.

There are my friend Anna's story and Jeffrey's story, and the standing ovation which I hear as multitudinous applause ringing down through the years from all the children whom the unsuspecting Mr. Joneses have helped.

Schools create memory pools through which we see our own reflections even now. We were all back there, and young, once. And as we see our own reflection superimposed on the image of one of our students, we see the magical connections schools make, one generation to the next, as they create and recreate the histories of our lives.

The poet William Butler Yeats, having spent the middle of his career inventing an elaborate, rather inaccessible superstructure of myth and symbol, returned, at the end of his career to the simple, direct mode he had started with. In "The Circus Animals Desertion," he wrote:

> *Those masterful images because complete*
> *Grew in pure mind, but out of what began?*
> *A mound of refuse or the sweepings of a street,*
> *Old kettles, old bottles, and a broken can,*
> *Old iron, old bones, old rags, that raving slut*
> *Who keeps the till. Now that my ladder's gone,*
> *I must lie down where all the ladders start,*
> *In the foul rag-and-bone shop of the heart.*

You, as teachers, know that rag-and-bone shop. You, as teachers, pay attention to the mound of refuse or the sweepings of a street. Can any work mean more than reclaiming a child from the refuse, or taking a castaway kid into your care?

I am here to give voice to you for all those children out there who, out of fear or meekness or shame, cannot ask and cannot tell. It is a quiet tragedy that has gone on for many centuries, the destruction of children. You, as teachers, are the single most valuable and effective check against that. You, as teachers, can save these kids.

I am here also to say thank you on behalf of those children, and on behalf of their parents, who wish they could have done better. Thank you for the time you took, the unnoticed, unpaid-for, unrewarded effort you put in. Thank you for risking rejection and embarrassment. Thank you for risking your own heart getting broken. Thank you for putting up with us in all our messy situations. Thank you for persisting and for being there.

A famous man was once asked how he had achieved so much, and his answer became a refrain in a song. He said, "In my mother's eyes, I only saw smiles."

For many, many kids, you provide those eyes and those smiles.

Who Do They Think You Are?
Transference in the Teaching Life
by Edward M. Hallowell

Scanning the tables, Marianne Constant knew exactly where she stood – or should it be said, where she sat? – for the first time since she took her job as head of Pilgrim Country Day School eleven years ago. "Eleven glorious years," her husband had said that evening as they were dressing. Not quite glorious, she had thought to herself, that's not the word, but how sweet of Jack to have said so, particularly considering the back seat he'd had to take so often. Not glorious, she'd thought, but, in sum, good. She liked the term "in sum," feeling that it gave a formal certitude to the word "good," which was after all, a word she'd only just then settled on. In a different mood, at a different time, she might have chosen something quite different, something like "just ducky," or, "a day at the beach," or, "a real gas," something that would take in, in an ironic way, some of the resentment she'd felt at times over the eleven years. But this evening, as she'd strung her pearls around her neck, she'd settled on the simple sturdiness of "good," knowing that it didn't tell the whole story, but what word possibly could? What can you say after eleven years anywhere? It was good, it was bad, it was just what I'd hoped for, it was nothing like what I'd expected, it drained me completely, it replenished me daily, there's more that happened than you'd ever believe, I can't believe it's over. She had all of these thoughts in mind and more as she settled on the words, "in sum, good," as her motto for the evening, words she'd turn over in her head as the farewell banquet made its way from cocktails to dessert.

Now she was between tournedos and baked Alaska, between Phillip Blakemore, head of the trustees on one side and Jack on the other, between farewell dinner and the next morning's moving van, which would take her family's belongings to Athens, Georgia, and the start of her tenure as writer in residence at the University of Georgia. She hoped the novel she would write there would also, someday, be, "In sum, good."

Around the room, others took in this moment for Marianne Constant in an array of inconstant ways. The special room in an old hotel near the Public Garden in Boston was full of the noisy chatter that can make these gatherings sound, from the outside, like a kennel. But inside people were lifting glasses and making passes and in general getting off their chests whatever they dared while saving the rest for well-wined reverie.

And the reveries were many. Charleston Montague, for a start, was chewing his meat with eyebrows raised at each bite as if the next one might be poisoned. Charlie Montague knew what it was to be betrayed, he could tell you, for betrayed he had been by the appointment of this woman he was on hand to honor tonight. The board of trustees had all but guaranteed that he would move from dean of students to head until, at the last minute, they'd come up with this forty-two-year-old woman, ten years his junior and ten generations of breeding his social inferior. Who did she think she was, this woman with the foolish last name, this pretender from South Carolina whose only claim to fame was that she'd written a novel nobody had read? And who did the school think it was, hiring her over him? What was she but a token, a blatant offering to those who felt Pilgrim was falling behind the feminist times? Well, hadn't he shown them, and her, what real character was by staying on, by not leaving in a snit when everybody else thought he surely would leave and have every right to leave and leave angry, too? But that was not the Montague way. One never quit. He, Charleston Montague, had stayed on in a valiant effort to maintain standards and uphold the academic rigor Connie, as he called her, so assiduously ignored. He accepted without rancor the demotions she handed him, knowing in his heart his cause was just. He felt she had never respected him, never even listened to him, really. But now, who was leaving? Who was attending whose funeral? He was attending hers. He had won. Now assistant to the director of development, he had positioned himself strategically. He had beat her at her own game. Bring on the new head, he thought to himself, inspecting his next bite of meat before popping it into his mouth.

At another table sat Billy Talbott, a relatively obscure member of the class that had just graduated. He was trying to join in the conversations around him as best he could, but, since he was quite shy, his attempts were halting. What was not halting, however, was his determination to attend this dinner, no matter how socially awkward he may have felt, because of his admiration for The Boss, as the students called Marianne. Although no one knew where the nickname came from, as far as Billy was concerned it didn't begin to describe what a woman she was, a great woman in his eyes, the best all-around person he'd ever met, the smartest, the kindest, the fairest, and the best. He liked to close his eyes in assembly and just listen to her voice as it rolled over him like a wave of good news. Even though he'd never really talked to her, even though, in fact, they'd never actually exchanged any words at all, he felt as if he knew her perfectly, knew her maybe better than anyone, certainly better than her stiff of a husband,

Jack. He had read all that she'd written, including her novel, several times. Some of the students didn't like her. Some of them thought she was just a figurehead, someone there just to raise money, to run the school like a business. Some of them thought she didn't really like kids, she just took the job for the prestige. But those kids didn't know her. He couldn't put it into words, exactly, and he didn't know just where the feeling came from, but he had a powerful sense that Marianne was with him, on his side and looking out for him wherever he went. And so tonight he was there, there for her, shy or not, to show in his own way his respect and gratitude.

In another part of the room Fats O'Malley was looking through the dainty portions for something he could call real food. Albert O'Malley, dubbed Fats by his brother at age ten, never stopped eating. Except to teach English. And teach English he did, with greater gusto, enthusiasm, and flat-out braininess than anybody east of the Mississippi, or so they said. Fats had come to this preserve of Paleolithic Protestants, as he thought of Pilgrim Country Day, at the invitation of Marianne, and he had stayed on for two reasons, one open, one secret. The open reason was that the students, offspring of the bountiful boring though they be, were bright, very bright in fact, and so he had a chance to stretch as he taught, and to rescue perhaps one or two minds every year from the permanent cerebral calcification their birthright entitled them to. The secret reason was personal, so personal that Fats himself could not bring it into conscious awareness without the assistance of so much bourbon that he would forget it the next day. But the fact of the matter was that he stayed on at Pilgrim to protect and defend its head, his secret paramour, one Marianne Constant. Since he could outwit and outthink, not to mention outeat and outdrink, any opponent that might sally forth, as long as he stayed around Marianne was safe. He had set off more than a few explosions at faculty meeting when he imagined someone beginning to attack the head. Once Miss Marianne herself, as he thought of her, had told him that as much as she enjoyed his loyalty, she was able to speak for herself. He took this not as a rebuff but as indirect encouragement to keep up his vigilant work.

Next to Fats – and it was physically difficult for anyone to sit next to Fats – but squeezed onto what little space was left on the chair to Fats' left was Lizbeth Ravenel, fellow English teacher and ardent admirer of Fats. Indeed, it wouldn't be unfair to say that Lizbeth loved Fats and would be in love with him if only he'd give her the slightest encouragement. But no, he had to devote all his prodigious romantic energy to mooning over that bitch at the head table. Didn't he know how obvious it was and how foolish it made him look? And couldn't he see through her veneer of cultured urbanity to the gross, ambitious troll that lay beneath? What a joke she was. Little Miss Marianne. Little priss Marianne. Couldn't fight her way out of a paper bag. Whenever anyone attacked her she looked down at the ground and folded her hands. What rot! What did she think life was, Quaker meeting? And to boot, she treated Lizbeth so politely it made her want to punch Miss Marianne in the nose. It set the cause of women back a hundred years having the first female head of PCDS be such a wimp. She reminded Lizbeth of her sister growing up, always doing the sweetsie-sweetsie act but getting away with murder while it was Lizbeth who'd gotten all the spankings. But if little Miss Marianne thought for one minute that Lizbeth didn't see past the wimpy pose to the conniving bitch beneath, then she was sadly mistaken. She'd tell her so to her face if she ever got the chance, which didn't seem likely now that, mercifully and to the great praise of all that's fair in life, Marianne was moving on.

Moving on, Maeve Harris thought to herself as she took a long sip of wine and looked down at Marianne. Maybe I should be moving on, too. There's a woman the same age as me and she's done more in a decade than I'll do in my lifetime. Maybe I should pack it in tonight, too. John wouldn't mind. God knows the kids wouldn't mind. Probably wouldn't even notice. Do they know their mother still teaches two classes of Latin? And would teach more if anyone wanted to take Latin? Marianne's kids know all about her work, I'm sure. Even though she jokes they don't, they must. What did Marianne do right that I did wrong? We both graduated from college in 1962. We both got married soon after that and started having children. But she had more confidence. She did new things. I haven't done a new thing since I don't know when. She still has more confidence. I hate her for it. No, I don't. I admire her. Do you have to hate everyone you admire? Why does Marianne bring out such feelings in me? Why am I such a petty old woman? Old? Fifty-two isn't old. You can be sure Marianne Constant doesn't think of herself as old. So why do I? Why couldn't I have some of her energy, her facility with things? In a way it's been wonderful having her around, almost like having her here makes her a part of me that I'm proud of, only she's not part of me, but I look to her at times as if she were and I feel her with me without knowing it. But having her around also reminds me of what I'm not. I don't honestly know if I'll be glad to have her gone or not. I don't know. What I feel about her is so complicated. Do I have any right to feel this way?

As Maeve Harris wondered over the complexity of her own feelings, Sam Rothman wondered about the school's. This place doesn't know her, never has, he thought to himself. Rothman, a trustee throughout Marianne's tenure, had seen her through much sound and fury. He was there for the great hiring controversy at the beginning, when many had opposed bringing a Southern woman to what had always been a Yankee man's job. He had stood by her through the challenges of the first few years when many parents, faculty, and alumni had wanted her to fail. He had helped her manage public opinion through the charges of sexual harassment that had turned the Upper School upside down. And it was Sam Rothman whom Marianne had called one night to ask if the school would be better off without her. "If I'm damaging this school, I'll get out right now," she'd said seven years ago.

"Don't do that," Sam said. "This school needs you badly."

"What should I do, Sam?" she asked.

"Take over," Sam said. "Be a bastard. These people need to know you're in charge." It was the same advice Sam's father had given him years earlier when his new business was faltering. Marianne had taken Sam's advice, so much so that most people thought of her as rather autocratic, even cold, very much The Boss, to use the students' term. But Sam knew better. Sam knew what a struggle it had been for Marianne, as it had been for him, to use authority, to take over. Once, when Marianne had said in an overheard conversation, "You know, I really like being in charge," Sam had known how insincere that statement actually was.

Also sitting at Sam's table were Will Ogden and Amy Baretti, both of the English department. The family backgrounds of these two teachers, both age forty-five, were quite different. The Ogdens were a wealthy family from the North Shore of Massachusetts. Mr. and Mrs. Ogden, Senior, began to disagree soon after they were married in the late 1940s, and they continued to disagree ever after. Marjorie Ogden seldom spent a happy day, losing herself for long periods in the throes of regret and sorrow for her life. Why was there nothing to it but children and life's demands? She often would talk to her little boy Will about the various shortcomings of his father while she wondered aloud if she wouldn't be better off dead. Will, in his grade school years, tried to reassure his mother, patting her forearm gently and telling her he loved her, while also trying to conceal his tremendous fear that she actually might kill herself. At night he would pray that his mother might be happy.

The Barettis, on the other hand, were a poor family from a different part of the North Shore in Massachusetts. Sylvia Baretti had five children. Her husband left her after the birth of the fifth, Amy. Sylvia worked two jobs and relied on friends and family to keep track of the kids while she was away. But, no matter what, she was home every night, and whenever she got home she would kiss each child, often fast asleep, goodnight.   When Amy was a little girl, she discovered one day that she was poor when one of her playmates explained to her that neither of their families had much money and so they were called poor. When Amy asked her mother about this she said to her, "It is true we don't have much money, but what we don't have in money we make up for in love."

The years had brought both Amy and Will into teaching and they are both at the banquet to say good-bye to Marianne Constant, but from very different points of view. Poor Marianne, thought Will, looking at his retiring head with sad, soft feelings. How hard she tried, but the school made it impossible for her. She could never put herself across and be heard. She always carried her sadness well hidden, but it was there, sagging within her like an empty dress on a hanger. I hope she'll be all right when she leaves. Without the school, hard as it was, she'll be so on her own. Can she make it? He shuddered, as if someone had just walked over his grave.

Simultaneous with Will's thoughts, Amy was looking at the head table and thinking, Marianne, you hot ticket. You've done it all here now, and you've still got time to go off and do a new gig in Georgia. You are so smooth. And you never made a big fuss about it, either. Just sailed in here, turned the place around, and now you're sailing on. Amy relaxed into a state of quiet good feeling about the departing head as she took in the conversation she was being fed by a diligent parent next to her.

As the evening wore on, the room continued to swell with the private feelings and fantasies of all present even as the spoken conversation waltzed along politely taking up tame topics that veiled the more heated feelings within.

The dinner had attracted such a crowd that while the school had expected to rent only a small room at first, they'd ended up with the largest room available short of the Grand Ballroom, such was the emotion aroused by the departure of the head – and occasionally around the large room a brush fire would burst forth and you could almost hear the water glasses rattle their ice cubes as some fresh news shocked the table or some opinion was rushed up like a spinnaker in the wind.

"Why do you suppose it was," asked Mrs. Harrington, putting her knife and fork down for a moment, "that Marianne went ahead and hired Lucinda to teach third grade the very day after I cautioned her not to? It is because the woman is so independent," she went on, answering herself, quartering up the word, "independent" with her tongue as if with a knife. "She thinks to take another person's advice, particularly another woman's advice, is somehow to capitulate or kowtow. I think this school will do well to have a more calming presence in charge."

At another table, Gretchen Downs was in the middle of the long saga of indirect criticism of Marianne which no one else at the table could quite understand because Marianne had always been good to the controversial Gretchen, protecting her from the frequent attacks she received from parents and students for her arrogant, condescending, and cold manner. "Of course, we've been so lucky to have Marianne," Gretchen was saying, "considering the alternatives with which we were presented. Now, perhaps, the school will be ready for – how shall I say? – a leader who can really lead."

"But Gretchen," interrupted Jay Phillips from mathematics, "don't you think Marianne really has led? I certainly do. Look at how the school has changed..."

"Precisely," Gretchen interrupted back. "Look at how the school has changed. Willy-nilly. At the whim of the winds and whatever trustee had Marianne's ear. Not to take away from Marianne. She did the best she could."

"I don't understand you, Gretchen," Sally Finley from Gretchen's own department spoke up. "Marianne has defended you right and left, and now on the night to honor her you are attacking her."

Gretchen turned red and squeezed her fist. "I can assure you that Marianne Constant has never defended me. It was never defense, I can assure you of that. It is an old trick, to disarm your adversaries by appearing to aid them. But I knew better. She knew I had her number, so she tried to keep me at bay."

"That's paranoid," said Sally.

"Paranoid? My dear Sally, my dear young Sally, it is perceptive, not paranoid. As the years teach you the lessons of life they have yet to teach you, you will learn not to trust those who seem most kind and solicitous of you. You will learn that those people almost invariably want something, as Marianne has wanted something of me all along. Rather, you will learn to trust people who spit in your eye, and keep company with insults more easily than with sweet words."

"Gretchen, I really don't want to get into a tiff with you, but I can't understand what you think Marianne has wanted from you. I mean what could she..."

"Possibly want from me?" Gretchen interrupted, cocking her eye at Sally.

"Well, since you put it that way, yes, what could she want from you?"

"She wants, my dear, what she knows she can never have. My admiration. My respect. She knows I see through her. She knows I know she is an intellectual sham. Early on, she had to decide whether to get rid of me or woo me.

She decided, in a rather cowardly fashion, not try to get rid of me, so she began to woo me instead. I am not easily wooed. Not by the likes of her."

While others at Gretchen's table intervened to change the subject, the emotion at Tony Capozzi's table ran quite differently. Tony, a parent of first- and second-grade boys, was recalling Marianne's readings to the lower school. Tony, a house husband, as he called himself, sometimes stopped by school to listen to the stories. Tony was struck by how Marianne read just like his great Aunt Lucy. She had the same way of looking up from the book to emphasize a detail, the same voice, the same way of almost singing the words. "I get worked up when I think about it," he said. "It's like when I was a kid and I'd want to hear the story one more time, one more time before I went to bed, it was my way of making time stop, and I'd look up at Aunt Lucy, and I'd say, 'Again!' and she would read the story one more time. They were the same stories Marianne reads, some of them anyway. Grimm's fairy tales, *The Wizard of Oz*. I'd hear them again and again and I wouldn't have to go to bed because I could say, 'Again!' and when I did go to bed her voice would stay with me. Now, when I listened to Marianne, it was like I was there as a kid again, and here were these stories, and I was wanting to hear them one more time, and Aunt Lucy, long dead, had given her work to Marianne Constant to cast the same magical spell over all the eager little heads and this one big head, listening as time stood still. It gave me the chance to connect back with that time and see my kids get it at the same time. What do I mean, 'Get it?'" Tony asked the air. "I mean get the magic, the magic of a story and the experience of being able to go anywhere and be anything anytime all in your mind. One more time, again! Here's a toast to you Marianne, again!"

At that, all the others at the table, moved by Tony's impromptu, unintentional speech, raised their glasses and said, without missing a beat, "Again, here's to you, again!"

The processes of mind by which we turn other people into beings of our own creation are, like Aunt Lucy's stories, many and magical. We concoct in our minds our own version of who the other person is. So often these feelings emerge from sources we can't quite identify, like Billy Talbott's for Marianne: "He couldn't put it into words exactly, and he didn't know just where the feeling came from, but he had a powerful sense that Marianne was with him." Our feelings originate not only in the bits of reality the other person presents us with, but also in our own pasts and in the unconscious part of our own minds.

We begin by "meeting" another person. In that moment of meeting, of coming together, we bring our entire past histories to bear. As we focus on the other person, the new person, the person we are doing this thing to called "meeting," we unwittingly see the new person in terms of all the other people we've ever seen before. We assign the new person a place in our minds almost immediately. We assign that place according to our catalogue of associations. There are some obvious categories that guide us at first: sex, age, appearance, accent, occupation. And then, as the meeting proceeds, wherever it may be, across seats on an airplane, on the dance floor, in a checkout line, over dinner, at a bus stop, or at a reception for a new head, and we gather emotion according to the details that emerge, a subtler system takes over, a system of categorization and rating that goes much deeper than the crude categories of age, sex, and job, and begins to ask and give answers to such fundamental questions as, Do I like this person? Is he on my side? Do I trust people with red-striped neckties? Where have I heard that accent before and did it make me fall in love or want to throw up? This subtle detection system and sorter of minute details is more sensitive and complex than any mechanical early warning radar system ever devised. It picks through the millions of details one could focus on when one meets another person, and it selects the one or two it will choose to remember and make judgments by. No, I do not like red-striped-tie people. In my experience, seven out of ten have been snakes. Yes, I do remember that accent, and it confused me the last time as well because the satin-tongued jerk who had it was so seductive I almost fell for his act, but no, I definitely hate the accent. No matter how we may try to meet each new person afresh, we do see people in terms of people we've seen before.

If an entirely new personality walked into our lives, a personality totally unlike any we'd ever met before, we'd probably be unable fully to comprehend it at first. We'd be unable to deal with the person and we'd inwardly recoil, dismissing him or her as overpowering or weird or even evil as we groped for some points of reference.

We deal every day with understanding and misunderstanding each other in terms of people we have known before and relationships we've had before. This is not to say there is no new person, no new relationship; this is not to say that we go on repeating the same relationships over and over again, meeting the same people over and over again, although sometimes we have to be careful not to. Rather it is to say that the newness of a person or a relationship is apprehended but slowly, as it emerges from the disguises of past patterns with which we initially enshroud it.

The process is perhaps like getting to know a new piece of music. The first time you hear it, as you are carried or jolted along by its melodies or dissonances, you are searching reflexively for a place to put this piece of music, a context, a frame of reference by which it can be known and apprehended. It sounds a bit like Mahler, you might say, with those mournful swellings in strings, or, if it's a different type of music you might say it sounds a bit like the Beach Boys, particularly the choruses. I play a game with my wife in the car on long drives where we'll tune in a classical station in the middle of a piece and try to guess the composer. As we zero in on it, we'll hit a stand-off. "Haydn," I'll say. "No, Mozart," she'll say. Neither one of us knows enough music to be absolutely sure. When we get the answer, sometimes the announcer names a composer neither one of us has ever heard of, let's say Antonio Piscalli, who thereafter will be known to us until, if ever, we get to know him better, as a composer who sounds a little like Mozart, a little like Haydn.

So, too, with people. As we encounter them we often begin silently guessing who wrote them, where they came from, who they are. As we listen to their melodies and their dissonances, we hear past melodies, past dissonances, and it is only gradually, if ever, that we let the new person take on his or her own identity. When I first heard Mahler I probably thought he sounded something like somebody else, and it was only over years that Mahler came to sound unmistakably like Mahler.

Psychoanalysts have various terms for the ways in which we distort one another in our own minds, or, to put it differently, the ways in which we create each other out of the raw material we see. Without dwelling on the terms, I simply want to call attention to the power of the phenomenon, because you all, as heads, teachers, counselors, or administrators, will be subjected to it from day one, even second one. In fact, you're being subjected to it right now by people at your schools who haven't even met you, but have learned a few bits of information about you. In their minds, right now, you are being created, conjured up, imagined in ways that I can assure you would surprise you. You might as well get used to being seen as someone who you think you're not because it is happening to you all the time.

Of course, it has been happening to you all along, in whatever roles in life you've had up until now. It happens everywhere, amongst everybody, all the time. But it is particularly powerful, this phenomenon of creating or distorting others in terms of what we have known before – in other words, in terms of who we are – when those others are in important positions, positions of responsibility, power, or authority, such as one's boss, one's teacher, one's department chair, one's head.

Such positions of authority and responsibility draw particularly strong feelings from people not only because of the power and influence they usually carry with them, but also because they tap into the primal reserves of emotion derived from our first relationships in life, our relationships with our parents. Our parental relationships often echo through our dealings with people in authority in adult life. Of course, there is not an exact correspondence; you don't feel toward your boss just as you felt toward your father and mother. But the phenomenon of distorting or creating others in terms of our own past histories has its roots in our original family relationships. We often repeat patterns in adulthood that were laid down in childhood. The authority figures in one's adult life become key figures in the drama, often serving as stand-ins for the key figures from childhood. Unconsciously we often look to people in authority in adult life for many of the things we looked to our parents or teachers or siblings for in childhood: approval and praise, regulation, discipline and even punishment, nurturance, guidance, security, reassurance, and protection.

A teacher might look to the head of a school for the approval he never received as a child, and so become pesteringly needy. An influential parent may treat their child's advisor abrasively, trying, unconsciously – this is all usually quite unconscious – to work out unresolved competitive feelings with a sibling or parent. A student may be terrified of a teacher, not because the teacher is very scary, but because the student is transferring feelings toward father or mother onto the teacher.

The head especially becomes the focal point of many eyes, some eyes trusting, others plotting, some eyes demanding, others wanting to serve, some eyes endorsing, others desperately seeking praise. Peering through these many eyes, it can be hard to discern who the head really is.

Look at the banquet for Marianne Constant. Who really is this woman? We know her age, her sex, her marital status, we know her occupation and her future work plans, we know her husband's name, and we know she came from the South originally and is headed back there. We know she is head of a large school called Pilgrim Country Day and we know that her retiring brought out a throng almost big enough to fill the Grand Ballroom at a hotel that sounds like the Ritz Carlton in Boston.

But what about all the rest we hear of her? Whom do we believe? Who is she? Other than her name, there seems to be nothing constant about her. And even her name changes. One person calls her Marianne, another The Boss, another Miss Marianne, another Connie, and others verge off into vulgar epithets. Everyone at the banquet seems to have his or her own version of who this head is.

Is she Gretchen Downs' sweet-talking intellectual fraud? Or is she Billy Talbott's best person there ever was? Is Sam Rothman right in saying she really didn't like power, or are the kids right who give her the name The Boss? Is she the ruthless incompetent Charlie Montague saw or the woman worth dying for, as Fats O'Malley imagined? Do her children keep up with her professional life, as Maeve Harris thought, or does she carry with her an inner sadness, hung, as Will Ogden saw it, like an empty dress on a hanger? Has her tenure at the school been filled with crises, like the ominous-sounding sexual harassment episode in the upper school with which Sam Rothman helped her, or was her time the smooth sailing Amy Baretti imagined? Is she the unfeeling bitch Lizbeth Ravenel felt her to be, or is she the presiding presence, the warm-hearted story-teller of Tony Capozzi's version?

She is all of these. And none of these. She is all of these, in that the members of the school community perceived her in these hugely disparate ways. Each of them created a Marianne Constant of their own. And she is none of these, in that each version derived from the subjective experience of its creator. No one version could be called definitive. Each version had in it bits of reality and bits of distortion depending on the point of view. Sam Rothman's father had told him to get tough at a key point in his life, and he had done so even though he hadn't liked it. So Sam assumed Marianne didn't like being tough either. We can only imagine what happened in Gretchen Downs' past to create her complicated feelings about Marianne. Maeve Harris, we might suppose, idealizes Marianne's life in counterpoint to her own depression. And so on down the list. Each person has his or her own reasons to see Marianne in a different way.

The real Marianne? That hardly matters to the assembled group, for they each have their own Marianne. It is striking how if you sit down and talk with the members of a school community, or any business or institution for that matter, about the person in charge you will get descriptions that are wildly at odds, shaded and distorted according to the pains and pleasures of the describer. And who is to say that the real Marianne isn't the sum of the distorted versions, as if they were drawn on transparencies and laid one over the other with the image that emerges being the one that is true?

But there is at least one person who needs to know who Marianne really is, and that is of course Marianne herself. As long as she can retain a sense that there is a person within her independent of and unaltered by the eyes of the community, a person who has some internal definition that cannot be changed by external representation, then she will bear up well.

But even if she has a solid sense of who she is, how can she deal with the many different versions of herself others have? How, for example, can she deal with Gretchen Downs, who hates her more the nicer she is to her? Or how can she deal with Fats O'Malley, who moons over her and insists on being her protector when she really doesn't want one? Or what is she to do with poor old Charlie Montague, who keeps hanging on thinking he should be head despite abundant evidence to the contrary? And how does she counsel Billy Talbott when he sends her love letters, or how does she fend off Mrs. Harrington who is forever trying to tell her what to do, and is it OK for Tony Capozzi to keep showing up at her reading aloud time and standing at the back with a wistful look on his face?

The general question becomes, How does a person in authority deal with the inevitable bits of personal craziness he or she will be thrown every day?

I have a few suggestions. First of all, don't take it personally. Recognize the phenomenon for what it is. Psychoanalysts call what we have been discussing transference, but you can just call it mishigas and leave it at that. Just know that everyone has their own mishigas, their own personal craziness, and when you get a face full of it, don't take it personally. As hard as it is to do, remember that the other person is coming from places you don't know about and is dealing with old conflicts and hurts you cannot know of. So, for example, when it gets back to you that Gretchen Downs thinks you are a fraud, don't think, 'Oh, my God, she's found me out.' Think instead, 'There must be some bomb in Gretchen that I detonate. Better watch out.' Or, when a Sam Rothman insists that you fear power, don't think, 'Is there something about me that exudes timidity?' Think instead, 'I wonder what happened in Sam Rothman's life to compel him to see me as someone who doesn't like power. ' Or when a Maeve Harris or a Billy Talbott treat you as if you're just about perfect, take strength from their support but believe them at your peril. Remember also, in not taking these perceptions personally, that there may be something to learn about yourself in some of them. That is to say, remember that they may be true.

A corollary to the suggestion not to take it personally is the following: You don't have total control over what people think of you. You have some control of course, but you don't have total control or anything close to it. If you are a female you will stir feelings in some people about that, regardless of who else you are or what else you do. And if you are a male you will stir feelings in other people, regardless of who else you are or what else you do. If you are unmarried you will draw some attention for that, no matter who else you are or what else you do. And if you happen to be that most politically incorrect of all species, a white male heterosexual Protestant, you will catch certain feelings about that, no matter who else you are and what else you do. You cannot control what people will think of you.

A second suggestion is to remember that in your role you are larger than life. As a teacher or administrator, and especially the higher you climb on the school's ladder of authority, you will be a special person, a strong and powerful person in the eyes of many, from first graders to parents to faculty as well. Even if you feel like an ordinary person, and I do hope you will retain your humility in this job, even if you feel ordinary, remember that others look at you as being larger and grander than that. You will understand their responses better if you keep that in mind.

Third, try to know the other person's pain. Everyone has pain. Try to know of it in those you deal with. Think of where they hurt, where they have hurt. You will then understand them better, help them better, forgive them better. As you wrestle with another person's craziness, try to know the pain from which it comes.

I would like to end not with my own thoughts but rather by paying a final visit to Marianne Constant. Some time after the farewell banquet she agreed to be interviewed by a man interested in the lot of a school head.

"I was always more of a teacher at heart than I was a head," she began. She was sitting in her backyard in Athens, Georgia. Her hair was up in a bandanna, and she had drops of yellow paint in the hairs on her forearms. Her half-painted porch backdropped the conversation. "Why I left teaching I really don't know," she went on. "It's like painting this porch. It needed to be done. I guess I felt a sort of 'duty calls,'" being the first woman offered the job at PCDS. I know when I got the job I felt a combination of elation and fear. I was thrilled, but I also started lying awake at night, thinking of parts of the job I didn't feel prepared to do, like budget-making and disciplining faculty. Fortunately, I had good people to help with the money, so that worked out OK. The faculty problems? To this day I don't understand why some people insist on backbiting rather than problem-solving face to face. I tried to learn not to take it personally. But that's very hard. You need a shoulder to cry on and there's none built into the job. Not the trustees, not the assistant head, not the faculty, and certainly not the parents and students. You are there to give to all of them. You can't ask them to prop you up, at least not directly, or at least not very often. You have to have supports away from work."

The warm Georgia wind blew a few strands of her hair in front of her eyes, and she brushed them away.

"The best of it was the kids," she went on. "Seeing them grow. I know it's a cliché, but it's true. The look of excitement and curiosity in their eyes every day made up for all the angry phone calls. It was harder being head, being that much more removed from the kids than I was as a teacher, but I was still like Conrad's secret sharer, there with them, on the sidelines, urging them on, making the place safe, or at least I like to think so. If there's a grandness to the job, it's that: You protect and you nourish, often behind the scenes, but it's scary when you think of it because you're everywhere. Your stamp is on everything. The school becomes tinged with your color everywhere. Of course it can all be wiped away, but for the time you're there, like it or not, it's you.

"Did I like it? Yes and no. How can you not? Despite what Sam Rothman thinks, I loved the power. The chance to get things done. Other days I hated it, all the headaches. The worst of it was being misunderstood, being betrayed. I'll never forget one of the trustees looking me straight in the eye and flat out lying about a matter that is now of no more importance than that ant on your shoe, but was of great importance to me at the time." Her voice drifted off.

Then she slapped her thigh and remembered a few stories which are too long to tell right here. "What advice would I have?, you asked," she said, taking a drink from a tumbler of iced tea she had poured. "First of all, I'll give you this recipe, since you asked for it. Mash up a lot of mint with a lot of sugar and lots of lemon juice into a sort of syrup, add a slug of whatever whiskey you have around, and stir it into a pitcher of tea and ice cubes.

"Advice for heads is harder. You know, I don't really like giving advice straight out like a wizard or something. But I guess since now I'm nothing but an aspiring southern writer I can tell you what I'd tell myself if I were still there. Keep the door open. Don't withdraw. There are so many demands on you from so many places that you can really feel like building a wall around you. But don't do it. Stay open. Let the people have access. That's all they really want. Do that, and get your own self taken care of in your own way, and you'll be pretty well off, I should think." She then pushed her hair back up under her bandanna, finished her iced tea with a long draught, gave me a water-pumping handshake and went back to her porch-painting, saying goodbye to all that for now.

Masochism in Teachers

by Michael G. Thompson

Masochism? Isn't that too strong a word? Perhaps. But no other word completely captures the range of self-denying, self-deprecating, and self-punishing behaviors that some teachers display and that I have observed in my school consultation work. Let me give some examples.

I once talked with a teacher who said that after twenty-five years of teaching he was ready for another career. He had, over the course of his teaching life, earned two degrees in other fields but had not followed those degrees into other possible vocations. Now he was ready to go. He said, "I'm tired of setting the stage for other people. I've been doing it for so long. Now I want to set the stage for myself." Can you guess what this man is doing four years later? Teaching.

A teacher who lives in a dormitory on the campus of a boarding school is unable to stop working during vacations. She feels a chronic need to work on class preparations. She feels this need most acutely every time she spots one of the school's administrators walking across campus to the office. She is overwhelmed by feeling that she must do as much as they do, even though she knows intellectually that they have contracts, vacation schedules, and pay scales different from hers.

A fifth-grade teacher works in a loose team-teaching arrangement with a colleague whom she regards as very limited and rigid in his teaching. The children often complain to her about him. Periodically, her colleague comes to her and asks, "Why don't the children like me better?" and she tries to coax him toward a more open and flexible style with students, but he cannot change. Other teachers are critical of this man, and the administration is aware of his limitations, but nothing ever happens because our teacher finds herself protecting, defending, and counseling her colleague, while a resentment grows inside her toward him and the school. After four years she begins to think about looking for a job at another school because she cannot bring herself to confront her colleague or betray him to the administration.

A teacher starts the year with a new girl in her class and is immediately aware that she has an unhappy student on her hands. The girl isolates herself socially, but alternates the isolation with sudden intrusive forays into groups or attention-getting outbursts in class. After a month, the teacher finds tacks in the bottom of her coffee cup that she is sure were put there by this child. At times the girl holds a sharpened pencil up to the faces of other children in a threatening way. Over the course of the year, the teacher comes to know the girl's family and learns of several recent tragedies. These events have been so heartbreaking for the family, and the mother has so obviously not fully recovered, that the teacher is filled with compassion and sympathy for them. Therefore, when the family fails to follow up on a recommendation of treatment for the girl, the teacher does not press the issue. So she endures the continuously difficult behavior of the girl and buffers the rest of the children as best she can. By the end of the year, she is exhausted and discouraged.

These examples are joined, in my mind, by the hundreds of teachers I have seen who work to exhaustion during the school year, who worry constantly about troubled students, who endlessly revise their lesson plans and preparations, and who, in meeting their obligations as teachers, seem to suffer a great deal.

Is "masochism" the right word? Shouldn't these behaviors be described as dedication, nobility, commitment, and self-sacrifice? Don't all teachers do these things, or don't we think all teachers *should* be self-sacrificing and hard-working?

Admittedly, the line between hard work and dedication on the one hand, and masochism on the other, is a thin one. People might not easily agree where the line should be drawn. I think that teachers are, in general, admirable people. I agree with my colleague Ned Hallowell who says that some of the best human beings he has met in his life are teachers. However, the gratitude of the former student does not obscure the observations of the present-day school consultant. What I see is many teachers in independent schools engaged in a kind of low-level masochism, embracing the more punishing and difficult aspects of teaching, taking a perverse pride in them, and feeling morally superior to others because of them.

As it relates to our subject, I would define masochism as any tendency in a teacher to participate in his or her own devaluation, to seek out and perpetuate the more punishing aspects of teaching, to accept and absorb the pain of others at considerable cost, and, finally, to take pride in enduring these painful aspects of teaching.

Teaching children is inherently difficult. As in farming and medicine, the teacher works with natural raw material that has immutable characteristics and limitations. Also, for complex economic and cultural reasons, teaching is undervalued in the United States. For that reason, teaching requires a high degree of economic self-sacrifice and daily personal struggle. These difficulties are easily recounted, and I shall do so briefly:

1. Teaching is a relatively low-status profession in the United States. Though virtually everyone in the country has been cared for and supported by teachers at some point, teachers themselves are not thought of as "doing well" in this society. The United States ranks twelfth among the fifteen major industrialized countries in what it pays teachers.

2. Teaching is emotionally demanding. To teach well, teachers must extend themselves to children and meet them in the "zone of proximal development." It is a constant stretch to perceive and meet the intellectual and emotional needs of children under the best of circumstances, and many teachers work in less than ideal situations.

3. Teaching is lonely. By definition, working with children all day isolates teachers from other adults.

4. Teaching has repetitive elements. Since the body of knowledge being taught is to a certain extent established by convention and by the age of the children in the class, much of the material is repeated for each new cohort of children that passes through the classroom. Repetition and sometimes boredom are the result.

5. Good teaching requires a high degree of personal discipline and consistency. Organizing, disciplining, and bringing the best out of children requires teachers to act "grown up" to a significant degree. They do not have the room to act childish, self-indulgent, or arrogant to the degree that is permitted in many other kinds of work because the children will punish them for it, painfully and immediately. As a result, most teachers are very controlled people.

6. Teaching results in no "product" and is very hard to measure. Success in teaching depends so much on the vagaries of student quality, family support, and educational resources that it is often difficult for a teacher to feel consistently successful.

In addition, there are some difficulties inherent in independent school teaching:

1. As poorly paid as all teachers are in the United States, independent school teachers are generally paid even less than public school teachers.

2. The economic gap between teachers in independent schools and the families of the students they teach is often enormous. Thus, in addition to the status gap between teachers and parents, the economic gap can also be painfully large. All one has to do is compare the cars in the student parking lot to the cars in the faculty parking lot of any independent secondary day school to see what every teacher feels every day.

3. Families in independent schools have power and leverage as paying customers that public school families do not. Thus, independent school teachers have proportionately less power in relation to these parents.

4. Without unions, independent school teachers have less collective political clout in dealing with salary, working conditions, and other issues than do public school teachers.

5. Independent school teachers are expected to take on much extra work that public school teachers are not – coaching, parent nights, sponsoring activities, field trips. Teachers who perform the most extracurricular work are held up as models for the rest of the faculty.

6. Although the situation is improving, new teachers in some independent schools receive relatively little training and support.

7. Independent school teachers labor under the universal expectation that they will do a better job than public school teachers. Whether this is true, or can be true, many independent school teachers subscribe to the expectation and hold themselves to it.

8. Independent schools spend relatively little money on professional development for teachers, so teachers are, in the main, thrown back on themselves to develop their skills and to understand the stresses of their work.

These conditions create difficulties with which every independent school teacher must grapple. Undoubtedly, one or more of them keeps many people from considering teaching as a career in the first place or drives them out of teaching in the early going. What combination of personality characteristics or life experiences keeps someone teaching in the face of these difficulties?

Having talked to many teachers about their lives and their reasons for teaching, I have developed some ideas about what kind of life experiences can propel a person toward teaching, and especially toward accepting the most punishing aspects of the profession.

Obviously, not all teachers are similar psychologically. However, common themes have appeared in my conversations with teachers and teacher patients. Perhaps the simplest way to portray these themes is through two case histories, which are fictionalized and combined for confidentiality.

Elizabeth

Elizabeth, forty-one, is a gifted and respected English teacher at a boarding school. Students love her; many literally fall in love with her because she is beautiful and puts such feeling into poetry classes. She always has time for students, talking to them about their concerns or helping the weaker ones master the material. She brings tremendous energy to her department and its intellectual life, but does not choose to lead it, though she has been offered the job.

For years prior to her marriage, Elizabeth lived in a dormitory as a dorm parent. After her first two years she had been promised that she would not have to live in a large, noisy dormitory, but she remained in the school's largest and most demanding one, not knowing how or whether she was entitled to petition for a change. She gave up many weekends to sponsor student activities, often picking up the pieces when less reliable colleagues failed to meet their responsibilities.

Over the years, Elizabeth's sense of burden and grievance grew. She had unhappy love relationships with a number of men and always ended up taking care of them as she did her students, all the while feeling deprived herself.

Elizabeth was the oldest of four children. Her mother died when she was ten, leaving her father emotionally devastated. Her father struggled to maintain the family's standard of living and raise the children, but he eventually succumbed to depression. Elizabeth's family became poorer; increasingly, Elizabeth became a caretaker child, trying to maintain her father as well as her brothers and sisters.

The one bright spot in Elizabeth's life was that she was a gifted student.

Before her mother died, she had attended an independent school. After her death, the school supported her with financial aid and helped her to obtain support at a fine secondary school. She had a brilliant career at school and won a scholarship to a good college.

There was a great discrepancy between Elizabeth's school life and her home life. She hid the facts of each from the other, often refusing rides to and from school so that she could keep these worlds separate.

After college, Elizabeth taught at several grade levels and ultimately settled at a boarding school whose academic excellence was reminiscent of the school she had attended. This gave her the opportunity to do for students what had been done for her by the teachers who had been so good to her.

Elizabeth loved teaching and her students, but she felt herself gradually worn down by the other demands of the job, which she could neither limit nor change. She allowed herself to be criticized by parents and used up by the very few most needy students. She could never get heard by the administration. While many of her colleagues complained incessantly, Elizabeth did not. Instead, she began to invest her spirit and imagination in planning trips and summer courses with her husband. This is where she was beginning truly to "live" – away from school.

George

George, thirty-one, teaches biology at an independent day school. His wife, Sarah, also teaches at the school, but on a different campus. George is a beloved and imaginative teacher; he has won prizes for his creative approaches to teaching, and his students have done well in science fairs and on advanced placement examinations. Other teachers go to George for advice about teaching, he is increasingly given responsibility for curriculum planning, and his word is heard in faculty meetings.

Clearly George is an asset to the school community, and the school's administration is hoping that he will stay for a long time. George and Sarah's first child is in second grade, and George is extremely grateful for the good teaching that their child is receiving, but there are tensions related to Sarah's teaching in the lower school.

Slowly George finds that more and more of his life and thinking revolve around the school and its demands. He throws himself into every challenge with energy that his colleagues admire and praise. Soon he expects himself to be a faculty leader in any activity he undertakes. Sarah and he begin to spend much of their conversational time discussing the school, its problems, its students, its parents, and its place in the world. Sarah begins to feel that the school is taking George over, though she herself cannot seem to resist the pulls of school life, George's success, and the all-encompassing demands of the community.

George was the youngest of three children. His father, a remote and severe man, never paid much attention to his family. George's mother devoted herself utterly to the children, but over the years the unhappiness of her marriage took its toll, and she began to drink. George, as the youngest child, experienced much of his mother's decline, and increasingly her alcoholism required him to be more competent, more giving, and more cheerful at home. He became his mother's mainstay and support. As his older brother and sister left home, George became the soul of the family enterprise.

It was only at school that George could really be a boy. He was smart, successful, and enormously popular. As the years went on, he stayed popular with the teachers, but found himself unable to take part in the more rugged and rebellious activities in which other boys engaged. After all, he could not become too rebellious with his family depending on him so much. Even so, school was the happiest part of his life, and the attention of his teachers nourished and supported him. After college, he never considered any profession but teaching. He could not wait to return to the kind of community that had supported him as a child.

Unhappily, by his eighth year of teaching, George had come to feel that he was "just a teacher" – in fact, more a teacher than a person. He felt that his identity and his usefulness were inextricably linked to his success in the school and that he was driven to do more and more for the school just to retain the respect he had achieved. His creativity and dedication were somehow "owned" by the school and his students, and he could not figure out how that had happened.

Readers of popular psychology will immediately recognize Elizabeth as displaying "codependent" behavior and George as an ACoA, adult child of an alcoholic. But they are also gifted teachers suffering in a profession that appears to be an excellent choice for them both. Why?

Here are two people who are doing what they should be doing – teaching – but enjoying it less and less. The prognosis is that they will burn out in teaching and eventually leave it, or stay and be unhappy, bewildered by the level of suffering they are experiencing in a profession they love.

The mystery is understandable if we realize that what has gone wrong is that both Elizabeth and George are trying to recreate the happiest times of their childhoods: the hours spent at school in the company of capable, attentive teachers. They feel great gratitude for what they received there and wish to repay it in some way. They are standing on the shoulders of the teachers who taught them. So far so good.

But what has happened in their pursuit of this dream is that they are recreating in their present jobs not the circumstances of their own schooling, but the troubles of their own families. And they find ample opportunity to do so because every school, like every family, is somewhat dysfunctional and has extremely needy individuals in it. Children who have been the bulwark of their family of origin can easily recreate that role in the larger school "family." The administration can become the impaired parents, and the students can become the needy brothers and sisters whom the teacher tried to take care of at home.

The stages of this reenactment are as follows:

Step 1: Childhood suffering. The parent does not understand/cannot adequately care for/asks too much of the child.

Step 2: School as hope. The school (as parent) loves and rewards and supports the child.

Step 3: Teaching as a reparative act. Child, now a teacher, loves and supports children.

Step 4: Adult suffering. Society, the administration, parents devalue, underpay, do not understand, cannot adequately care for, ask too much of the child, now a teacher.

Step 5: Teacher masochism. Child, now a teacher, accepts and absorbs the excessive demands and exploitation of teaching because it is the familiar childhood situation of step 1.

This sequence shows how gifted teachers, in the right profession, doing right by children, the school, and parents, can end up feeling as helpless, inadequate, and exploited as they may have been in their family life. I call it "masochism" because, in psychoanalytic theory, masochism always involves the reenactment of some disappointing aspect of parents or caregivers.

In teacher masochism, the school is allowed to become the dysfunctional family that disappoints the child/teacher and the family that the child/teacher must save; students may become the hurt siblings the teacher must save. Recently a veteran teacher told me, "Now, whenever I hear the words 'So-and-So must be saved,' I run in the opposite direction." She works hard, she cares, and she is a good teacher, but she is out of the business of saving.

This series of steps does not account for the life histories of all teachers or perhaps even a large minority. But in my experience it does represent something that happens to teachers, often very good teachers, who allow themselves to be eaten alive by their jobs or cannot set limits on the demands of parents, administrators, or children, and who suffer from feelings of being overwhelmed, of having too much asked of them, of having the school take over their identities. To the extent that teachers endure too much or suffer in a profession in which they should thrive, the term "masochism" is appropriate. I want to fight teacher masochism because it reduces the effectiveness – and the well-being – of good teachers.

Teachers who display too much tolerance and endurance are often the kind of people anyone would want to work with. Masochism has long been associated with such virtues as discipline, loyalty, selflessness, and humility as well as humor. But too much masochism can result in rigidity, morbidity, alienation, and vengeful self-satisfaction. The first set of traits can make schools great places to be; the second can make schools horrible places for adults and children alike.

What habits of mind and behaviors give evidence that teachers are too self-sacrificing? Here are some:

Inability to give oneself permission to enjoy things. Many teachers who routinely encourage children to enjoy things are unable to do this themselves. An example is the lunch I once had with three teachers. I was the out-of-town speaker, and the school had chosen to treat us to a nice lunch. We sat surrounded by business people, suffering over the menu. When not one of the three teachers would order a salad in addition to the entree, I could not bring myself to, either. What I realized, and later confirmed by talking with the teachers, was that everyone there had decided to "take it easy" on the school's budget. In other words, no one could relax and enjoy the treat; everyone felt too guilty or responsible to accept even something nice being done for them. Many teachers have difficulty in giving themselves what they recommend for children every day.

Inability to set limits. Some teachers have a hard time saying no even when they obviously should. Whether it is giving a child extra time, taking on another committee assignment, or talking to a parent who has called at home at dinner time, teachers often believe that they should, or absolutely must, extend themselves that extra bit. Many do not believe that their feelings are valid, that they are entitled to say no, until they are on the edge of physical exhaustion.

Accepting negative characterizations of themselves. It is admittedly difficult to be in a profession that is devalued by segments of society, and we have all read the reports of studies in which children say that their teachers are not, in their opinion, successful people. That kind of depreciation is hard to bear, but too many teachers accept or echo it. A teacher I know ran into a college acquaintance who, upon hearing that she was teaching, said, "Oh, you're still teaching...but you were so bright!" It is painful to hear people treated that way; what is more painful is that many teachers do not confront or counter such remarks. Or, worse yet, they say the same things themselves, often in an ironic way.

Accepting as normal one's chronic feelings of guilt, shame, or inadequacy. One reason that people – not just teachers – are willing to accept negative views of themselves is that inside they share others' low opinion of them. Often when people feel downtrodden, they are the ones doing the most treading. Chronic feelings of shame or guilt are a signal that a person's self-esteem is too low. We all worry about children's self-esteem. We should also worry about teachers' self-esteem and do something about it.

Compulsive caring and over-control. When people feel that they are the only ones who can do something and do it well, when they are convinced that everything will fall apart if they are not personally and totally in charge, it is a signal that perfectionism is out of hand and unnecessary suffering is on the way. We all want to be important and imagine that we are very important to our beloved enterprise – and sometimes we really are as important as we feel – but not nearly as often as we think. Having to do everything for one's class or department, having to lift up every child or go to extremes for a certain child at great cost to oneself, is initially noble and impressive, but ultimately masochistic.

Rationalizing. Rationalizing bad treatment, poor working conditions, and especially one's own style is only a temporary solution. In the long run, the effects are felt, and the body and the mind rebel.

Taking pride in suffering. The last stage of teacher masochism is easily recognizable: comforting oneself, either overtly or silently, with one's righteousness in suffering.

When I mentioned to two school administrators that I was going to write about the masochism of the independent school teacher, both said, only half in jest, "Don't get it published in late winter or spring" – contract renewal time for teachers. Even as a joke, the message was clear: To a certain extent, independent schools run on the self-sacrifice, nobility, and masochism of teachers.

Can people be "cured" of masochism? Probably not, because the dedication and nobility with which it is associated is so needed by children. However, I hope that teachers who want to stay in teaching can learn to treat themselves better so that they can stay. Acting in self-denying or self-depreciating ways or not setting limits on one's perfectionism leads to bitterness and self-righteousness – neither of them good traits in a teacher – or to leaving the profession, actually or psychically. Treating oneself badly and accepting bad treatment or overwhelming assignments from others leads to burnout. As W. B. Yeats said, "Too long a sacrifice makes a stone of the heart."

I hope that people who work in schools, who love schools, and who want to stay can recognize their own tendencies to give too much, to take too much flak, to drive themselves, and to rationalize the demands made upon them. If they can see that they are letting themselves be overburdened by their work, I hope they can change their work or their own styles before their teaching hearts become stone.

How Can Teachers Cope?

by Edward M. Hallowell

A few years ago I was talking with my friends Maria and Bill about a presentation I was trying to prepare.

"So, what are you going to talk about?" Bill asked.

"I'm not sure what I'm going to call it," I said, "but what I really want to talk about is that teachers and schools are being asked to do too much and that too many parents don't seem to have the time to be parents. Kids don't have a childhood anymore."

"Do you think it's true," Maria asked, "that parents don't want to be parents?"

"Some," I said. "They're too wrapped up in themselves and their careers to be bothered. They see kids as narcissistic extensions of themselves, not as growing individuals. Some parents only see children as being around to reflect well or poorly on themselves. What happens is that these parents get very hyped up in their expectations – how they want their children to perform and achieve – but they are quite uninvolved in the day in, day out, work it takes to help their children reach those goals. For example, I have a patient in the sixth grade whose mother flat-out said to me, 'Look, I'm a lousy parent. I just don't have time. I want you to make up the difference. I don't care what it costs.'"

"But if she doesn't care what it costs," interrupted Maria, "doesn't that show some willingness to make sacrifices?"

"Sure it does. But not a willingness to sacrifice time, which means sacrifice career."

"Are you implying that mothers shouldn't have careers?"

"Not at all," I said. "The same goes for fathers. I just don't think the big social change we've seen where everybody wants a bang-up career is allowing kids to get the parenting they need."

"That's too reactionary," Bill said.

"I'm not opposed to careers, Bill," I said. "I just think we need to find something better than understaffed day care centers and soccer camps to take up the slack. Plus which, lots of single parents and dual-career parents do a great job with their kids, and lots of traditional nuclear families don't. I'm not saying turn back the clock. I'm just saying let's be more inventive in the alternatives we create, and let's put more emphasis on loving kids and less on finding fancy forms of babysitting. Don't you see this problem as a teacher, Bill?"

"Yes, but it's hard to know what to do about it," Bill answered. "You can't just walk up to a parent and say, 'Spend more time with your child.'"

"Why not?" Maria asked. "If you do it in a way that isn't too guilt-provoking, it could be really important."

"How can it not be guilt-provoking?" Bill asked.

"Well," Maria looked gently at me, "I disagree with Ned. I think these parents really do love their children as unselfishly as parents ever have. There's always an element of pride in any parent's love. I think a lot of parents simply don't know what they should do. They see other kids being sent here and sent there, and they think they should do the same. If you as a teacher can say, 'Don't waste your money, keep them at home,' that can help."

As I sat there, feeling guilty about all the wonderful selfless parents I knew, she went on.

"Not only that. Some of them who are so apparently devoted to their careers work so hard because they want to make things as good as possible for their children. I know plenty of mothers whose jobs pay the tuition for a child's school or college, and plenty of fathers who very happily would turn in their briefcases for a baseball glove if they could afford to."

I was beginning to interrupt, but she put out her hand to stop me and went on.

"You have to understand, some parents just need a little permission, a little encouragement, to go have fun with their kids. I have a patient, a wealthy single-parent working father, who, when I pressed him, confessed that he was simply too embarrassed to coach his son's Little League team. 'You don't know what a trauma baseball was for me as a kid. I was such a lousy hitter that I used to get special instructions on how to work the pitcher for a walk. Now you think I should be a coach?' I pointed out to him that, as far as being a coach went, he was uniquely qualified precisely because he had been a poor player as a kid. He would understand what not to do to his players, and for that age group you don't have to be Babe Ruth to be a good coach. Well, he summoned up his courage, and now he loves coaching. I think the same is true for a lot of overextended parents. They need to be nudged in the right direction, given permission to play. It's not that they won't; they just don't dare, or they don't know how important it can be for their kids – and for them."

"But do you think teachers can offer that kind of advice?" Bill asked. "I don't know about your school, but at our school some parents would choke if I started telling them what to do."

"Not telling them," Maria said, "suggesting. Encouraging. With fathers, if you preface it with a little flattery, you can usually say anything you want, and most mothers are interested to begin with."

"I don't disagree with you," I said. "I was just talking about a certain group."

"You don't have to be defensive, Ned. I knew what you meant."

"Not to put you back on the defensive," Bill piped up, "but the talk was supposed to be about kids and teachers, and you seem to want to focus it on parents. You know, as a teacher, and maybe this is bad, but I just don't have all that much to do with parents, and I'm not completely sure that I want to."

"You shouldn't have to," I said. "The agreement that makes sense is for you to teach, parents to parent, and kids to – well, whatever the verb is that encompasses all that kids do. My point is that the agreement is breaking down. I see schools and teachers being asked to take on much more than they possibly can, and I think it's imperative that schools not let this happen. It may seem like passing the buck, but when a child is having a problem, the first person, and not the last, to know should be the parent. A teacher will often talk to other teachers, guidance counselors, psychological consultants, deans, heads, even other kids, before talking to parents. There is almost a reflex reaction on the teacher's part that the problem should be solvable at school. Or that talking to parents might just create more problems. When a teacher is worrying more about a child than a parent is, then something is out of whack, and balance should be restored. Call the parents in, or call them up. Let them know your concerns.

"It doesn't happen as often as it should, for a lot of reasons, not the least of which is 'Out of sight, out of mind.' You tend to think about the people who are in the same room, not the people who are somewhere else. Another reason is just what you alluded to, Bill. It can be a royal pain in the neck to get in touch with parents. And another is that you can feel like you ought to handle it yourself. And, of course, there are times when you absolutely should not get in touch with parents. But those instances are more common with adolescents than with middle schoolers. Parents and teachers are not adversaries, after all. The more the teamwork can be promoted, the better."

"I agree," Maria picked up, "but I think there are specific classroom measures you can take to promote moral growth or whatever else you want to call it. First of all, let the teacher set a good example. You know, be a decent person. Second, run the classroom in such a way that people are encouraged to listen to each other, beginning with the teacher listening to students and then promoting that among students. After all, within the classroom the teacher really does become a kind of parent. Well, take advantage of it. Be a hero. But that's where the school really has to know what its values are, what its philosophy is, what it wants to impart. You need to stay away from mixed messages. Do you want to promote individualism and competition, or more affiliative kinds of behavior – that sort of thing?"

"Too theoretical, Maria," said Bill.

"No, but it plays itself out in practical ways. We live by certain principles and values. Whether we know what they are is another question. I'm just saying that it can be of great practical assistance to teachers to have the values and principles of the school spelled out. And by 'spelled out' I mean more specifically than through slogans, such as 'Work and courage,' 'Veritas,' or whatever."

"But wouldn't that suppress diversity?" Bill responded.

"You're going to have diversity no matter what," Maria went on. "That's just in human nature, particularly the human nature of independent school teachers. It's whether you want to have diversity amidst chaos or order. Chances are, if the school has a well-articulated philosophy, the work of encouraging moral behavior will be greatly assisted."

The themes we were getting at in that conversation have only grown larger since we spoke those few years ago. The social network is coming unstitched.

I think our social system is in flux, in dialogue, so to speak, as we talk to each other, civilly one hopes, rancorously so often, trying to figure out how to get what we want while we go where we're going. I do see children not getting what they need from parents, even though, if you look at the history of childhood over the past 500 years, children are far better off now than they have ever been. But I do not mean to blame parents. The problem is not so simple as that; it is not so simple as good guys and bad guys. The problem has to do with a society in transition.

I do see teachers being asked to do far, far more than teach. I suppose that this has always been the case as well. Good teachers always seem attuned to percolations of the little psyches that surround them; they are certainly my best source of information on children.

Specifically, then, how can teachers cope?

"There can be no moral education," wrote Alfred North Whitehead, "without an habitual vision of greatness." School is a time when children begin to define greatness for themselves. But where are they to look? Where are the models? What are the values? Is there greatness in the silent, unnoticed heroism of a decent life, or must everybody be a star? Is there, as psychologist Anne Nash suggests, something formative, pattern-setting, and ultimately enabling over a lifetime in finding satisfaction in cooperative behavior, stressing the importance of friendships, or are we finding that kids look to models of individual achievement and isolated struggle?

In answer to those questions and to the general question "What can teachers do?" let me propose four specific answers, answers alluded to in the dialogue with Bill and Maria.

First, involve parents.

Second, take a day off.

Third, take an active role in calling attention to and promoting the two key developmental tasks of this period: moral development and making friends.

Fourth, preserve childhood.

When I say "Involve parents," I may sound like the psychiatrist who treats his depressed patients by telling them to cheer up. I know it is not that easy.

I have observed, however, that teachers, and mental health professionals for that matter, are not looking to parents often enough as the court of first or second resort. There is something forbidding about picking up the telephone and making that call home. It carries with it the possibility of setting in motion a process of God-knows-what – a parent who overreacts, or who hangs up on you, or, worse, won't hang up, or who causes you to overreact – so that it often seems easier and more sensible just to handle the problem yourself. Yet there is an old axiom in psychiatry that applies equally well to teaching: "Never worry alone." If you are worried, parents should know it.

I have a recurring Orwellian negative fantasy of the day in the not-too-distant future when children will be thought of as genetic extension units, or something similar, conceived to satisfy parents' curiosity about what they might produce, and raised in pre-adult behavior centers called schools.

It is only on my gloomy days that I have this fantasy, and I hear tell that teachers have the odd gloomy day themselves. But to the extent that parents are taking themselves out of the experience of childhood, teachers and schools can help to bring them back in. Being a parent is no more a high-visibility glamour job than teaching. But it is fair to say that they are the two most creative, formative, and decisive careers in our society.

Teachers cannot and should not do it all for kids – everything from monitoring personal hygiene and dress to table manners, to lessons of common courtesy, to values education, to sex education, to day care, to summer activity planning, to family therapy, to dietary counseling, to money management, to sibling management – and still somehow fit in something about reading and writing and that other thing.

Teachers can do a lot of that, but they can't do it all. We need to involve parents more. In my experience, even the most self-absorbed parent will respond if invited. Ironically enough, most parents I have talked to even agree with my general thought that parenting is a dying art. These parents say that they would like to spend more time with their children, that they feel overcommitted to careers, but once the subject is opened up and they are given support they begin to make changes that benefit them and their children.

It can be a tricky business, though. Here are a few suggestions of ways teachers can deal with defensive or overbearing or skittish parents – not that they ever encounter such people, but just in case.

Ballroom dancing is one approach. It begins with an invitation. You may have to ask more than once, but that's OK. Once you're out on the floor, you begin to learn each other's moves. It's awkward at first, for both of you. You don't know each other's style. But bear with it. Rely on your instincts. Follow the music. The music is provided by the child; the variety of melodies, rhythms, tempos, and beats is endless. But don't give up. Stay out on the floor. If you get tired, take a break, but ask again. Listen to the music, move to it. Don't analyze it so much as get into it. If the parent makes a move you don't get, try to follow it anyway. If you're shy about dancing, risk it anyway. Give your partner a break. Let him or her enjoy being out there with you. Over time even the most unpredictable, disjointed music can be danced to. And once you get the swing of it, how good you'll be!

To me, this is the essence of working with parents – and children, and people in general, for that matter. Let yourselves move with each other. Once you've found the right distance, the right step, what began as awkward and tense becomes expressive, athletic, spontaneous, alive.

It does take some time, some risk, some patience. But there is no one, absolutely no one, who deep down doesn't want to dance.

A teacher's invitation, then, need not be an accusation; instead, it can be an opportunity to join the parent in helping the child.

Second, take a day off. A good teacher works harder than practically anybody else. The hardest I ever worked in my life was when I did my internship in internal medicine. I was on call every third night, which meant thirty-six hours on, twelve hours off, twice a week. But it sounds much tougher than it actually was. Nurses did most of the work; I had time to sleep, and I spent many hours over cups of coffee making friends.

Teachers have no nurses to do most of the work. They are on call all day, not only on call but being called, on stage. From teaching to activity clubs, to sports, to administrative meetings, to grading papers, and, in boarding schools, to dormitory duty, a teacher's work is never done. And this takes in only tasks, leaving out the vast amounts of time spent in concern, in thought, in planning, in worry.

The children of the 1990s, needier than ever, add to the energy required to do the job well. Even the best kids on the wrong day can drive you crazy. In order to cope, and do more than cope, and to find the work as rewarding as it can be, you simply must find ways to renew yourself on a regular basis. Whether it's exercise, the symphony, or bagpipe lessons, you need to find something you can do on a regular basis that you really enjoy and can relax doing.

But no one should do what a friend of mine did in his first year of residency when confronted with the same problem. To get away from the emotional and intellectual drain of work, he signed up for the relaxing activity of learning Japanese. Find something that is fun, something you can look forward to, something that you can build into your life. And once you find it, don't cancel or put it off, ever: whether it's season tickets to the basketball game or bird-watching or a shared ski lodge or a regular dinner group or chamber music. Whatever it is, give yourself permission to take care of yourself.

Third, take an active role in calling attention to and promoting two of the key developmental tasks of this period: moral development and making friends.

As much as I endorse schools not taking on too much, and as much as I endorse greater responsibility on the part of parents, I do believe that school teachers can and should play an active role in promoting moral behavior and making friendships. In reality, it is unavoidable, for children are figuring out who they want to be, who they admire, what they value and how to be friends, and how to deal with competition, jealousy, possessiveness, rejection. They act out every day a veritable melodrama of who likes me, who hates me, who I like, what teacher is a wimp, what teacher is neat, why the kid didn't sit with me, whose table I'll sit at today. It is a cauldron of courting behavior that has very little to do with Eros and very much to do with establishing a sense of self-esteem, security, and connectedness away from home. This is the other side of the coin of my parent involvement argument. Parents cannot and should not hover over their children at school, shepherding them from attachment to rejection to attachment, telling them who to like, who not to like, who to admire, who to reject.

Children do this mainly on their own, but under the eye of teachers.

Teachers, while not hovering, can encourage talk about the whole business of picking and choosing friends. General discussion of the issues and feelings that surround friendship becomes animated very quickly among children. And moral behavior then becomes not a dry book of precepts, but a topic emotionally fused. "Jimmy used to be my best friend, but now he's a wimp, and I'll never talk to him again. No one can make me like someone." Or, "It's not fair that I have to play against Jennifer for the last spot on the team. She's my best friend." Or, "Why shouldn't I have cheated on the biology test? My dad says that getting into Superschool is the key step for the rest of my life, and sometimes 'a man's gotta do what a man's gotta do.'" Or, "Everybody drinks. You either get in trouble with your friends for not doing it, or you get in trouble with the school for doing it. You know what I think? The same thing Brian Holloway says about defensive holding: it's only bad if you get caught." Or, "Why should I stick up for myself? It doesn't matter what you say. The teacher is always right."

It is in the mediation of these kinds of conflicts that the schoolteacher plays a decisive role in every child's development. And in the presentation of these conflicts in all their untidy detail, children keep teachers and psychiatrists young – and alive.

The school itself can help in this work, as I suggested earlier, by knowing what it stands for, articulating a philosophy that can guide teachers and stimulate them, even to disagreement. Schools do have distinct personalities, traditions, tones. It can be helpful for the school to examine what it is and let its teachers – and parents and students – know.

Fourth, preserve childhood. I worry that childhood is disappearing. I think teachers can assist in preserving it.

Children will do their best to hold onto childhood. They will fight it out for a while, but they can be worn down. If too many times a parent turns to a child for psychotherapy, if too many times a child is brought to an admission interview for soccer camp, if too many times a father lectures his fifth-grade son on the importance of getting the big picture and getting a leg up on the competition, if too many times a mother lectures her eighth-grade daughter about not making the same mistakes she did, if too many times the psychotherapist asks the child why he or she isn't getting better grades, if too many times a teacher reminds a seventh-grade class that their record will follow them for the rest of their lives – in short, if too many times we interject into childhood the concerns and preoccupations of the adult world, then sooner or later a child will give up being a child and begin the ungainly charade of being an adult too soon.

The skirmish we are seeing in so many schools may be in part an inborn bristling on the part of children at being asked to give up childhood before its term. If we are not careful, childhood may even disappear and be replaced with problematic pre-adulthood. As child advocates, we are obliged not to let this happen; we don't want to let this happen. Who are the guardians of play if not children? Who are the liveliest, if not children? Who are the most honest among us, if not children?

In coping with the children of the 1990s, I would urge you all first to preserve childhood in the 1990s. Remember that time of life, that state of mind, when you were lord of all the fields and king or queen of all the stars and feel now how much your will to love and dream and risk and create depends on your having had that once, having had that time when everything was new and possible and impossible all at once.

In our efforts to impose organization upon childhood, let us remember that a little anarchy is a good thing, that the normal prelude to a new idea is a bit of chaos, and that at times it may be more valuable for us to learn how to tolerate some degree of disorder than to irritably insisting upon control. The best classroom structures are those that have built into them cubbyholes for chaos, openings and outlets for the unpredictable.

As the breakdown in various social structures and institutions, from family to religion to agreed-upon values in general, has led to a disruption of childhood, let us not overreact by rigidly attempting to stamp out "bad behavior." We do need to set limits, and heaven knows children need structure. But they also need that favor life does us called childhood, with freedom and the chance to be whimsical and bad and good, to try the new as well as learn the old – to be children.

It is our first job to preserve that, at least.

Understanding School Culture

by Michael G. Thompson

I once visited four different schools in the Washington, D.C., area on four consecutive days. On the last day someone asked me, "Don't they all start to look the same to you?" My reaction to the question was disbelief, even astonishment. For a moment I couldn't imagine that someone could have such an idea about schools. Then I realized that the questioner was not involved in school life. Viewed from a sufficient distance, of course, schools do look the same. They are schools, not airplane factories or dairy farms; they look like schools and they are run as schools. But viewed close up they are extraordinarily different, and the closer you get the more different they are. Each has a distinctive feel.

This sense of feel is so pervasive and powerful that we can experience it immediately when we walk into a school. In fact, I worry about a school that seems to lack a particular flavor; somehow it hasn't been lived in, doesn't have a history or a personality. I am not yet experiencing its culture.

Once we do feel a school's culture, however, it leaves a strong imprint on us. The combination of architecture, symbols, and artifacts, the look and behavior of the people, our conversations, the treatment we receive, all this and much more leave an indelible set of memories in the visitor.

The paradox of culture is that it is often difficult to articulate exactly what we have experienced in a school. Of course, some anecdotal events are easy to describe, some artifacts stand out, but the deeper levels of culture are sometimes tough to capture conceptually or to put into words. There have been notable efforts to describe school culture, such as those in Sarah Lawrence Lightfoot's *The Good High School*, yet engaging as these portraits were, I was left with a feeling of incompleteness in all of them. The fault lies not in the observer, but in the nature of culture. Culture is pervasive, obvious, omnipresent, and at the same time invisible, ephemeral, and terribly complex.

There are two times when we feel the presence of a culture most strongly. One is when we are strangers, particularly in a foreign culture. As travelers we welcome the experience of a foreign culture; it wakes us up and makes us question our assumptions. I never go to a foreign country without having the feeling that as an American I do certain things wrong, that I need to change my life. The longer I stay, of course, the more complicated my response to the other culture and the more homesick I become for my own familiar cultural assumptions.

What shocks and pleases us about an outsider's observations of our culture is that we get to see ourselves in a fresh light. That is why we respond so strongly to Lorene Cary's vision of St. Paul's in *Black Ice,* and why we still teach Alexis de Tocqueville's *Democracy in America.* De Tocqueville's outsider status lends weight to his observations, even observations we might have made ourselves. When, for example, he writes, "I know of no other country, indeed, where the love of money has taken stronger hold on the affections of men," it has more validity than if an American had written it.

I talked recently with a woman who had become head of a coed boarding school which had been all-male in the relatively recent past. Like a foreigner, she was shocked by the depth and extent of male culture and the unexamined male assumptions that dominated such topics as student discussion about the relations between boys and girls.

The other time we most strongly feel the presence of a culture is when we try to change the way people do things. Seymour Sarason points out that it is only when you challenge people's bedrock assumptions that you come to see what these assumptions really are and how ferociously their possessors will fight to defend them.

What, then, is school or organizational culture? In *The Principal's Role in Shaping School Culture,* Terence Deal and Kent Peterson point out that culture is only one of several ways of viewing a school and that each alternative point of view arises from a separate discipline. To look at a school from the point of view of the needs of the people in it, be they students, teachers, or administrators, is essentially a psychological analysis of a school. To focus on the structure and operations of a school is sociological. To analyze the governance structure and the school constituencies is to view it through the lens of political science. Schools are open to economic analysis as well. The cultural view arises from anthropology.

If asked, anyone might be able to give a quick definition of culture. The definitions would certainly include a number of nouns: beliefs, values, patterns of behavior, art, and climate. Students of anthropology might more easily give a complete definition, as I found when I began studying the literature of culture.

For Deal and Peterson, to focus on culture means to look at an institution's "deep pattern of values, beliefs, and traditions that have been formed over the course of its history." For anthropologist Edgar Schein, on whose *Organizational Culture and Leadership* I rely heavily through much of this essay, culture in organizations exists at three levels. At the most immediate level are the art and technology of an organization, and the visible and audible behavior patterns. These patterns are not, however, easy to decipher.

At the second level are values, testable in the physical environment and testable by obtaining social consensus. Values are the enshrined solutions to organizational and human problems that arose in the past and were solved. The solutions became beliefs and prescriptions: "You ought to do it this way. This is the right way to do it." When Joseph Tobin and his colleagues interviewed Japanese preschool teachers about class size and student-teacher ratios – in Japan there is typically one teacher for twenty-six preschool students – the teachers expressed envy of American teachers, but were in agreement that American student-teacher ratios were not good for children. As one teacher said, clearly expressing consensual Japanese educational values, "Well, maybe you could say [the American class size] is better for the teacher, but not better for the children. Children need to have the experience of being in a large group in order to learn to relate to lots of kinds of children in lots of kinds of situations."

According to Schein, if you only see the two top levels, you miss the most important aspects of culture that "operate unconsciously, and that define in a basic, 'taken for granted' fashion an organization's view of itself and its environment. These are basic unconscious beliefs about the nature of people, the nature of the environment, and the nature of human relationships. These beliefs are so deeply ingrained in us that we very rarely are conscious that they are beliefs. We generally express them as 'truth' or 'the way things are.'"

One of the things we take absolutely for granted is the existence of schools themselves and the order of things in schools. Sarason professes to be confused by why we teach reading and numbers to first graders. He asks teachers and administrators, "Why *must* first grade children be exposed to such instruction?" He finds that his intellectual questions are experienced as an attack on the culture and workings of the school, and the answer he gets is finally, "The way things are is the way things should be because alternative ways of structuring school life are seen, clearly or dimly, as requiring changes within individuals and within the culture."

At the deepest of Schein's three levels, culture is experienced by individuals as the natural order of things. Or as a business consultant said to Deal and Kennedy, culture is "the way we do things around here." Can you feel the conservation and resistance inherent in that statement?

Why is it necessary to understand culture? "Mainstream" American culture is under assault from both within and without. There are many subcultures within this country that do not experience mainstream cultural assumptions as natural or valid – and are saying so. Most particularly, women and people of color are challenging the assumptive basis of white male culture. As one of the members of Lorene Cary's Third World Coalition group said to the others about St. Paul's School, "This community has the feeling that everything's just fine, and it's not, and we need to keep saying that, by any means possible." Persistent, insightful, and angry subcultural challenge is the near future for our society and our schools, not to mention the attacks from abroad on U.S. cultural domination.

Many of us have accepted the rightness of the challenge and have embraced the necessity for change. However, change is going to challenge our most fundamental assumptions and some of our oxen are going to be gored in the process of change. (By "our" I mean those of us who are white, male, or simply fully acculturated to the independent school world.) For our schools to become more multicultural we are going to have to give up familiar notions to which we are more wedded than we know.

Recently I was sitting as a member of the board of trustees of my daughter's school, listening to two candidates for board chair outline their different visions of the school. One was a brilliant white woman, an accomplished attorney who practices law and teaches at a major law school, the other a gifted and persuasive male African-American professor of education at an equally prestigious university. What extraordinarily different visions they had for the school, what very different assumptions about the role of a school! What a choice for the rest of us on the board!

As schools try to change, try to become more multicultural, it will be necessary to understand one's reactions and resistances. It will be necessary for the head of a school to be able to articulate the process to members of the school community, and for the community to be able to understand its own assumptions and resistances. Only a greater understanding of school and organizational culture will permit us to do that.

What is the function of culture in an organization? Schein maintains that organizational culture has two purposes: to define the group's response to its major problems with the external environment, and to help maintain internal relationships within the organization.

For independent schools in particular, the central external problem is defining why they are there and what they offer that no one else offers. In public schools, this takes the form of defending the school against a host of critics who challenge its effectiveness and its very nature. This group consensus on the "survival problem" is the central pillar of group culture. Much of the school community's identity and purpose arise from a shared vision of what the school is doing. Without such a vision of the external problem the group will fall apart. When a school begins to lose students, or to lose the confidence of the community, the culture is threatened. Its goals and means are called into question. It is failing according to its own criteria for success, and if its efforts to correct its course and become successful again do not succeed, the group will begin to fall apart and so will the culture. A demoralized faculty is one whose culture has begun to collapse.

Every member of a school community is either part of the cultural mission of the school, an obstacle to that mission, or part of a subculture with a different mission. We can see this in George Orwell's description of his school, Crossgates, and its head, Sim, in the days prior to World War I:

> *Sim had two great ambitions, one was to attract titled boys to the school, and the other was to train up pupils to win scholarships at public schools, above all, Eton....I did not at first understand that I was being taken at reduced fees; it was only when I was about eleven that [the head and staff] began throwing the fact in my teeth....Over a period of two or three years the scholarship boys were crammed with learning as cynically as a goose is crammed for Christmas....your job was to learn exactly those things that would give an examiner the impression that you knew more than you did.*

Here Orwell illustrates Schein's list of cultural functions: the mission, goals, means, and criteria for success. It would not seem that everyone, students included, could become emotionally involved in such a mission, but the power of culture is that it enlists everyone, even in such a horrible place.

A group also needs cultural guideposts to achieve internal consensus, to speak the same language, to harness individual aggression into well-recognized stratifications of power and status. Cultural guidelines for love and intimacy are also needed. If aggression and sexual strivings are not bound by cultural rules, the entire community can feel unsafe. One only has to be at a boarding school where an affair begins between two people married to others living on campus to realize how radically unsafe everyone can come to feel. I know of two schools that had such incidents; on both campuses these incidents are still much discussed even three years later in an effort to repair the cultural fabric that was torn.

A faculty member at one of these schools said to me at the time of the incident, "Oh, how I wish we still had religion to back up our moral stands, so that the head could do something about this affair!" This teacher beautifully illustrated Schein's point that for the group, religion "explains the unexplainable and provides guidelines for what to do in ambiguous, uncertain, and threatening situations."

It is also significant that this teacher looked to the head as the one to "do something." All of the writers on organizational and school culture are of one voice with respect to the role of the leader. They agree that the person in charge must be, first and foremost, a cultural leader. As Thomas Sergiovanni says, "What a leader stands for is more important than what he or she does....Leadership acts are expressions of culture."

It is around the leader as stable "center" that the culture can grow. If there is no official cultural center, there will be no cement to hold the group together and "wild" centers will spring up as a natural response to group needs. It is up to the leader to domesticate such "wild" centers. As Sergiovanni writes, "Recognizing that organizations often resemble multicultural societies and that subgroups must of necessity maintain individual and cherished identities, the domestication process seeks minimally to build a cultural federation of compatibility which provides enough common identity, enough common meanings, and enough of a basis for committed action for an organization to function in spirited comfort."

Schein writes that leaders embed and transmit culture. They do not have a choice about whether they communicate; everything they do is a communication. They only have a choice about how and what and how consistently they communicate. Leaders shape culture most often by paying attention to and measuring some chosen aspect of school life. If the head is consistently interested in one thing, it will become a centerpiece of school culture. If the leader is inconsistently interested in many things, or unclear about why they hire and fire, people will spend a lot of time trying to figure out what interests the leader, and his or her inconsistency will be a central feature of the school culture.

According to Deal and Peterson, a leader acts in five ways to shape school culture. First, the school head is a symbol who affirms the values he or she espouses through behavior, routine, what she pays attention to, and even how he dresses or how she decorates her office. Second, the school head is a potter who shapes and is shaped by the school's heroes, rituals, ceremonies, and symbols. Third, the school head is a poet who uses language to reinforce the school's best image of himself. Fourth, the head is an actor who improvises in the school's inevitable dramas and in so doing dramatizes his values and vision.

These dramas, called critical incidents by others, are extremely important in setting out the fundamental values of the school. Finally, the head is a healer who presides over the life transitions that affect the school community, helping all to express the pain or grief or joy that attend the inevitable deaths and births and retirements. At a mid-year meeting for new school heads, I was struck by how many funerals these first-year heads had already attended, and how it had affected them personally and simultaneously established them firmly in charge of the cultural lives of their schools.

Culture contains the "shadow" aspect of school life. School culture is where the skeletons are buried. No school admits its troubles in its mission statement; no school acknowledges problems in its formal governance structure. It is the culture that contains the secrets, conflicts, contradictions, hatreds, and uglinesses. As my brother, an organizational consultant in Chicago, says, "Even Saddam Hussein could write a wonderful mission statement." But every school has some conflicts and some schools have many contradictions alive and at work. Listen again to Orwell's description of his school:

> The various codes which were presented to you at Crossgates – religious, moral, social, and intellectual – contradicted one another if you worked out their implications....On the one side were low-church Bible Christianity, sex puritanism, insistence on hard work, respect for academic distinction, disapproval of self-indulgence: on the other, contempt for braininess and a worship of games, contempt for foreigners and the working class, an almost neurotic dread of poverty, and above all, the assumption not only that money and privilege are the things that matter, but that it is better to inherit them than to have to work for them. Broadly, you were bidden to become at once a Christian and a social success, which is impossible.

This strikes uncomfortably close to home. I have spoken to parents at an independent school in an extremely wealthy suburb, who asked me how they could help their children with values. They told me that one girl in seventh grade had been ruthlessly and cruelly teased because she was discovered to be wearing clothes from Sears. They asked me how these attitudes could be changed. My answer was, "with great difficulty," because the children's attitudes are part of a cultural problem. I observed that the parking lot was at that moment filled almost exclusively with BMWs, Saabs, and Mercedes. It is hard for children not to be label-conscious when their parents are label-conscious.

Ned Hallowell has said to me that class, wealth, and power are the dirty secrets of independent schools and that it is necessary to be more open about them. What is clear is that they are secrets only to those in the school; they are obvious to outsiders. As Jung wrote, someone standing looking toward the bright sunlight does not see their own shadow, but others can see it right behind them. As with individuals, schools often try to hide from consciousness that which is painful, conflict-ridden, contradictory, or ugly about their deepest realities and beliefs.

One school I consult to was founded in the 1960s by a group of counter-cultural parents who intended it to be the most progressive and open school in the area, a protest against the more traditional local schools. The school's mythology says that it is open and warm, a wonderful, loving community of learners. But the original anti-authoritarian aspect of the school is deeply imbedded in its culture, making it almost ungovernable. Although they claim to want strong leadership, most of the faculty and parent body reflexively oppose any head's efforts to provide such leadership. One head solved this problem by simply giving up trying to govern and becoming the darling of the most anti-authoritarian parents. The next head, a stronger leader, provoked profound ambivalence with every move she made.

I see this anti-authoritarian flavor whenever I give a talk to parents. Perhaps my mistake is wearing a jacket and tie. At any rate, before I am three paragraphs into my talk, some parent is lecturing me about how male-biased psychology is or how categorical and nonindividualistic my approach to psychology is.

In fact I prefer consulting to schools like this one, schools that are different from the ones I attended. If I am somewhat the outsider I can see the cultural assumptions more clearly. For example, I consult to a bilingual French-American school where not only are the clinical problems of kids somewhat different, but the Francophone teachers frame problems differently than American teachers do. By contrast, Ned Hallowell has consulted to both the schools he attended. He might argue that he has a gut sense of the deepest level of culture in those schools. *Chacun á son gout*, as we say at the École Bilingue.

Every school has a shadow side that must be denied by the members of the community. If a leader, whether school head, board chair, or other administrator, runs into resistance to change, bad behavior on the part of faculty or parents, or some other puzzling and unpleasant aspect of community life, he or she is probably encountering the behavioral manifestations of some deep belief about people or the school. When parents bully teachers in an attempt to win something for their children, they show their belief that their children are not being taught in a loving community; they demonstrate that they really understand the school to be a dog-eat-dog environment. When faculty speak harshly of children, it is often because of envy or anger that they are not as supported as the children.

When these assumptions are brought to light, the typical reaction is defensiveness and denial. None of us likes to have our pessimism, our prejudices, or our fears revealed or questioned. Understanding a school means understanding the dark assumptive world of its community members. For a school to be multicultural, its leaders and faculty must understand the assumptions of its subcultural groups. Ned and I consulted to the head of a school in New York who said he was consistently accused by the Czech and Polish families of favoring the Russian parents!

The leader of the school is most often the one who confronts and articulates the shadow aspect of the school, giving permission to the community to confront unhappy aspects of itself. However, many faculties have a gadfly or truth-teller who may also perform this function. The difficulty for school leaders is to be honest about their schools while simultaneously holding an inspiring, idealistic vision of what the school can be. The tension between the two is great, as is the probability that the leaders will have personal blind spots about their school's culture, particularly when they have been at a school so long that the culture has come to embody many aspects of their personalities.

As I have said, it is difficult to come to an understanding of an organization's culture. Cultural analysis must be conducted in part by an outsider, in dialogue with a motivated insider. In a way, therapy is a model for cultural assessment; individuals cannot truly analyze themselves because, as Freud said, in self-analysis the analyst always falls in love with the patient.

In fact I know of no school which has conducted a thorough cultural analysis along the lines of Edgar Schein's ten-step process. It is time-consuming and expensive, and an organization has to be ready for such insight into itself. Without a perceived need and a psychological readiness, the task will be incomplete or superficial and will result in no change. Only a school which feels its culture is so troubled that it threatens the survival of the organization is likely to see the need, and in that state the chances of achieving consensus on undergoing the process are slim.

Nevertheless, a reading of some of the materials on organizational culture, group discussions about the deep assumptions of a school community, and perhaps such activities as the Multicultural Assessment Program of the National Association of Independent Schools may provide some insight into a culture. Many times such insight begins with discussion of a specific problem within the school. As we begin to discuss the issue, the assumptive worlds of teachers become evident to each other. Everyone is startled by the range of differences and the power of certain beliefs. And everyone can see how people's assumptions affect the jobs they do. Such discussions make for interesting faculty meetings and provide material for consideration for months afterwards. Whatever method you use, an attempt to understand your school's culture may explain many things that previously baffled you, though the process may never be completed.

What Do You Want for Your Children?

by Edward M. Hallowell

Over the past few years I have talked with several hundred adolescents from around the country. Some of these conversations have been in social contexts, others as part of my research, others in the context of psychotherapy, and a few in psychiatric hospitals.

On the whole I find young people these days to be enthusiastic, energetic, full of questions, full of answers, and full of life. I find them to be pretty happy, much happier than the worries of the world would have one predict.

Before I bring up some concerns I have, I want to remind you what the older generation often forgets about their children – that we were that age once, that we were just as moody and disruptive and self-centered and incommunicative, that we caused our parents as many, if not more, worries and sleepless nights, and that, in spite of it all, we didn't destroy the world; in fact, we thought enough of the world to go ahead and bring children into it ourselves.

Our generation, the generation that is now parents, the baby-boom generation, should give ourselves an especially large, ironic wink when we look at ourselves in the mirror. Who ever thought that we would be parents? Certainly not us. Who ever thought we would be middle-aged? We thought we would be young forever, disencumbered, disenfranchised and disenfranchising, alienated and alienating, passionately committed and lazy all at once. We thought time would wait for us as we took another swim in the river; we thought time would wait, as every generation does, I guess, before time grew us old, before time turned us into what we never thought we'd be. We even thought the world would change, and change it did, I guess, but not just exactly as we thought it would. We have been surprised, and we have surprised ourselves, in so many, many ways, some delightful, some frightful, but all in the course of the blink of an eye. Where has the time gone? Where are the days and nights we spent with each other being young, being so opinionated and aware and unaware all at once? Where have the days of earnest irresponsibility gone? I'll bet most of us, in our hearts, don't feel old at all, and don't feel that those young days have really passed. I'll bet that most of us could close our eyes right now and be back in high school in a flash – and see the blades of grass beneath the tree we leaned against and watched the one we first loved slowly walk by. Those days are not so long ago – and yet they are.

Believe it or not, years have passed. Who would have believed what we've done? Who would have thought we would become parents, authority figures, limit-setters, guardians of tradition, believers in social structure, seekers of such mundane prizes as good baby sitters, effective financial planners, and safe sex?

So as we wring our hands at times and wonder what to do with our children, we should remember that we are all just passing through parts of life others have passed through before. Not every problem must be fixed; not every crisis must have a solution. You and your kids are doing the best you can. There is enough trust in the world, still, to get us through.

With that introduction, let me raise a few concerns I have for kids these days, and ask you, their parents, what do you want for your children? We grow up asking what do we want for ourselves, but as we round the turn we're rounding now, we ask more and more what we want for those who will follow us. What do you want for your children? It is a question whose answers you act upon every day in the choices you make, but at the same time it is a question parents don't ask themselves often enough.

Andrea was a twenty-year-old college freshman who came into psychotherapy because she was feeling at loose ends. "I know what I want," she said. "I want to be rich and I want to be famous. But I don't know how to get there. And I don't feel happy inside."

As I began to ask her about her parents, she quickly interrupted, "Don't blame any of this on them. They've been great. They've given me everything."

The oldest of four children, Andrea had moved around the country as her parents' careers had demanded. Her father, a research scientist for a drug company, and her mother, a tax attorney, were both highly successful in their fields and had provided very well for their children. Andrea, an attractive and bright young woman, had a special talent for tennis. She had worked hard at it since an early age. Although she wasn't good enough to turn pro, she almost was. "That's the hell of it," she said. "All that work and all I've got to show for it is a lot of trophies. If only I were just a little bit better."

Because of all her moves, she didn't have many old friends, and no actively involved extended family. Religion was not a real factor in her life, nor was she attached to her most recent community, a town outside of Boston. She had always done extremely well in school, in spite of all her hours devoted to tennis, and so she had gained admission to Harvard. "But big deal," she said. "As soon as I got there I found out that everyone else is just as smart or smarter than I am."

As I got to know her I found that she was a very nice person. She treated other people well and, at least superficially, she liked them and they liked her. But she didn't feel a part of anything larger than herself, and so it was to herself and her achievements she repeatedly turned to find support and self-esteem.

In psychiatric terms Andrea was depressed. But in more human terms she was one of many in her generation who had done all the things they'd been told to do only to find something essential was missing.

Andrea's story is suggestive of a world that is changing both for children and their parents. Some of the vital statistics have received a lot of press. We all know that there is a drug and alcohol problem among young people, and we know that family structure has changed over the past few decades. What is perhaps less well-known is the high incidence of depression among young adults. One would expect depression to be highest among old people, those who are dealing with death or serious illness. In fact, the incidence of depression is highest among young people, higher than the incidence among those over sixty-five. Christopher Lasch has written about the parents' generation as narcissistic, and David Elkind has characterized their children as hurried. This generation of children may be the first that cannot reasonably expect to surpass its parents economically, while at the same time pressures to succeed seem more intense than ever.

Even among children who are doing all the right things and have all the best advantages, such as Andrea, there is malaise, even depression. And parents who are working hard to provide all that they can often find something troubling about their children's lives.

As we begin to consider why this is, and as we begin to consider what we do want for our children, let's look for a moment at the context of adolescence these days. From simply listening to many adolescents and their parents I have compiled a list of factors that combine to create special pressures upon young people in the late '80s and '90s. I have found among the predominant factors: 1) the change in family structure, including the emergence of many dual-career parents and single-parent families and the disappearance of the extended family as a daily, vital force; 2) the breakdown of communities, villages, and neighborhoods such that one often lacks a home base or meeting place and the shared values and support found there; 3) the decline of religion as both a spiritual and social force; 4) ambiguity as to the roles of men and women, mothers and fathers, sons and daughters; 5) ambivalence around accepting the role of nurturer or caretaker by either parent; 6) the influence of media; 7) the cynicism about post-

Vietnam, post Watergate, post Contra-Gate government; 8) the decrease in a sense of security or permanence of jobs or close personal relationships and a corresponding decrease in a sense of loyalty to institutions or loved ones; 9) an explosion of information that creates constant anxiety over one's capabilities; 10) a lack of respect for old people, who are seen as dinosaurs rather than sages, and with this disrespect a fear of old age; 11) an absence of mentors, heroes, or tradition; 12) the decline of authority or power figures in the family, and with this a heightening of ambiguity around moral decisions; 13) an over-reliance on the self to find meaning in life; and finally, 14) an increase in the level of worry among children due to the number of global concerns they become aware of early on.

That's a long list. I would like to focus for a moment on a major theme that runs through it, in different ways. It is that the individual self is more on its own now than ever before. Supports that used to be there – from family to community to religion to loyalties and shared values – have eroded. Guiding principles have given way to a kind of free-for-all of self reliance in which one finds one's way on a day-to-day basis.

Day to day this hardly matters and is barely noticeable. But over time a child growing up begins to absorb his surroundings and become part of his culture. I am concerned that the current generation of children in independent schools is missing out on what I call a connected life. The essence of a connected life is feeling in your bones that you are a part of something beyond yourself: other people, institutions, or ideals. It need not be a conscious sense; indeed, it often is not. But the connected person takes strength and support by belonging to and feeling a part of something larger than himself.

A generation ago, when I was an adolescent, we spoke of feeling alienated from society and we rebelled, in the manner of the '60s. I do not think this current generation feels alienated. They buy into what we call the system. They want to be successful. They want to make it. But they are not quite sure how to join or where they fit. They are not sure all their hard work will pay off or have meaning. Without knowing it exactly I think they are having to deal with what we tore down in the '60s: tradition, shared values, social structures, clear roles. As we created greater freedom for ourselves and our children, we also severed a number of attachments we found burdensome or meaningless: attachments to the church, to the traditional family, to sex roles, to small communities, to constricting systems of values. But as we shed those burdens, we did not anticipate how we would drift apart in our individual lives.

As businesses have grown and merged into huge impersonal conglomerates and as rapid communication has shrunk the world, those pockets of connectedness called communities have been threatened. While we may be globally connected by phones, computers, and fax machines, paradoxically we are often locally disconnected, even isolated.

Maybe it is different elsewhere, but in Boston people live in condominium buildings without visiting each other, they work together without knowing each other, they join clubs together without talking to each other, they move out of town without saying good-bye. These are good people, people with all the right intentions who simply find that their work and their children leave little time for building that sense of interconnectedness that once was called community.

The children pick up from their parents, and from television and video and each other, the importance of making it, of work and achievement, and the best and the brightest children, your children, do track themselves for success. They make friends, too, because it is in their nature to do so. But what they don't plan for, what they cannot plan for because they don't even know it's missing, is the sense of purpose and meaning and support derived from long-term affiliations: with each other, with institutions, with groups, with community, and with ideals beyond personal achievement.

I have a seventy-year-old friend who grew up in the Depression. A second-generation Italian named Joe, he runs a mom and pop store in my home town of Cambridge. He thinks I'm nuts. "You think kids these days have it tough?" he yells at me. "They don't know what tough is. Tough is having no shoes. Tough is stealing a quart of milk so your baby sister won't starve. Tough is watching your father beg for a job. These kids have it made. They come into my store and I want to slap 'em up side the head the way they throw away money."

"But, Joe," I say, "there's more to life than money."

"Sure there is," he says. "Sure there is." And he winks at me and rolls his eyes.

But what Joe doesn't say is that he's lived in the same community since he was a boy, that his father and mother and priest pretty much told him what was what from the moment he could think and he did the same for his kids, that he has no doubt but that we all live our lives in God's hands, and that his little store now functions as a clubhouse of sorts in his neighborhood in Cambridge. Joe's life is a paradigm of a connected life.

Do you want for your children Joe's life? Probably not exactly, but they could do a lot worse. If, as I have suggested, your children are growing up in a world lacking in connectedness and the security that engenders, what does this imply?

For one thing, it implies a greater burden than ever upon schools. Schools remain an active, vital force in children's lives, for many kids the only social institution to which they belong. It has become, for many children, much more than the place where they get what used to be called book-learning; it has become their home away from home. It has become a place where they learn everything from sex education to table manners, from dating protocol to team loyalty. It has become a place where they acquire and test values as well as acquire and test friends. It has become their marketplace, their hang-out, their clubhouse, their dating bar or day care center, depending on their age. At times teachers become substitute parents and the school a sort of extended family. The school experience can make or break a child, not only academically but in terms of self-esteem and self-confidence.

The problem is that, if you are like most independent school parents these days, what you want from the school teeters on the brink of impossibility. Basically you want what our generation – yours and mine – has wanted all along: You want it all. For independent schools, this request boils down to the following: Nurture my son and daughter, fill my children full of warmth and goodness and high ideals, teach them to value beauty and scorn all that is ugly and corrupt but at the same time give them a competitive edge over everyone else, get them the highest achievement scores, teach them to excel – and, for the amount of money I'm paying you, get them into Harvard at least and extract from them any residual neuroses that the process (or I) may instill.

But before asking schools to do it all – and schools, being schools, are most willing to try – it is best to ask yourself what "it all" really is so you don't coerce schools into trying to perform contradictory tasks.

So I return to my question, What do you want for your children? I have suggested that they need more attention not to getting on the success track but to forging a connected life, making and sustaining connections of all sorts. I have suggested that schools, as a last vital social institution, can help in this regard but cannot do it all.

So what remains? What is childhood supposed to be? My friend Joe would spend a long time talking about what he didn't get – money, money, money – and yet, if you look at his deeds instead of his words, what he gave his own children was pretty much what he did get: love, emotional security, and a frequent kick in the pants.

Think back to your own childhood. What was there that was good? What did you miss? Can you see the sun slanting into your, say, fifth grade classroom at eleven in the morning? Can you remember your teacher then? Can you see the main street of your town? Did you ever go to a band concert? How about snakes – when did you see your first one? And the opposite sex, remember hating them and being curious, too? How about amusement parks? That combination of organ-grinder music, screams from rides, and the texture of cotton candy. Maybe you remember none of that, but something different instead.

It's a safe bet, though, that you all did have a childhood, a time of life, when, if you'll let yourself remember, you had big hopes and big worries that seem quite small now but were your world then. You had stolen five dollars and didn't know whether to give it back. You had peeked at someone's underwear and didn't know whether to peek again. Or you had seen something genuinely bad and wrong, as did one of my eight-year-old patients who witnessed a murder, and you didn't know what to do. No matter what the particulars were, you remember that time of your life and you know that the memory of that time is special, essential, of the essence of your life, though long ago. Time was different then, time was slower. And worries were different, in some ways more treacherous, in some ways tamer. Plans were long and bold and an afternoon could take in several lifetimes.

That's part of what a childhood is supposed to be, don't you think? A slow time for important planning, for building dreams. To do this kind of work you need a backyard or a swimming hole or an empty field or a corner store or a tree house and you need a friend or two – actually you don't need one, it just usually happens that way. But you do need time. You need to be left alone in your tree house with your friends. That means you need time away from school, homework, soccer camp, tennis lessons, riding lessons, tutoring, chores around the house, computer camp, and whatever other obligations you have to meet. You need to be left to your own devices. You need free time. What a wonderful phrase: free time. It's almost as good as play time. Well, to do the important business of childhood you need plenty of free time and play time. It is the time for stoking the imagination.

As important as free time is, you'd be amazed how hard it is to come by in the lives of independent school children these days. Their schedules are dizzying. I don't know how some mothers do it who have to transport several children from one enriching activity to another all afternoon and into the evening. I sometimes wonder why they do it. Is that what they really want for their children, or did the frantic schedule just silently, unconsciously evolve, as if it had a life of its own?

What else goes into childhood? Worms, baseballs, dolls, Mother's make-up, hide-and-go-seek, fairy tales, grandparents, school, spaghetti, or is it now pasta? Dirty clothes, siblings, parents, stepparents, pets, having to stop the car to go pee, the question "Are we almost there?"

That's the question of kids: Are we almost there? Always looking ahead to the next step. Discovery at every turn. That's part of what is supposed to be in a childhood. Discovery. Discovery has to be one of the three or four defining words of childhood, along with play and innocence and maybe loss. Loss, definitely loss. The losses of childhood can extend, like a recurring melody, throughout a lifetime. But so can the discoveries. Everything you do, as a kid there was that once you did it for the first time. The first breath. Imagine that. The first step. The first word. The first kiss. I remember at age nine walking up the ramp into Fenway Park for the first time and beginning at that moment an enchantment that has lasted my lifetime. I didn't know what I was discovering then, but I knew by my eyes as they widened taking in the green, green field that I was onto something big. As my mouth encircled and let out that one word of youth, "Wow," I was hooked.

And how many other discoveries, some forgotten, some not? I don't remember my first pizza, but there must have been a first. I do remember the first time I saw a dead man, flat on the main street of Chatham during a hot Fourth of July morning parade. "Is he taking a nap?" I asked my mother. And I remember my discovering injustice, when I told the truth but was disbelieved by my second-grade substitute teacher.

All these discoveries, their poignancy long passed, seem to define another word of childhood: impressionable. That is for sure: As kids, the world impresses us. We take impressions, our brains do, like a key pressed into hot wax. Those bits of reality, those keys, unlock the poignancy of the associations years later, as even now the dead man on Main Street does for me. Kids' brains are hot, and although one cannot control what keys will be pressed into them, we must never forget the primacy of those impressions. We therefore have the chance to build into our children's lives a richness and variety for a lifetime.

As children discover and learn, so too do they watch. They look up, as the phrase puts it, to one or another adult, imagining how they want to be when they grow up. And they look at each other and they look into books and they watch movies and TV and they absorb whatever is in the air as they begin to identify what they admire and what they value. Subtly, slowly, and with deliberation they concoct their own idea of what is great. "There can be no moral education," wrote Alfred North Whitehead, "without an habitual vision of greatness." Part of the adventure of childhood is finding your own vision of greatness. Part of the test of adulthood is trying to stay with that vision.

Beginning with superheroes or fictional characters in early childhood and ending with some real-life role model in adolescence, children concoct their ideal selves from all they're exposed to. Feelings of breathless admiration – so common in childhood – fuel and extend the process. On the stage of the imagination, where the process takes place, many figures come and go, both real and imaginary, from fairy tale princes to knights and Mutant Ninja Turtles to All-Pro quarterbacks and international ballerinas to discoverers and poets and novelists and statesmen and warriors. Many figures walk across that stage at night as the child is falling asleep dreaming of greatness someday, someday striking down the pretenders to the throne with one strong stroke or someday leaping across a stage with feet lighter than the break of day or someday staring down the bad guys like Gary Cooper in *High Noon* or someday rising up like Clarence Darrow in a stirring courtroom-size debate. These nighttime reveries are a universal part of childhood, and with any luck they don't end there. But in the childhood dramas, among the men and women who walk across that stage, there is almost always in one disguise or another Mom and Dad. It is an inescapable fact: We teach them by what we do. They take it in, metabolize it, change it, and challenge it, but it is their starting point.

I think it was Goethe who gave a young man the following advice: "Be careful about what you want when you're young, because before long you'll have it."

I wonder what these kids want, while they're young. I wonder about the vision of greatness they are developing. Are they really learning what we want them to, or are they receiving a more cynical message?

Let me share with you a poem by Robert Frost that parodies what I fear is the message many kids receive these days not because parents, or anybody else, wants them to, but because the invisible forces that make the times we live in conspire to make it that way:

PROVIDE, PROVIDE

The witch that came (the withered hag)
To wash the steps with pail and rag
Was once the beauty Abishag,

The picture pride of Hollywood.
Too many fall from great and good

For you to doubt the likelihood.
Die early and avoid the fate.
Or if predestined to die late,
Make up your mind to die in state.

Make the whole stock exchange your own!
If need be occupy a throne,
Where nobody can call you crone.

Some have relied on what they knew.
Others on simply being true.
What worked for them might work for you.

No memory of having starred
Atones for later disregard
Or keeps the end from being hard.

Better to go down dignified
With boughten friendship at your side
Than none at all. Provide, provide!

This brings me back to my earlier mention of the connected life. With so many children and their parents lacking sustaining connections to other people, institutions, or ideals, with so many of us living together in relative isolation unbuttressed by supports greater than the individual self, what comes to matter more and more is the individual self on its own, the self and its various means of assertion, achievement, and advancement. Individualism, ambition, social mobility – these are terms very much in the American grain. But are our children hurrying toward a life of achievement without paying enough attention to the spiritual, moral, and emotional dimensions of such a life? Surely we do not want for our children a life of achievement without satisfaction, or advancement without moral conviction, or an individualism made pale by loneliness.

Schools, our last, most vital social institutions, offer the best forum for keeping our children in touch with each other, as well as for preparing them educationally for the world out there. If you ask most adolescents what really matters to them, they will usually give you a few flip answers like sex or cars or money or music, but if you pin them down the honest answer time and again is some variation on the theme of friendship. It is only when the connected life fails that the vision of greatness becomes overly self-serving and cynical.

The challenge for us adults, us parents, I think, is daunting. We cannot be expected to revitalize what has gone flat in our society so our children can grow up healthier. But we can, I think, act within our own communities to support and endorse not only the achievements of our children, but their attempts to create for themselves an interconnectedness that is durable and vital, a morality that makes sense, and a recognition of the importance of their spiritual lives. In short, we can support and endorse our children's efforts to renovate their world rather than simply adapt to it.

Looking into the eyes of a child is like looking into the world as we want it to be. Looking into the eyes of a child we see enthusiasm and trust and hope and a look that says, "What's next?" As a child looks up to us, little does he or she know how longingly we may look back. We may, as we look into those eyes, yearn for our own lost innocence or our own lost radiance, our own lost childhood with its simplicity and trust, and as we yearn for what now seems long ago we find it once more in the eyes of a child, and finding it, we swear by whatever we can to make it last, to give this little one the eyes of a child forever.

Looking into the eyes of a child we yearn for what cannot be, for time that is lost and long-since grieved, and yet, through some mystery of life here it is again, reborn, looking up at us, giving us what can be so hard to come by – hope and trust and love. What happens after death I do not know. I hope there is rebirth and eternal life for the soul. But there is one miracle on earth I surely believe in because I see it happen every day: the miracle of the rebirth of the human spirit through a child. As we grow old and tired and our ideals fade away, our children rush in and fill our lives with energy, warmth, and renewed belief in the possibilities of things. As we hold the children in our arms and as we look into their eyes and see their trust in being held by us, let us remember always that the best thing we will ever do is live up to that trust. Let us give, despite whatever other pain or despair we may know, the best of ourselves to our children so they may begin their lives by knowing they have our love.

What do you want for your children? The answer, really, is simple: You want the best. You want for them all that you didn't have and you want for them all that you did have. You want dreams to come true for them that didn't come true for you and you want them to take the best from you and go on from there. You want to leave them, at whatever point you finally have to leave them, feeling strengthened and inspired by you and remembering you as you remember the best of what you were given. You want for them strength and wealth and health and most of all you want for them love, for themselves and for each other. You want for them to pick up where you left off and change and improve the story so that one generation's mortality interrupts but does not destroy the tale.

In wanting for your children, the best part of you wants, but there is also a part of you of which you must beware. There can be selfishness at work as well as pride, revenge, greed, and vanity in their many forms. Your children will ask you, Did you want what you wanted for me or did you want what you wanted for you? You will someday need your children's forgiveness for some of the ways in which you've wanted for them, and for some of the ways in which you haven't wanted for them, much as your parents have needed yours.

Your children will soon leave home. Your hearts will break a little bit, and you will be relieved and frightened too. How short it's been since they were babies and you were up in the night looking over their cribs, wanting for them, dreaming for them. Now they have those dreams in their hands, more and more to do with as they please. Remember, as I said at the start, you have done your best, as was done for you. Let yourselves love them now as you did at the crib. You are the only people who know that part of them, the baby, the innocent, and the dreams you filled them with. Keep that part of them alive, as they move away from it. Never forget the child within them and the dreams that child carries. Keep that alive for them, as they will just as soon forget it as they mature and move away. Let them grow up, but never let what you – the best part of you – has wanted for them grow old.

Try to be wise for your children. Try to remind them of what you've forgotten or maybe never knew and didn't grasp until your child asked and then you found such counsel in your soul as you didn't know you had. Rise for your children beyond what is petty and selfish and small, rise beyond yourself and become something greater, something wiser, something larger than you may think you are. Let your child surprise you (as he or she has surprised you all along) by leading you to see beyond yourself to the time when you are gone and from that height decide what part of you you want to leave behind.

Normal Sexual Feelings Between Children and Adults

by Michael G. Thompson

In the summer of 1969, I did my first student teaching, as part of a master's degree program, in a fifth-grade classroom. At one point I was reading aloud to a group of children, with some of them leaning against me. Suddenly I realized that one girl was rubbing against my leg. I could tell that she was totally unconscious of what she was doing, but I was filled with anxiety, embarrassment, bewilderment. As soon as I could, I changed to another activity.

I felt I couldn't talk about this to anyone. It was as if I had witnessed or participated in something that should not have happened, that some line had been crossed. Quite simply, it seemed like a sexual encounter, not one that I had sought or initiated, but one in which I was somehow implicated. I felt guilty and embarrassed.

Finally, I had a chance to discuss it with my master teacher. He and I agreed that such things happen and that the girl must be very lonely or emotionally abandoned in some way; perhaps that was why she had been sent to summer school. We made it into a rarefied psychological problem, and I felt much better. But I didn't feel totally right; there was something incomplete about our explanation of what had happened.

Some years later and somewhat wiser – fortified with a couple of years of teaching experience and a master's degree – I took a job as a psychology teacher and school counselor. During my first two years, two girls developed intense crushes on me. One would come to her counseling sessions wearing a thin Indian cotton blouse with nothing underneath. Another kept getting into difficulties that required late night telephone calls. Once, when she was in an apparent suicidal crisis, I went to her house, to find her dressed provocatively and alone in the house. By that time I had supervision from a child psychologist and was able to talk about these things with him.

My discomfort around talking about sexual feelings was not unique to me; it stemmed from the deep cultural, social, moral, and personal inhibitions we all have about even thinking about sexual feelings between adults and children. Most sexual feelings remain unconscious, especially ones affected by the incest taboo and other powerful social sanctions. Our defenses against such feelings becoming conscious are often formidable.

I have discovered, while doing psychotherapy with adults who have children, that most adults worry about telling a stranger, particularly a psychologist, about how much physical contact – normal, warm, loving physical contact – they have with their own children. Patients often "confess" that their children still crawl into bed and look at television with them at age twelve and thirteen, or that they bathe with their younger children. Many parents are embarrassed and ashamed about their physical intimacy with their own children, fearing that society will see it as too close or unhealthy.

The reticence and uneasiness go on, and so, almost one hundred years after Freud's early discoveries about infantile sexuality, after close to a century of increasingly open discussion of sex and sexual feelings, I am here to say that children are actively sexual from birth, that they have a "sexual" life throughout childhood – though not genitally centered – and that they have sexual feelings toward adults. All adults are sexual beings. They had a sexual life in childhood, now mostly repressed in the unconscious, and they respond to children as sexual beings and have sexual, or at least sensual, feelings toward them.

Those people who, by virtue of comfort with sexuality in their own upbringing and culture, feel at ease with having such impulses can acknowledge that they exist and peacefully coexist with them. Other people, for whom such thoughts have been forbidden by family or culture, may need to keep them always unconscious for fear of shocking themselves.

When anything internal or unconscious that is this powerful must be denied, we usually project it outside ourselves. We use this common psychological mechanism to protect ourselves against acknowledging thoughts, wishes, and impulses that our conscience cannot abide or come to terms with. The problem then exists in the other person: "they" have bad thoughts, "they" are morally corrupt, "they" are attracted to children, "they" need to be controlled.

Thus when Vladimir Nabokov wrote *Lolita,* the classic story of an adult-child sexual relationship, the book was banned, burned, and censored. Nabokov was excoriated for being a pervert and, probably, for having made conscious what is unconscious in many people. "Yoo-hoo, not *me,* buddy," we say. "That's *you; you're* sick, *you're* weird, *you're* wrong. Children aren't like that. I'm not like that." Nabokov even protects us by taking the responsibility and saying that his character is not normal.

However, it wasn't just the Humbert Humberts in our society who made Brooke Shields a sex symbol from the age of ten. How many sexually charged pictures of her were run in national magazines when she was between ten and fourteen? It is children of middle school age who are the main targets of sexual abuse. Abuse drops off after fourteen. For every sexual encounter, there must be a great deal of fantasy and impulse going on that is denied, projected, or lived with, but not acted upon.

Everything I have said about sexuality in children and in adults was said by Freud. Still, it is not necessary to believe or accept Freud's notion of infantile sexuality and its central place in the formation of the personality to accept the fact that children come into the world already sexual. It has been conclusively demonstrated that both boys and girls are capable of orgasms as infants. All parents know that, by three or four, children touch their genitals from time to time and that many actively masturbate from an early age. While Victorian-style sanctions against masturbation are no longer in fashion, children do sense the discomfort of the adults in their world with masturbation, and so it soon becomes private.

Throughout childhood, children remain intensely curious about the bodies of other children and of adults. Nudity is of constant interest, even in families where it is commonplace. Children also exhibit themselves spontaneously. My daughter, almost from the time she could walk, would, when getting out of the bath or having her diaper changed, run around the house naked, laughing and shouting.

Adults tend to regard this as innocent and somehow nonsexual – unless the situation becomes too overtly like an adult sexual situation. My daughter and I love to jump on the bed together and hide under the covers. We sing, "Five little monkeys jumping on the bed, one fell down and bumped her head..." It is great fun. However, when she was littler she would want to play this game when I was otherwise occupied. A couple of times she walked into a group of adults, took my hand, pointed upstairs, and said, "bed?" when it wasn't her bedtime. A couple of Christmases ago, a relative took me aside and told me how uncomfortable this made him.

When a young child meets a stranger, smiles, and then buries her head in her mother's shoulder, people invariably say, "What a little flirt she is" – an example of adults defining certain childhood behaviors as sexually tinged. Innate or potential sexual behaviors are reinforced through such social learning. Children learn to discriminate between things adults regard as seductive or sexual that are pleasing and sexual things that are displeasing. What is acceptable and what is not varies enormously from family to family and from culture to culture.

Temperament plays a role here, too. Some children are born more sexually inclined than others. Not all young children masturbate; it doesn't occur to some. Some percentage of children experience orgasms early in childhood, but most, apparently, do not; it is obviously a difficult phenomenon to study. Probably children, like adults, are more or less sexual and are distributed on a normal curve, with some children being extremely nonsexual and others being highly sexualized. Other factors, such as social learning, then serve to suppress or accentuate these innate tendencies.

We still call the period between six or seven and twelve "the latency period" because Freud believed that the very obvious sexuality of young children goes away during these years while they concentrate on skill-building and pleasing adults.

Freud was wrong about this. During the latency years, a child's sexual interest becomes hidden from adults and is either a private matter or is displayed only in the company of trusted companions. This is, after all, the age of "playing doctor." Some children, usually from families that intensely disapprove of any show of sexuality, may be prevented by anxiety from participating in such games. As adults, these children tend to have a harder time allowing themselves to experience sexual pleasure than those who engaged in more sexual activity or exploration during their childhoods.

Physical sexual development explodes in early adolescence and with it comes a growing sexual exhibitionism in adolescents. One of the major developmental tasks of adolescence is adjusting to having an adult body with adult sexual potential. Once they adjust to body changes, young people must then, to use Harry Stack Sullivan's concept, integrate lust and intimacy. Differentiating between sexual feelings and affectional needs and understanding how these work inside oneself, is a long and difficult process that reaches well into adulthood.

The adult world starts to look at adolescents as sexual beings, and children are aware of this. One way they learn about their own sexuality is to show it to other people, particularly older people, to see what reaction they get. They may lack language for what is going on inside and outside of them, and they may feel overwhelmed and ashamed by their impulses.

If this picture of childhood sexuality is accurate, then when you look at an eleven-year-old you are not seeing a sexless, innocent creature. You are seeing someone with an active sexual fantasy life, perhaps a masturbatory life, and perhaps even some sexual experience with other children. The condition of being innocent, as the Norwegian psychologist Thore Langfeldt says, is not a question of not having the sensations or experience, but rather of not having a name for it or not wanting to reveal it.

Why, if children have sexual lives, is there not more sexual activity between adults and children, especially if sexual feelings always exist between adults and children?

Adult-child sexual contact is bad for several reasons. First, small children are not biologically ready for sexual contact with adults. Second, it destroys the generational and role boundaries in a society and creates generational chaos. Third, for evolutionary reasons an incest taboo is desirable; psychological barriers are needed to prevent family members from reproducing with one another. Fourth, because of the power discrepancy between a child and an adult, a child can never truly give informed consent to having sexual contact with an adult. And fifth, most child-adult sexual contact has been demonstrated to be harmful to the vast majority of children.

Perhaps the most powerful developmental argument against child-adult sexual contact is that children do not need it. The aim of childhood sexuality is not the same as that of adult sexuality. For adults, the aim is consummated genital sexual expression. Developmentally speaking, younger children do not need that level of sexual expression. They require care, protection, guidance, and education from adults, not a sexual life. That they can get very satisfactorily from fantasy, from other children, and from masturbating.

Therefore, when a child and an adult have sexual contact, the sexual need is in the adult. The child, up to eighteen, does not need to have an adult sexual partner. We need to give children, all the way through adolescence, time to develop independent judgment, their own sense of what they truly want and need. And, with respect to sex, we need to give them time to grow out of the automatic obedience to adults we spend so many years training them into. Until they outgrow that obedience, their choices with respect to sexual behavior will not be truly consenting. That is the philosophy behind the age of consent law, and while it is true that some adolescents are psychologically and physically mature before the age of eighteen and fully able to consent, lawmakers have had to set a protective age after which the average adolescent is able to give informed consent.

Adults who sexually abuse children often have grown up in homes with little emotional or physical affection. They lack the experience of having their own dependency needs met, and so they are unable to recognize the dependency needs of the child.

When the child is an older adolescent, it may seem to the abuser that the child is at least as grown up as he or she. While abusers are not often mentally ill in the psychotic sense, they usually have unsatisfactory sexual relationships. A failed marriage in which the mother implicitly or explicitly hands the daughter over to the father as a substitute wife is a classic abuse situation.

Children who are surrounded by such isolated, unhappy, immature adults may themselves be starved for affection. Their wish to try to please their parents, to make them happy, to get whatever affection is available may prompt a child or an older adolescent to go along with an abusive situation in hopes of saving or comforting the parent or caretaker and gleaning a bit of affection for themselves through the sexual contact.

What about normal and happy children, and normal and happy adults – adults who are not compelled by reason of background, emotional deprivation, or marital distress to sexually abuse children?

Why should adults who have been cared for in their childhoods and who live nourishing and full adult lives feel anything sexual toward children? If children have no developmental or biological need for actual sexual contact with adults, why should adults have sexual feelings toward children at all? Why shouldn't adults be able to make a firm, clear boundary between themselves and children, know that children are children, and have no complications about sexual feelings? We aren't made that way, and neither are they. Why? One reason has to do with things intrinsic to children, and four things have to do with matters internal to adults.

First of all, children need to practice on us. They test our good will, our patience, our anger, our consistency. They push us in every conceivable way, so why shouldn't they bring to bear the full force of their developing sexuality on us? They do. That is the essence of the Oedipus Complex. All it means is that the child tries out, mentally, the idea of being the partner of the opposite-sex parent. Why not? Children try out cooking and driving a car and everything else in fantasy before they are able to do it. It only makes sense that they would try to fill all adult roles in fantasy, including sexual roles.

For adolescents, on the verge of being adults themselves, it becomes that much more important for them to practice the roles of adulthood. And so they do. But they rarely mean – really mean – what they appear to mean when they lead with their sexuality.

Children need to see our public reactions and private feelings in order to know what is inside them. The only way they can do this is to evoke our feelings so that they can see them. When you are driving a carpool full of kids telling smutty jokes, you know, as weary as you may be in your heart, that they need you to react, at first with humor and acceptance, later with limit setting, and perhaps finally with anger.

Inevitably, children need to flirt, excite, seduce, and arouse. They need to be charming and alluring. Who else are they going to practice on? Our sexual feelings are evoked from time to time because children need to evoke them, and they need to see them. Trying to keep from having a response is like trying to stop the tide.

Nor is the absolute refusal to have a response healthy for children. A major complaint I hear from adult patients is that their parents were not affectionate with each other or that their parents stopped being physically affectionate with them when they reached puberty. One patient reported that her father, who had been playful before she turned twelve, suddenly became wooden and distant when she became an adolescent. This felt like an abandonment and loss to her and left her feeling that men could not deal with her full self, including her sexuality. So the question is not one of having or not having a response to children, but rather of having a response that is appropriate.

The first reason intrinsic to adults that causes them to have sexual feelings toward children is what I call the "whole person response." People come to be physically attracted to people they work with or are close to. I once saw a woman teacher distraught and crying over the graduation and the departure of a twelfth-grade boy. Her grief over the departure of this boy from school was real, and it resembled distress over the breakup of a love relationship. I am not saying that it was a consummated sexual relationship; I trust it was not. The feelings displayed, however, were consistent with a love relationship. There are, no doubt, many good reasons for not allowing a close relationship with a child or adolescent to become so strongly felt, but there is no way that I know of, except through the use of rigidity and denial, to prevent feelings from wanting to go that far.

A second reason adults respond to children with sexual feelings has to do with the quality of love we experience, or imagine we experience, that comes from children to us. The love of children seems so much purer, easier, and more accepting than that of adults.

The idea that love with a child, especially love complicated by sex, would be easier than love with another adult is an illusion. But sometimes the love between adult and child can appear simpler than the complex, ambivalent, and at times ungratifying relationships of adult life.

The third reason that adults may feel sexually attracted to children contradicts that illusion. Children are in fact so demanding, so needy, and so omnipresent that raising them, teaching them, or caring for them is such hard work at times that we want something back. The yearning for sexual contact with a child is often the expression of the wish to be paid back: "Look at all I've done for you. Now it is time for you to do something gratifying for me." Most of us have made our peace with the fact that we will never be taken care of by children in anything like the way we take care of them, but that doesn't stop the wish from arising.

The fourth and final reason that adults can come to have sexual feelings toward children has to do with lost parts of the adult's own personality. In the process of growing up, we inevitably lose some of our spontaneity, playfulness, and imagination. We become disciplined and responsible, and we are both the better and the sadder for it. One of the great pleasures of working with children is to see over and over again their freshness and life force. Even a children's psychiatric hospital, where the patients are truly disturbed, has an air of vitality and optimism that is lacking in almost every adult institution.

Many of us fear that we can never again feel as we did when we were young, that we can never again experience the intensity or playfulness we once did. Children embody these lost aspects of ourselves and enable us to see the world again through fresh eyes. Yet we can also come to envy children because of their optimism, and envy can lead to the desire to possess: "If I could love and possess this child, I could recover what I have lost in myself."

I don't believe that a given boy or girl is what casts the spell for most people. Rather, what casts the spell is the intensity of experience that one had as a child and the loss of playfulness and spontaneity that is the lot of too many adults. Charles Kingsley wrote: "Depend upon it, a man never experiences such pleasure or grief after fourteen years as he does before."

Our attraction to children is based so often on what we are afraid we no longer can have or be within ourselves. J. M. Barrie, the creator of Peter Pan, was a man who lived a sad and lonely life. Unhappily, he had an intense sexual interest in boys. Yet one only has to read *Peter Pan* to know that he believed that growing up is a catastrophe, in the process of which we lose much that is wonderful about us; hence Peter's wish never to grow up. The attraction to children was, for Barrie, the embodiment of the sadness of growing up and losing the childlike and happy parts of the self.

When I go to consult at a school, twenty years after that first experience of practice teaching, I see sexual feeling as simply one form of communication in the school environment. Teachers and children bring their whole personalities into school: their energy, their commitment, their love, their sense of duty, their ambitions, their power needs, and their sexuality. All of these drives are brought to bear on the educational process.

My headmaster at Millbrook School, Edward Pulling, defined teaching as "the transmission of knowledge through personality." And the fuller the personality, the better the transmission; a lively, full-blooded teacher is like having a radio with brand-new batteries – you hear everything clearly.

In the course of ordinary teaching, teachers try to "seduce" students into loving the subject that they are teaching, and students "seduce" teachers into caring for them and wanting to teach them. A wit once described Oxford University as an institution filled with tutors in love with English literature and students in love with their tutors. Because of the reality of sexual harassment, that must not be literally true at the college level and certainly not in a school for younger children. However, good schools are suffused with a loving atmosphere between teachers and students. To try to prevent students from loving certain teachers or even having crushes on them, or to deny that teachers have loving feelings toward certain students, would be to deny the humanity of the educational process.

I would hate to see fears about sexual abuse and sexual abuse allegations frighten teachers into remaining distant from students, emotionally or physically. Teachers need to hug and hold smaller children; they need to let children gather around them and lean against them for reading. Children have to be allowed to sit on their laps. Older children need to be patted on the back, they need an arm around their shoulder, they need to be in physically cozy group situations. Adolescents also need some physical contact with teachers – a pat on the back, the congratulatory hug on a public occasion, the encouraging physical contact between the coach and the players on the team.

The guidelines cannot be specific, because the external actions are not a sufficient guide to the dangers. Many cultures permit much more touching and physical affection, without any sexual meaning, than does ours. Two Chinese adolescent boys may walk down the street in Beijing holding hands or with their arms around each other's shoulders, and this has no sexual meaning whatsoever. In this country, that signals something entirely different and highly sexual.

The ultimate test must lie in the adult's understanding of his or her intentions. If the adult is meeting sexual needs by touching a child, then the physical actions, no matter how innocuous, are potentially dangerous; if the teacher is only showing affection, then even effusive gestures are not problematic. Sexual feeling may also be present in both parties in the most affectionate gesture, but the important distinction is between the existence of simple sexual feeling and the adult's sexual needs being met. Any teacher who feels that he or she is having sexual feelings toward children that are too intense should certainly seek some counseling.

Sexual feeling is one of the coins of the realm in any school. It has to be acknowledged and controlled, like hate, jealousy, or any other passionate feeling. But it is to be found in every school, in every child, in every teacher; and I would not want to see children or teachers cut such feelings out of themselves because of guilt or ignorance. It grieves me to see teachers become less sexually alive than they could be either as a defense against their feelings or out of principle, believing that sexual feeling has no place in school. It does have a place, because children bring their sexuality to us, and they need a warm, loving, controlled, and most of all, genuinely human response from us.

Connectedness

by Edward M. Hallowell

Things fall apart; the center cannot hold.
The best lack all conviction
While the worst are full of passionate intensity.

When William Butler Yeats wrote those lines over half a century ago, he might have been describing the feelings many people have in the 1990s as they look around and try to get their bearings. We live in a time of remarkable connectedness on the one hand. Globally, we are joined by fax machines, telephones, computers, supersonic transport, and all manner of electronic communication such that we are only seconds away from the other side of the planet. Yet, paradoxically, locally, at our home base, in our home town, we are in many ways separated, disconnected, even isolated. The connections that sustain and uplift, the connections that make life buoyant have for many people, come unplugged.

The topic of this essay, human connectedness, is a simple idea, rich in its ramifications. Let me suggest these ramifications through image and anecdote by painting a few scenes at the outset.

I was in the post office the other day in my home town of Cambridge. It was just before Christmas. Everyone was bustling about under the slate gray skies that so often portend snow at that time of year. There were even a few flakes, I think. A Christmas carol could be heard from a Salvation Army street corner band while worried shoppers tried to balance Christmas generosity with hard economic times. I hit the P.O. about 3:30 and, much to my surprise, it was all but empty. A small miracle that wouldn't last but a minute or two. I handed my packages to the elderly postman behind the counter and watched as he weighed my bundles. I didn't say anything and he didn't say anything except, "First class?" I nodded. He weighed. I waited. He stamped, thump, thump, on each package.

I flashed back for a moment – how our brains can reproduce an entire scene from decades ago faster even than a fax machine – I flashed back to when I was four, holding onto my grandmother's ink-blue overcoat as she handed packages across the counter at Christmas, and I asked her where we were going next. "Over the river and through the woods," she said, taking coins from her purse, "to grandmother's house we go. And when we get there you can help me make eggnog and scrape the nutmeg on top."

Now as I took coins from my own pocket the smell of nutmeg seemed to emanate from the brown paper packages before me, despite the intervening years.

"Christmas at home this year?" the man behind the counter asked.

"Yes," I said, somewhat astonished that he had spoken. "And you?"

"I'll be with my grandchildren," he said with a smile.

"Oh, really?" I said, my grandmother still in mind. "That's great!"

"Seven grandchildren," he said.

And then, since the place was empty, we stopped and talked. I asked about his grandchildren and got a sentence or two on each one. Those extra few minutes we took with each other made all the difference as I went on with my various errands.

A chance moment of connectedness with my past and with a man I'd probably not see again.

Connectedness sustains us invisibly. It can be come by in unusual ways. In another Christmas season I was interviewing a man - let's call him Charlie - who had been brought into a state psychiatric hospital for evaluation because he had been found wandering the Boston Public Gardens muttering to himself. He was admitted to the state hospital because he had no funds. In fact he was homeless.

He looked older than his actual age of fifty-four. He'd had a hard life and had creases and lines in his face to show for it. But his eyes also crinkled when he smiled and his bushy gray and white beard made me think he was jolly inside. Diagnosed with manic-depressive illness in his twenties, he'd been in and out of mental hospitals ever since. Medication controlled his illness pretty well, but when he stopped taking it, which he would do now and then as if to tempt fate, he would fall apart. Never married, he loved children. Unfortunately, although he had seven nieces and nephews, his sisters did not like him visiting because they were afraid of his psychiatric illness.

Of the many odd jobs Charlie had managed to secure for himself over the past thirty years, by far his favorite was playing Santa Claus. Every Christmas season, when he was not in the hospital, he would find some department store or shopping mall that needed a Santa Claus and sign up for the job.

"They usually have a sleigh or something fancy for me to sit in," Charlie explained. "Then the kids line up. It's such a kick. I really get into the role. When

I put on that red suit I feel like I actually become Santa Claus. I believe in him. I am him at those moments. Now don't think I'm crazy, Doc. I know I'm not Santa Claus. It's just that when I dress up I feel like I am. And when the kids come up. . . it's the closest thing I get to being a dad. You know, they sit on my knee and tell me what they want, and I smile and tap my head and tell them I'll do my best to keep it all up here and bring them what they want. I can sit there all day long and never get tired of it. The floor managers are always amazed. 'Don't you want your break?' they ask. 'Naw,' I say, 'Christmas only comes once a year.' Sounds pretty silly, huh? I mean I hear all kinds of stories. It makes me feel like I'm part of their lives, all over the city. I even describe to them my workshop up on the North Pole. It has all the latest stuff, you know. Is that crazy, Doc?"

"No," I said, "I don't think that's crazy at all, Charlie. If you ask me it's pretty goddamn ingenious." We worked together to get him out of the hospital quickly so he could go be Santa Claus for another group of children.

Imagine what it must have felt like for Charlie, unwelcome in the homes of his own family due to an illness he couldn't control, finding makeshift connections with children by playing Santa Claus. For a certain time, under the lights and hubbub of a shopping mall, Charlie would become a special person bringing the gift of Christmas to children he wanted to be with, but didn't know.

In another vein, I think of a five-year-old girl, whom I shall call Sophie, who connected through imagination to the world she wanted to find. She was brought to see me because she had no friends, and her parents thought she was pathologically shy. In fact, as it turned out, she had a host of friends, friends that emerged as Sophie and I played together on my office floor, friends who were created by Sophie in her mind and transported through the medium of play to the outside world.

Over time, her parents told me of their considerable troubles. Each of them was maintaining a fast-track career with a multitude of social and business obligations that left very little time for Sophie. Additionally, they blew off steam, as they put it, by drinking heavily and often having riotous arguments that included much yelling and breaking of things. "We're both very high-intensity," Sophie's father said.

"We don't mean anything by it," her mother added. "It's like something we do. We always make up."

But Sophie was terrified. So she withdrew. In her own world she found the safe, soothing connections she couldn't find in the world her parents gave her.

The unifying theme in these anecdotes, and in this paper, is the theme of connectedness. My thesis is this: We live in a time that conspires to disconnect us, one from another, from institutions, from ideas and from ideals, so that the individual is precariously alone. I would go on to contend that the implications of this disconnectedness for children are enormous.

I think of the two major tasks of childhood as the development of competence and the development of connectedness, both of which contribute, in different ways, to the overarching goal of developing a sense of confidence and self-esteem. If we do not pay close attention to our children's developing sustaining connections, connections of all sorts, then they will always be at risk of not finding satisfaction and meaning in life, no matter how competent they may become.

What is connectedness? It is a sense of being a part of something larger than oneself. It is a sense of belonging, or a sense of accompaniment. It is that feeling in your bones that you are not alone. It is a sense that, no matter how scary things may become, there is a hand for you in the dark. While ambition drives us to achieve, connectedness is my word for the force that urges us to ally, to affiliate, to enter into mutual relationships, to take strength and to grow through cooperative behavior.

One of my adult patients, a highly accomplished and successful man of thirty-five, said to me recently in reference to his feeling lonely, "What I really want to do is walk up to people and say, 'Will you be my friend?' But that makes you too vulnerable. It immediately puts you at the bottom of the inherent power differential that is in every relationship."

My patient lives in disconnection and so can easily feel one down. In order to handle the tension of the power differential he so readily perceives, he works harder and harder for success, feeling that if he achieves enough he can be on top all the time. Having all the power, he will not have to put himself in the vulnerable position of asking, "Will you be my friend?"

"But no matter how good you are," I say, "there will always be someone better. Then what do you do?"

"Work harder," he says wryly.

"But don't you think it's good to have friends where maybe you're helping each other along, on an equal basis?" I ask.

"Nice idea," he says. "But it always comes down to who's on top."

We have always had to deal with the tension between individual achievement and the alienating envy it can spawn. None of us has everything. We all find reasons to envy other people. There is no point in trying to moralize or lecture oneself out of envy; it arises spontaneously and is not "bad," but rather natural.

However, the best antidote to the corrosive force of envy is not, as my patient suggests, more achievement, the success cure so many seek these days, but rather the best antidote is to have in place meaningful and sustaining connections to other people, institutions, or ideals. These connections act as internal supports that pick one up from failure, disappointment, or rejection. The connected person can never fall very far because there are the life lines of support to break the fall. The disconnected person, on the other hand, dangles precariously, held in place only by the strength of his own arm.

In developing this idea of connectedness I would like to look at six different kinds of connectedness and consider a few aspects of each. They include:

1. Familial connectedness
2. Historical connectedness
3. Social connectedness
4. Institutional/Organizational connectedness
5. Connectedness to information and ideas
6. Religious/Transcendent connectedness

First there is the connectedness we are born into, familial connectedness. Whoever has been a parent or a child knows of the primal strength of the parent-child bond. In some ways, we might argue that the entire stories of our lives can be written in the terms of this bond, how it affected us, how it shaped us along the way.

We live our lives amidst the voices and memories of mother and father, sibling and kin. From the biological connecting that conceived us in the first place to the graveside where our loved ones bid us farewell, we are, most of us, never long unmindful of one or another of our parents or relatives. That there is much conflict in the family story only indicates how much energy it contains, how much we infuse it with our basic hopes and expectations, while at the same time lashing to it the disappointment and destruction that are our birthright as humans.

If you go back and look at families in dramatic literature, you read in the Greek tragedies the sparest of dialogue, the sinews of human experience. The plays center around families, their connections and disconnections. Murder, revenge, jealousy, incest, self-mutilation abound. Royal families torn by passionate misunderstanding, woeful self-deception, what Aristotle called the tragic flaw. And if you leaf through Shakespeare, and his contemporaries for that matter, you find more of the same: great families warring within, murdering each other, taking revenge, all against a backdrop of passionate familial connectedness. It is as if these characters, instead of taking their fundamental complaint against life up with God or wrestling with an angel, go after each other, pounding out on the anvil of each other's bodies and souls their attempt at retribution and justice.

In modern drama by the likes of Chekhov, Ibsen, and O'Neill, there is less murder, but equal intensity of the family drama. We see the beginning of the drama of the disconnected man in the plays of Beckett, Brecht and Sartre. Our peculiar twentieth century, with its wars and bombs and relativity and psychological-mindedness, seems to have done something to have disconnected us, from one another and from larger ideals and sustaining systems of belief, and from the family. If you look at the great plays – and art in general – of the later part of our century, you find shadows of disconnectedness, man alone, with no exit, waiting, listening to music without melody, reading books without plots, reciting prayers without conviction.

Familial disconnectedness is perhaps best represented in the fact of homelessness. Homelessness, which is not a metaphor but a stark fact, can be seen as a kind of metaphor for the homelessness within us all. Homelessness has become such a compelling phenomenon, one which even the cynic is hardpressed to ignore, in part because, I think we, to some extent, identify with the homeless. How far is each of us from homelessness? Only a serious illness or an accident or a bad call by the referee away, perhaps. And we know this. And it scares us half to death. Were we more connected as a society, were the extended family the active, vital force it once was, the homeless would be taken in by their own. Instead they are disowned, on their own.

That connectedness within families strengthens children – and that disconnectedness weakens them – has been demonstrated time and again. Psychologist Mihaly Csikszentmihali and sociologist Eugene Rochberg-Halton in a study done in Chicago in the late '70s found that children of warm families, families whose members were connected and attentive to each other, were more sympathetic, helpful, supporting, and caring. The children from cool or disconnected families were less loyal, warm, friendly, sociable, and cooperative than the children from warm families. And Judith Wallerstein, in her study of children of divorced families, found that many of those children were set adrift in their twenties, underachieving, failing to make lasting relationships, not finding a secure place for themselves in the world.

As we shuffle and reshuffle the family and the roles within it, I think it is critical to keep in mind the primary importance of familial connectedness. We trivialize it at our peril. While one's ability to separate from one's family of origin has received a lot of attention in the psychological literature as a sign of mental health, the ability to preserve meaningful but not engulfing ties to one's original family can sustain one's sense of rootedness, tradition, and security in an increasingly rootless, traditionless, and insecure world.

The mention of rootedness and tradition brings me to the second kind of connectedness, which I call historical connectedness and which our current generation of children is in danger of losing altogether. Without reading books, without having family stories told around a dining room table over and over again, without listening to folklore from Grandma or Grandpa, without participating in various rituals, ceremonies, or repeated outings that include evocations of the past, it is hard for a young person to learn about his or her personal past, to develop, that is, a sense of historical connectedness.

In a completely different context, T. S. Eliot wrote a famous essay about originality and tradition in the development of the young poet titled "Tradition and the Individual Talent." The essay lends itself to our consideration of how each new generation finds its place in history. "Tradition," wrote Eliot, "is a matter of [wide] significance. It cannot be inherited, and if you want it you must obtain it by great labour. It involves in the first place the historical sense which we may call nearly indispensable to anyone who would continue to be a poet beyond his twenty-fifth year; and the historical sense involves a perception not only of the pastness of the past but of its presence. . . ."

I would suggest that this historical sense is essential not only for the poet, but for anyone who would like to know who he or she is. We need to understand and feel the presence of the past, as Eliot says, in our own lives – how prior generations turn up in our current soup, not only genetically, but through customs, traditions, rituals, even feuds passed down over the years.

Eliot goes on :

What is to be insisted upon is that the . . . [individual] must develop or procure the consciousness of the past and that he should continue to develop this consciousness throughout [his life]. What happens is a continual surrender of himself as he is at the moment to something which is more valuable. The progress. . . is a continual self-sacrifice, a continual extinction of personality.

A continual extinction of personality? Can you imagine a statement more antithetical to the message of self-focus and self-promotion our children receive in the media every day?

I hope it is not too much of a reach to relate T. S. Eliot's essay on poetry, written in 1917, to the current scene, but to my mind it applies perfectly to the idea of the development of historical connectedness. Each generation is altered by and alters the past. In order to know and feel this, each generation must connect with the past.

I am not championing the study of history, although I do certainly think that it is a very good thing. Rather, I am stressing, for the sake of mental health and human growth, not to mention good poetry, the importance of knowing what has come before, and how you hook up to that, quarrel with it, change it, renew it.

Let me give you a personal example. My two-and-a-half-year-old daughter's name is Lucy. Right now she is a bouncy bundle of energy, curiosity, and most everything that is right with life. As she grows older, she will learn that her real name isn't Lucy but Lucretia Mott Hallowell. She will know where the Hallowell came from, since Mom and Dad have that name, but she will probably wonder where such strange first and middle names came from: Lucretia Mott. Then I hope her mom and I will be able to tell her stories about her namesake, her great, great, great, great, great grandmother, Lucretia Mott, a little Quaker lady with a stout Quaker heart who worked to free slaves and advance women in the second half of the nineteenth century. Lucy will want to know about Lucretia Mott, why she got stuck with her name, what it meant back then to be an abolitionist and a feminist. Lucy will get this bit of history up close, as part of family folklore, and she will take it in and do something with it – I don't know what – as she develops a sense of who she is. It is my hope that this bit of historical connectedness will be sustaining for her; I know it will be meaningful, as names always are.

Regardless of who your ancestry has in it, it is your ancestry, and it has done much to create you. The family lines sustain us more the better we know them. Seeking personal definition, it can be just as useful to look back as to look within. Children need to hear the folklore of the family.

When we lack historical connectedness, when we have only the present and only the individual personality, then we lack so very much. We lack the reverberation and echo of the past, the sense of largeness and sweep that a feeling for the past instills. Without the past, we sit alone in the great house and listen to the clock tick. But if we know that the very clock ticking now was ticking at our mother's birth, then we are not so alone, and if we see in the hallway mirrors not only our own reflection but the faces of generations past and their stories, conflicts, habits, and customs, then we are less alone still. If we pass on those stories to our own children and keep the past alive for them and us, even as the present changes the past as it does in our telling of it, then we keep alive much more than old stories; we keep alive the historical connectedness that our children, and we, so richly warm to.

Within the framework of historical connectedness I should mention another kind of connectedness which we do not have to work to acquire, but which accrues within us every minute of every day. This is the connectedness of memory, the connectedness to our own personal past which memory automatically wires up. Richer, deeper, more mysterious and complex than any bank of computers or any library's archives, the human brain stores details and records events far beyond what we consciously control. Through a complex and personal language of associations, our memory offers up little jewels, constantly matching this place and that, this time and that, this person's face to that, this lyric in a song to that dance we once had, this chance aroma to that breakfast scene, this sprightly cadenza to that original score. Our memories are stitching and knitting all the time the fabulous tapestry of our associative inner lives so that we are, in our present lives, always connected through memory to the vastness of our pasts, in all the details and arresting vividness of the original events. Just as the man in the post office took me back to the nutmeg in my grandmother's eggnog, so we are transported daily back and forth across that chasm in time that divides the here and now from the past, the then and there we look back to. As memory's cousin, anticipation, connects us to the future, so does memory keep us in touch with where we've been, ferrying us into the land of what is no more but once was so. Memory and anticipation change our landscape all the time. As we live in the present, anticipation carries us into the future and memory conveys us into the past, so that we are suspended, as if in a hammock, by the poles of the past and the future over the whoosh of the ever-vanishing here and now.

This special kind of connectedness with different parts of time, probably the fullest and richest connectedness we have, gives us the heartache of knowing what has come and gone, the comfort of reminiscing, the knowledge of growth, the fulfillment of taking stock, and the wisdom of perspective. Memory and anticipation keep us connected with ourselves.

From familial and historical connectedness, which define the rugged aspects of one's backbone, one's biologically received self, I take up the social connectedness we establish during a lifetime, the connectedness with other people, mainly of one's own choosing, and with one's community or locale.

We live in a time when neighborhoods, villages, and communities have broken down, so that the on-street, built-in ways of making friends and establishing a local support network are not as at-hand as they were, say, two generations ago. Nowadays, one must work hard to make and keep friends over time.

For children, not having a viable neighborhood is less isolating because they still have the built-in village called school. The friendships children make in school, rough and tumble though they be at times, over time draw the child into the world of affiliation and relatedness, in counterbalance to the world of achievement and individualism school also offers up.

If our children are growing up, as I believe they are, in a disconnected world, it is of great importance that we pay attention to helping them forge different kinds of connectedness early on. I think one of the great challenges of the coming decades will be to create and preserve connectedness in the face of the disconnectedness our technology and social structures often encourage.

Of the many points that could be made here, I wish to focus on one thought. It is by way of trying to answer my patient's question, Why don't we solve the problem of connectedness by just walking up to one another and asking, "Will you be my friend?" I would like to describe the psychological challenge we all contend with as we try to connect with each other.

While there is within us all a kind of drawing force, a powerful magnetic pull that leaves us leaning toward each other, reaching out, there is also a force in the other direction, the opposite pole of the magnet, pushing us apart, pulling back the hand before it reaches out, saying, "Do not connect, keep your bounds, play it close to the vest."

Where does this pulling away originate psychologically? What keeps us from finding greater protection through one another, instead menacing each other, attacking, or finding fault? D.W. Winnicott, the British pediatrician and psychoanalyst, said that the most difficult task in all of human development was coming to terms with our destructive feelings toward others. He said that in any close relationship there appears, in fantasy, sometimes unconscious, sometimes not, the wish to destroy the other person.

Destroy may seem too strong a word, but a relationship perforce destroys one's hope of the other person being under one's total control, at one's beck and call, all-giving, all-caring. In this sense, we destroy the other person; we destroy our infantile version of the other person as all-gratifying en route to our being able to tolerate and then enjoy the other as an independent being.

In simple terms, the child – or adult for that matter – inevitably gets disappointed in any relationship because he or she does not have complete control over the other person. The other person is at times frustrating, in some way not giving what is wanted. This leads the child, or adult, to destroy the other person in fantasy. If the relationship can survive this process of repeated destruction, then what results is genuine and useful connectedness. What so often happens, however, is at the moment of frustration the subject pulls away and withdraws. Rather than bearing with the tension, the subject pulls back, thus avoiding frustration. However, the subject is now alone and disconnected.

How common it is, this wish to destroy the other, and how often we back away from a relationship rather than deal with the unpleasant, destructive feelings we encounter. Getting past, or learning to live with, such feelings is a necessary prerequisite of genuine connectedness. There is more to being friends than being nice. One must tolerate very un-nice, aggressive feelings. Once a child or adult can do this in a friendship, then the relationship can be meaningfully reciprocal. We need to get comfortable with our destructive feelings – not too comfortable, mind you, just comfortable enough not to have to hide them all the time.

The fourth kind of connectedness is connectedness to ideas and information. I include ethical and moral thinking within this domain, although the roots of moral and ethical behavior extend to connectedness in all domains.

Let's start with information. There is more information now than there has ever been. Only a few centuries ago, it was possible for a person to aspire to know all that was known. Now, with what is known increasing exponentially, it is a major task just to keep abreast of even a very small field. The idea of knowing everything is obsolete.

Stores of information have grown so vast that, I would contend, our very connectedness to information itself is threatened. It is a paradox that while we know more now than we ever have, illiteracy is rising, the ability to use language is declining, and our children are disengaging from study at an alarming rate.

I think this relates to our connectedness to information. By connectedness to information I do not mean just the having of information. I mean the feeling of being comfortable around information, of feeling supported, fed, and informed by it, rather than feeling threatened, starved, or smothered by it. How many of us, and how many of our children, react to a new piece of data or a new technique with a sigh, a half-hearted camel's groan of one more straw being piled upon our heavily laden backs?

Similarly, in the world of ideas, one can know many thoughts, be able to recite the laws of thermodynamics or the principles in Aristotle's *Poetics*, but not feel helped or at home or happy with ideas in general. On the other hand, one might know no famous ideas, but still feel drawn to ideas and feel at home and warmed by thought. Curious children are a good example of the latter.

I worry that our children are growing up disconnected from both information and ideas. While they are surrounded by information, they do not know what to do with it. While they may peruse ideas, as if browsing in a store, they do not connect with them in a meaningful way; they do not buy them and take them home and make them their own. The subset of the world of ideas we call ethics and morality can seem strangely alien or quaint when the only meaningful morality appears embedded not in ideas but in expediency, luck, class privilege, or force.

With so much information available – the skies are raining enough new information to drench us daily – and with new ideas growing up to contain the information, there is a chance for young people to be knowledgeable and thoughtful as people have never had the chance to be before, and with that knowledge and thought to wield the power that naturally accompanies knowledge. But in order for young people to take advantage of this opportunity, they must feel comfortably connected to ideas and information. Ideas and information should be brought into their lives in such a way that they feel at ease with them and confident and eager at the prospect of new ones. Their exposure to ideas and information should not be like taking a sip of water from a fire hose. Rather it should be in a context that stresses mastery, manageability, and fun.

From ideas and information, I move to institutions and organizations. Much of one's satisfaction day in and day out depends upon the degree of involvement and at-homeness one feels where one works – or in the case of children, where one learns. Our degree of connectedness to institutions and organizations often reflects in a concrete way the degree to which we feel valued and appreciated by the society we live in.

The last few decades have seen great changes in the individual's relationship to institutions and organizations, from the work place to local and national government to clubs and societies. Since Vietnam and Watergate, the cynicism and disconnection many feel toward government has been growing. On the other hand, philosophies of management have been shifting toward a more democratic, involving style, a style that invites participation by workers on all levels. In education, many universities are trying to become what Zeldam Gamson, a sociologist of education, calls "learning communities," with the emphasis not on hierarchy, but on collaboration. Schools, one of our most important social institutions, are stressed by the increasing demands put upon them and are looking for ways to involve parents, community, and whatever other resources can be marshalled to increase the connectedness within the school world.

Robert Bellah and his associates, in their two books *Habits of the Heart* and *The Good Society*, point to the need for fostering and developing affiliations and attachments within our institutions and organizations. And futurists Alvin and Heidi Toffler in their book *Powershift* contend that as knowledge is shifting toward universal availability and ownership, so is the power that goes with it shifting toward a broad base, with emphasis on small cottage businesses that can be maximally creative and, if I may stress the word, connected.

The institutions and organizations that do best are the ones that pay attention to the connectedness within them. They nurture their people. They attend to them. They listen to them. They know that they *are* their people. It makes no business sense to have the people of the organization feeling cut off or left out. It makes much better business – and psychological – sense to connect them into the whole.

Yet the complaint that fills the hearts of so many who work in institutions, and this certainly includes teachers in schools, is one of feeling unappreciated, undervalued, even unknown. Teachers, who work so hard and do so much, are often left paying cheerful lip service to the good will of their schools, while underneath the chipper veneer they feel spent, at loggerheads with an administration that talks a good game but does not deliver the goods, and upset within themselves at the withering of their work ideals. Often they say, "If only just once in a while my boss would walk through that door, look me in the eye, and, really meaning it, tell me, 'You're good.'"

What I am talking about here is not complicated psychology. It is really no more than an extension of what we were all brought up calling politeness. You say hello when you pass someone. When you are waiting for the person behind the counter to hand you your bundles you might comment on the weather or the handsome new curtains they've just had installed. When you are paying your toll on the turnpike, you make a remark to the person taking your money even if he or she looks the other way. You make a little chit-chat in the waiting room with the other person who looks uncomfortable being there. No matter what you are doing, you put aside everything else to make the other person feel comfortable and at ease first. You allow perhaps for there to be laughter before there is serious work, connectedness before productivity. In a world that is itching at every turn to dehumanize us all, you insist on being human first.

Until the rest of our society restores or recreates its interconnectedness, institutions in general and schools in particular will have to work hard to stay human. I believe, however, that schools have a unique opportunity to lead the way in recreating the social connectedness we so disjointedly seek.

It is said that the coming decade will see the cocooning of the American family. Technology will allow most of the family's business to be conducted from home. Everything can be done at a keyboard: Order groceries and shop for other goods, write checks and conduct other banking business, consult a physician, rent a videotape, play games, run a business, even campaign for political office.

If we are to be increasingly cocooned, then, more than ever, schools and other institutions will have to respond to the tremendously increasing need for the sort of human connectedness that the cocooned family will inevitably – and already does – lack.

Finally, I take up my sixth and last category of connectedness, connectedness to what is beyond, call it religious or transcendent connectedness. Whatever it is called, it means a sense of being a part of the largest of all things, the cosmic universe, and in that connection a fundamental feeling of being a part of something, rather than feeling alone. Such connectedness, whether it be Buddhist or Hindu or Christian or Jewish, whether it be one's personal system of belief or a miraculous sense felt once in a lifetime during a cloudburst, joins the individual with the unknown and unseen, with what happens before and after death, with what is eternal. If there is nothing before and after life, if the universe is a meaningless void, if human life is a biochemical coincidence signifying nothing beyond happenstance and chance, then religious connectedness is nothing more than an ironic joke, a wry smile upon an indifferent universe, a hallucination contrived by humanity to make sense of things.

But if it is the case that there is an energy behind the mystery, a meaning beyond existence, then the intimations we may feel that connect us to our god, whatever that being may be, serve to focus our faith and create the connection found in prayer, meditation, or other transcendent devotion or cogitation.

Though unseen and unprovable, this connection can be felt as the surest connection we have. Take as an example of this, from the tradition that I know best, the extraordinary statement by Paul in his letter to the Romans in the New Testament:

Who shall separate us from the love of Christ?
Shall tribulation, or distress, or persecution, or famine, or nakedness, or peril, or sword?

Nay, in all these things we are more than conquerors through him that loved us.
For I am persuaded, that neither death nor life, nor principalities, nor powers, nor
things present nor things to come,
Nor height, nor depth, nor any other creature, shall be able to separate us from the
love of God.

Whether or not we feel the absolute connectedness Paul feels, I think most of us have felt at one time or another a murmuring in our hearts that bespeaks a possible connection to something beyond.

However, we must be careful. As our methods of discourse and discovery change, it is important to know of our capacity for and need of spiritual connectedness. Particularly for our young people, who are at risk of being more a lost generation than the generation Gertrude Stein intended that term for, we need to help them watch out for those who would exploit their spiritual hunger for financial or political gain or for power and control. The list of charlatans and crooks posing as ministers to spiritual need is alarmingly long of late. While we certainly do not want to dictate how or what anyone worships, still we do not want to condone the appalling financial and spiritual rip-off that is the big business of fad religion. From Scientology to Moonies to satanism to the ministries of Swaggart and Bakker, these sects take advantage of the power of the need for connectedness and commit the most awful deception in the process.

But if we look past the deceptions that have been committed so often in the name of God and consider spiritual connectedness as the genuine human concern that it is, we see there is an undisputed mystery that surrounds our lives on this planet. We don't know for sure why we're here, where we've been or where we're headed. We don't know why we suffer or why we thrive or why we were born or why we die. But we do wonder about these things.

How we engage this mystery defines our spiritual connectedness. Whether we do it alone or in a group, whether we do it under a banner or without formal ties, whether we do it systematically and at a scheduled time or spontaneously when we are so moved, whether we do it out of fear or obligation or love or curiosity or hunger, whether we do it with full faith or full of skepticism, whether or not we know what we're doing when we do it, we all engage somehow, at some time, with the mystery of life. It is at times embarrassing in this very scientific century to talk of things like mystery and faith and God, because most of our intellectual tools seem geared up for other things, and yet even as we turn away from them we find ourselves face to face with them once again.

This brings me to the end of my discussion of different kinds of connectedness. The list is meant to be suggestive and is by no means exhaustive. There are as many kinds of connectedness as there are people, places, and ideas to connect with. My categories have sketched in just a few. I have tried to emphasize what I think will be a central problem for children and adults in the coming decades. While we are prepared to attend to children's competence, I think we must equally prepare to address their connectedness in its many spheres.

Let me close by going back with you to where this paper began, in Harvard Square, in the P.O., late on a graying afternoon just before Christmas.

Leaving the P.O., I blew air into my cupped hands to warm them. The lights of the city decorated what otherwise would have been a drab sky. Shoppers hurried in and out of stores while other people just sort of milled about, not quite sure what their next move would be. There was the Salvation Army band, and I wondered why I got so moved at the sound of that humble brass ensemble, but I did. The present was staying just one step ahead of my past as memories weaved around me as if they were other pedestrians, bumping into me, politely excusing themselves, moving along.

Until one grabbed me by the shoulder. A pedestrian, that is. "Aren't you..."

"Yes," I quickly answered. "Amazing just to bump into you like this!" It was Mr. Magruder, my fifth-grade history teacher, one arm full of bundles and all of him full of memories. We gabbed a little bit. I don't remember what I said because I was preoccupied with recollection. He must have thought I was addled. I wanted to take him and walk right back to our schoolhouse or out onto the soccer field where he taught me to kick with my instep instead of my toe. The moment was cut short, of course, by time, and we said goodbye.

The next stops were Reading International, Crate and Barrel, and the Loeb Drama Center to pick up some tickets. This was an area of town I knew well, having gone to school here and lived here for twenty years.

I stopped for a minute and looked above the roofs at the sky. There was just enough contrast to give a difference between the gray sky and the black roofs, all offset by the neon signs and city decorations which glowed, like footlights, below the skyline. Here we all are, I thought to myself. For at least this one minute, we're all here, now, together.

How many people are there around the city who are alone? I wondered. Who's having a fight, who's breaking up, who's making up, who's looking for a way to start off fresh, who needs a friend? What is the glue anymore that holds us all together? Was there ever any?

So much of my glue came from my teachers. I have loved my teachers, so many of them, from grade school on up. Bill Alfred, professor of English at Harvard and my tutor when I was there, used to have me into his house on Athens Street and we read plays, and I felt drawn to him and to the plays and to the words and to the larger world that seemed to grow before me as I lived on into it. Fred Tremallo, my old English teacher at Exeter, was like a father, getting me to look up words in the dictionary when I didn't want to and telling me about his Italian ancestry. And Mrs. Eldredge, my first-grade teacher, who found out I had dyslexia, kept me close to her, right near her side, near her dresses with apples on them and her powder I can still smell, as she did what would now be called tutoring me but which then felt like love. I could never tell them all how much they meant even if I spent a lifetime trying. Would they want to hear? Just the facts. Nothing cheap.

As I heard the Salvation Army band still playing its tromboned carols, I thought of how much pain there was in the city that night, any night, and how much we needed each other to stave it off or take it in and put it behind, again and again. We've all been hurt. We need to know how to find a place to take us in.

I heard the band die out at the end of a chord. Then silence, like the moment after you say goodbye. They must have reached the end of their day. I could imagine them packing up their instruments and pot-bellied donation cannister and saying goodbye. They would be back, I imagined, I hoped. People return. People come back to give what they gave before until they can't do it anymore. I caught a glimpse of myself in a storefront window, dimly reflected, passing by.

"Only connect," E. M. Forster said. That evening, under the chilly skies of Cambridge, I understood what he meant.

About the Authors

Ned Hallowell

Edward M. Hallowell, M.D., is in the private practice of child and adult psychiatry in Cambridge, Massachusetts. He also consults at various independent schools both locally and nationally. In addition, Ned has a specialty in attention deficit disorders in children and adults.

© Koby-Antupit

Michael G. Thompson, Ph.D., is a child and family psychologist in Cambridge, Massachusetts. At one time, he was a middle school teacher; now he consults to and has run more than one hundred workshops for schools from Seattle to Miami. He is the father of two children, Joanna and Will.

Michael Thompson